Unlocking people's
creative forces

UNLOCKING PEOPLE'S CREATIVE FORCES

A Transnational Study of Adult Learning Policies

Paul Bélanger   **Paolo Federighi**

UNESCO Institute for Education

Cover Illustration: "La Réflexion" by Enrique Hojman

First Edition 2000

ISBN: 92 820 1104-6

Production: Lithotec Oltmanns, Hamburg
Printing & Binding: Robert Seemann GmbH, Hamburg

Printed in Germany

To

Alessandra
Anouk
Louis
Sophie

Contents

Introduction

In order to survive and improve their lives, adult men and women on every continent are striving to develop the means to enhance their capacity to act and understand the ways of the world. Adult learning also has strategic importance for economic actors today. Risk management strategies, economic policy, environmental and health policy all invariably rely on continually raising people's competencies and skills. Similarly, traditional and new types of popular movements and national liberation projects call for strengthening and spreading the capacity for initiative so that people can deal with the challenges facing them, bring about change and take an active part in economic and social development.

It is no coincidence that the crisis in industry has led most countries to invest in adult learning. Nor is it happenstance that, after winning independence or autonomy, Namibia, South Africa and Slovenia have hastened to launch adult national literacy campaigns and major adult learning programmes to unlock the urban and rural population's creative and productive capacities.

National educational scenes are changing dramatically. While yesterday initial education completely dominated the stage, now it is being redefined as a preparatory phase of a learning itinerary that, especially if properly begun, can carry on throughout life, amidst a rich variety of pathways.

It is impossible to grasp the importance of recent trends without adopting an expanded vision of adult learning[1] and reconstructing its fragmented reality. Redefined properly, this field has become a new space for the development of key social dynamics, including diverse negotiations over the expression of learning demand and the organisation of educational responses. The difficult challenge of liberating the creative forces is the main subject of this book. In particular, the content and dynamics of adult learning policies and strategies are closely examined. We hope that we have succeeded in conveying a sense of the significance of the boom in adult learning demand and the growing number of policies and strategies being forged to deal with it grasp and meet it.

---

[1] "Adult learning denotes the entire body of ongoing learning processes, formal or otherwise, whereby people regarded as adults by the society to which they belong develop their abilities, enrich their knowledge, and improve their technical or professional qualifications or turn them in a new direction to meet their own needs and those of their society. Adult learning encompasses both formal and continuing education, non-formal learning and the spectrum of informal and incidental learning available in a multicultural learning society, where theory- and practice-based approaches are recognized." (Hamburg Declaration, para. 3., in: UNESCO 1997)

1

This publication is the fruit of five years of empirical research conducted in 24 countries from every region of the world (see Appendix II, tables 1 and 3). The UNESCO Institute for Education worked with 24 national teams and researchers (see Appendix III), who took part in three research seminars organised by the authors. The two initial meetings, in May and October 1994, decided on the study framework and tools and a sampling plan for the policies to be studied. At the third seminar in 1996, national analyses were used to develop a preliminary transnational analysis. One hundred and twenty-two policies (legislation, govern-ment decisions and policy statements) dealing directly with adult education or closely related areas were systematically studied using a common analytical frame-work (the Appendix contains three tables giving the source and the target sectors of the policies analysed)[2]. In addition to this basic material, there is a more recent list of policies from the 24 countries in question and documents from other countries and organisations (see sections 1 and 3 of the Bibliography), as well as all other sources and references (see section 2 of the Bibliography) and the documents and analyses produced for the Fifth International Conference on Adult Education (Confintea in Hamburg in 1997), the Conference reports, and the subsequent debates, discussions and policy programmes.

This book does not pretend to be exhaustive. The field is too highly fragmented and losely institutionalised. Neither is our aim descriptive. We rather endeavour to identify basic trends and analyse their underlying dynamics. Our goal is to provide analytical and operational reference points for the various actors in-volved in developing and implementing new adult learning policies.

This is a transnational study. It is not a comparative analysis based on some uni-versal standard model, which in any case would be meaningless. The reader will also search in vain in this publication for "the best formulas" or for model legis-lation and policies to copy. We have chosen instead to identify trends that, however common, can only be understood in their own national context, and, conversely, to situate national policies in the framework of the global trends that influence national decision-making. The three above-mentioned seminars, like the entire post-Confintea process, created a setting conducive to studying the relationship between global and local, understanding the national impacts of various policies and hence identifying basic approaches.

Although we believe that international co-operation and exchanges are impor-tant to avoid reinventing the wheel and that there are basic trends influencing every region in the world, we are also convinced that the best practical guidance

---

[2] The analytical framework, the 122 policy files and other basic documents can be con-sulted through the UIE documentation centre (see the introduction to section 2 of the bibliography).

does not simply attempt to transplant "successful solutions". Each country will succeed best when it redevelops the policies it needs in its own environment based on dynamics rooted in the particularities of its own historical and social development.

The structure of this book does not follow the order of analysis. After presenting a reconstructed and expanded view of current adult learning in the various regions of the world (Chapter 1), we identify several basic trends in the process of developing and implementing policy and outline the subject and functions of adult learning policy today (Chapters 2 and 3). The middle of the book, Chapters 4 and 5, deals with the changing socio-economic and cultural dynamics that are reflected, sometimes explicitly, sometimes contradictorily, in today's adult learning policies. This new "problematic" gives meaning to the concrete measures and policies to promote the expression of learning demand (Chapters 6 and 7) as well as to the specific policies to organise and co-ordinate different educational responses and support learning continuity (Chapter 8). All this has led to changes in the role of the state and other actors. Adult learning has witnessed the rise of new organisational models and even educational synergies (Chapter 9). In Chapter 10, we take a closer look at the impact of these epistemological and policy changes by presenting and analysing the basic trends in the specific field of adult basic education. The conclusion sums up and raises questions about possible future orientations.

This book would not have been possible without the help of researchers from the 24 participating countries, whose names appear in the Appendix. We would like to thank them for their hard work, patience and solidarity in carrying out a transnational empirical study that would normally have required means well beyond the reach of this project. We were also helped by the entire team at the UNESCO Institute of Education, especially our two efficient research assistants, Uta Papen and Wolfang Jütte, and the documentary expertise of Ursula Giere. And we could not have managed without financial assistance from the German government, the Norwegian government and the Catalonian authorities to co-ordinate the 24 teams.

Finally, we would like to give special thanks for the unflagging efforts of our researcher Michael Hein, who revised the entire manuscript, compiled a complex bibliography and finalised the technical appendices. This meticulous work in the final phase of the book has hopefully rendered it a useful, accessible reference tool. We would also like to thank Patrick Hamm for having done more than just translated the manuscript into English. He has worked with Michael Hein to check the technical terminology and track down the original bibliographic references.

We hope that this collective effort has provided a sound sociological analysis of trends and a practical and effective tool for social actors, decision-makers and researchers alike. Hopefully, following in the steps of so many others, we have succeeded once again in showing that practice bereft of theory is all too-often blind, and that theory is only meaningful if it guides and is illuminated by practice.

10 December 1999
Paul Bélanger and Paolo Federighi

Chapter 1
Reconstructing the Fragmented World of Adult Learning

It is impossible to understand recent adult learning policies without first reviewing and reconstructing this new highly fragmented field in all its national forms and configurations. A proper understanding of the importance and different orientations of the policies and strategies being developed in various regions of the globe entails looking at the extent of the social demand for adult learning, observing the growing consensus on the need to learn new skills throughout life and highlighting the gap between this demand and the actual participation of people in organised learning activities.

The purpose of this first chapter is to reconstruct the fragmented world of adult learning by overcoming both the semantic exclusions engendered by the usual or conventional definitions of the field and the epistemological borders erected by such dichotomies as vocational versus general, work versus leisure and economic versus socio-cultural. The chapter seeks to transcend the bounds of ministerial preserves and reductionist visions of a learning scene where only satisfied demand is visible, where only what is institutionalised seems real, and where the immediate aims of the actors and their inevitably strained relations with current adult learning policies and organisations all too often fade into the background.

1.1. The boom in adult learning demand and its diversity

The demand for adult learning has shot up over the last two decades, albeit quietly until recently. Men and women everywhere increasingly aspire to improve their quality of life and living conditions through self-improvement and new skills. This is happening in different ways on every continent.

1.1.1. The boom in learning demand

In Canada, the participation rate in organised adult learning rose from one adult in fourteen in 1969 to one in six in 1974 and one in five in 1983. By 1994, about 40% of the adult population were participants in some form of adult learning (Bélanger and Valdivielso 1997: 2). In Sweden, the figure for those taking part in adult learning activities each year rose from one adult in five in 1975 (Rubenson 1989: 130-132) to 50% in 1989 (Abrahmsson, Hultinger et Svennigngson 1990) and over 50% in 1994 (Bélanger and Valdivielso 1997: 2). More than two-thirds of the adult population in Japan intend to take part in organised education, and more than half of adults were already doing so in 1992

(Okamoto 1994). In Germany, organised adult learning covered about 40% of adults in 1991, compared with 29% in 1982 and 23% in 1979 (Nuissl 1994). The same phenomenon can be seen in Australia, Ireland, New Zealand, the Netherlands, Switzerland, the United Kingdom and the United States (OECD and HRDC 1997; see also Table 1.1).

Table 1.1
Percentage of Adult Population* Participating in Adult Learning
Activities in 1994 - 1995.

Country	Participation Rate
Sweden	52,5%
New Zealand	47,5%
Switzerland (germ.)	44,7%
United Kingdom	43,9%
United States	39,7%
Australia	38,8%
Canada	37,7%
Netherlands	37,4%
Switzerland (franc.)	33,7%
Ireland	24,3%
Belgium (dutch)	21,2%
Poland	13,9%

* 16 to 65 years-olds excepting those 16 to 25 years-old who study full-time (i.e. more than six hours per week)

In the developing countries, adult participation in basic education[1] or post-literacy education and post-primary education was already significant in the 1970s (UNESCO 1972; Coombs and Manzoor 1974; Dave, Ouane and Perera 1989) and has grown steadily despite repeated economic slumps. Ecuador, Namibia and India are particularly good examples of the adult population's strong

---

[1] Adult literacy policies will be dealt with in Chapter 10.

demand for basic education in recent years. In Ecuador, between 1989 and 1992, more than 70% of adults with a low initial educational level, i.e. half a million adults, have signed up for literacy programmes. In 1994, the national literacy programme in Namibia was already reaching more than 33,000 adults in its third year of operations, i.e. more than 10% of the total number of adults with difficulties in written communications in this small country of only 1.5 million (Lind 1996: 72 f.). In India, the national literacy programme reached more than 73 million people in its first years of operation, with more than two-thirds of participants attaining the first skills level (National Literacy Mission 1999). This kind of social demand is also visible in Brazil (P 5)[2], where the authorities state that about 20% of the adult population need basic education, without counting the 25% school-age children who are declared "illiterate". Widespread demand for basic adult learning was and is an indisputable fact in the developing countries, just as it is now in the industrialised countries (UIE 1992; OECD and Statistics Canada 1995; Hautecœur 1997).

Policymakers are now turning their attention to adult learning, particularly in relation to vocational retraining and skills upgrading, unemployment and economic recovery in general, as well as the fight against poverty and for literacy. Participation in training programmes has become an integral part of many workers' lives in the post-industrial countries and in industrial zones in other regions such as Colombia, India and Venezuela (Ozaki et al. 1992; Psacharapoulos and Velez 1992: 583). New adult training policies have been adopted or at least proposed in Australia (P 7), Brazil (P 3 and 6), Canada (CS: 15 f.), the Czech Republic (P 2 and 8), Ecuador (P 2), Hungary (P 6), Italy (P 13), Lithuania (P 6), Slovenia (P 3, 4 and 6), South Africa (South Africa 1997), the United Kingdom (P 1-3) and the United States (CS: 182 f.). In Belgium, participation in work-related adult learning doubled from 1980 to 1986, although the budget allocation was temporarily halved over that period (Leroy 1990; Belgium, CS: 12-14). The current transition phase in Central and Eastern Europe has generated strong demand, again linked to current economic readjustments and the slump in employment. For example, in 1995, Slovenia published a white paper on vocational training emphasising the working population's needs (P 6). These historic changes have also generated learning demand that is related not so much to work as to changes in civil society and its relationship to the state (The Czech Republic, CS: 22-24; Hungary, CS: 70 f.).

Demand for adult learning is also being expressed strongly in relation to the

---

[2] Throughout this publication the reader will see these references: country CS or country P 1, P 2, etc. They refer to the country studies (CS) produced for each of the 24 countries studied and to the different policies (P1, P2, etc.) analysed in each of them (see Appendix II: Table 1). Some of these studies were published in a special issue of the *International Review of Education*, Vol. 42 (1996) Nos 1-3.

quest for quality of life, the revival of urban life, the strengthening of participation in community organisations and local community life, and the revitalisation of previously repressed cultures. Learning aspirations and the need for new competencies go well beyond work-related training and overlap with many other interests and skills.

Learning a second or third language is also growing rapidly around the world. Meeting this need currently accounts for about a third of the total work of adult general education centres in Germany (Nuissl 1994). The United Kingdom and Australia are posting growth in programmes teaching the official language, such as the "English for Speakers of Other Languages" programmes (ESOP), aimed at minorities and immigrants. The same trend can be seen in Asia, prompted by economic globalisation, in Hungary and the Czech Republic, due to the trend to replace Russian with English, and in the Philippines and Lithuania, due there to movements to revive languages. In 1993, Lithuania, where the native language was suppressed until recently, passed a law on language learning programmes, making citizenship contingent on mastery of the language. The language learning programmes receive substantial funding from the diaspora.

Second to vocational training, learning a second language is the sector where private education firms have moved the fastest to take advantage of the growing demand for continuing education. One Australian study (CS: 20) noted that from 1984 to 1994 the amount of space one large Australian city's "yellow pages" directory devoted to continuing vocational training and language learning had risen by 20 times and 7 times, respectively. The number of national and international private language-learning and computer training firms grew to such an extent that, in 1991, the governments of the new German Länder (CS: 23) had to lay down minimum standards for these establishments or at least clarify their status. Greece (P 1) followed suit in 1992, as did Ecuador and Hungary (CS: 67 f.).

Adult general and community education, previously threatened with being replaced entirely by work-related training, is now in great local and national demand in Australia (CS: 24 f.), Canada (CS: 7-9), the United Kingdom (P 5-8), and the United States (CS: 177-181). The situation is similar for adult literacy in the Philippines (P 7) and, more recently, in the Ivory Coast (P 3). An un-published OECD report on continuing education in Hungary describes a similar situation there too.

Rapid changes in social life have in turn prompted training activities within organisations. Millions of people in the voluntary sector, women's groups, environmental groups and co-operatives have joined together to strengthen their ability to take individual and collective action. In 1994, the Civicus network published a report on common trends in this "third sector" in different parts of the world (Darcy de Oliveira and Tandon 1994). A recent survey (EAEA 1995: 42 f.) estimates that one citizen in every seven engages in learning activities organised by voluntary groups in the European Community each year.

1.1.2. Official, though unequal, recognition of learning demand

Although social demand for adult learning has been rising rapidly and steadily for decades, national and international political authorities have only recently taken note of it. It was not until the early 1990s that demand for adult learning was incorporated into official discourse, and not until the end of the century that it became the subject of political debate and legislation.

In 1990, the Jomtien Conference on Education for All, organised jointly by UNESCO, the World Bank, the UNDP and Unicef, adopted a declaration stating that, "Basic education should be provided to all (...) adults." (Unicef 1990: art. 3, para. 1). The Conference emphasised that adult literacy programmes are crucial to meet the diverse needs of adults (Unicef 1990: art. 5). At a December 1993 summit on Education for All, these same partners echoed this point with the support of the heads of state of the nine most populous countries. They called for "an increase and improvement in literacy and education programmes for young people and adults" (UNESCO 1994). Since then, this theme has been taken up by governments in many countries, including in a Royal Appeal for adult literacy in Morocco (CS: 101), a statement on national policy in India (CS: 91), a 1993 declaration by the Party in Vietnam (P 1; CS: 5-8), and a national action plan in Namibia (P 1; CS: 15). All the adult basic education and literacy policies analysed in this study were indeed adopted following the 1990 Jomtien Declaration. "The Segou Perspectives" (Mali 1995), adopted in March 1995 by eleven countries in Western and Central Africa, gave adult literacy programmes a significant boost and marked a major turning point in the use of local languages in this field. Budget cutbacks, worsened by structural adjustment programmes, subsequently led several countries to again restrict basic education to young people. This setback was a central issue at the 1995 Forum, which made a mid-decade review of the implementation of the Jomtien action plan (UNESCO 1995).

It was also in the 1990s that this subject really began to be discussed in the industrialised countries, with a proliferation of national and international reports and conferences on adult learning and the continuing development of human resources (OECD 1996). The European Community has held six successive conferences on adult education since 1994 (Athens in June 1994, Dresden in November 1994, Madrid in November 1995, Florence in May 1996, Manchester in May

1998, Turku in September 1999). They emphasised the important role of adult learning for human resources development and reiterated "the need to give all adults the opportunity to improve their skills throughout life". In 1993, the Commission of the European Communities published a white paper along the same lines: *Growth, Competitiveness, Employment – The Challenges and Ways Forward into the 21*[st] *Century* (European Commission 1994b). The paper stated that growth and competitiveness are so important that education, particularly work-related adult learning, should be deemed a "catalyst for changing society". The same principle featured in a second white paper (European Commission 1996).

By the end of the century, politicians and business leaders alike had integrated the "learning solution" into their analyses of the crisis in work. It is now standard for any discussion of economic globalisation and the introduction of new technologies to mention that the productivity gains needed require a continuing increase in skills levels. In the United Kingdom, this was the subject of a series of reports by the Manpower Services Commission: *A New Training Initiative. A Programme for Action* (P 1), *Education and Training for the 21*[st] *Century* (P 2) *and Employment for the 1990s* (P 3). In this last statement, particular emphasis is given to the role of employers in further education and to how refusal to invest can hold back economic growth. This same plea can be found in a more nationalistic version in Australia (Keating 1994), where the Prime Minister of the Commonwealth stated that, to compete and prosper, his country needed to harness all its resources and most importantly the talent and energy of the Australian people.

In the United States, *A Nation at Risk* and *Work Force 2000*, published in 1983 and 1987 (Hudson Institute 1988), established a link between the development of human resources and international competition. In *The Work of Nations*, Robert Reich, the former US Secretary of Labor, stated his belief that the main strengths of his country on the eve of the 21st century were the abilities and skills of its people, and that continuing to develop this strategic resource must become a top priority (Reich 1991). The Canadian reports *S'adapter pour gagner* (Canada 1989) and *Les chemins de la compétence* (Canada 1992a) as well as the statement from Quebec *Partenaires pour un Québec compétent and compétitif* (Quebec 1991) also emphasised that it would be impossible to meet the challenge of the North American Free Trade Agreement without developing continuing education, adopting an active policy towards the labour market and reorganising unemployment insurance for this purpose. 1997 and 1998 saw even more statements on adult learning policy in the industrialised countries: *A Nation Learning* in the United States (Commission for a Nation of Lifelong Learners 1997), *The Learning Age* in the United Kingdom (1998), *The Joy of*

Learning in Finland (1998), *New Competence* in Norway (1998), and *Vers une politique de formation continue* in Quebec (1998).

Likewise, the 1991 medium-term development plan for the Philippines (P 7) set as a key objective "improving the population's skills to be able to compete globally by the end of the century". A similar argument is found in the reasoning of the National Literacy Mission in India. In 1997, the new government of South Africa adopted a detailed 300-page statement (South Africa 1997) on adult learning, as did Morocco in that same year (Morocco 1997). In response to dominant trends in global economic centres, proposals were made in Latin America and Asia to restructure the so-called peripheral economies to prioritise knowledge-intensive production with a higher technological content so as to improve the terms of international trade.

Although these policy statements on demand for adult learning and its public and private management tend to focus on economic factors, some of them – and some governments – recognise other learning aspirations, including second-chance education, personal development projects, civic education, community education, general and formal adult education, popular education, and language learning. The titles of two Australian reports, *Come in Cinderella: The Emergence of Adult and Community Education* (Australia 1991) and *Beyond Cinderella. Toward a Learning Society* (Australia 1997), are indicative of the difficulty of bringing demand for non-work-related learning out of the shadows.

Recognition of the demand for adult learning is sparking intense debate over lifelong learning, i.e. at the OECD, in its action plan launched in January 1996 (OECD 1996), and in the European Union, where the Commission proclaimed 1996 "The European Year of Lifelong Learning". In 1995, and again in 1996 and 1997, UNESCO made lifelong education one of its central concerns (UNESCO 1995 and 1997). Moreover, it placed lifelong learning in a context that takes into account the vast range of individual aspirations and economic and socio-cultural necessities in the different parts of the world. The Organisation, which has reoriented its actions along these lines, published a report by its International Commission on Education for the 21st Century (UNESCO 1996) and held the International Conference on Adult Education in 1997.

Despite this progress, the amplitude of social demand is still underestimated – only the visible, explicit part of demand is considered. This excludes those who do not take part in the programmes offered, but are no less likely to want to improve their capabilities, albeit probably in a different way (Sirvent 1994; Bélanger and Tuijnman 1997). Based on the "Declaration of the Right to Learn" adopted by the Fourth International Conference on Adult Education (UNESCO 1985) and more recently on the "Hamburg Declaration on Adult Learning"

(UNESCO 1997), several organisations have pointed to unequal trends in existing programmes and expressed the demands of excluded populations at the global level (Darcy de Oliveira and Tandon 1994), in particular in Africa (Minedaf
1998), Asia (Unicef 1990; UNESCO-APPEAL 1997), Latin America (Ribero
1993; Sirvent 1999), Germany (Nuissl 1994), England and Wales (Sargant 1991
and 1997), Australia (Australia 1995), Canada (ICEA 1982; Doray and ICEA
1995), Sweden (Rubenson 1989) and Switzerland (FSEA1998).

At the above-mentioned 1997 UNESCO conference, some 1,500 delegates from
more than 140 countries officially and unanimously recognised this rise in adult
learning aspirations and the need to invest in this field to ensure that all can participate actively in the development of their communities. The UNDP report on
human development published in 1993 is explicit about the relationship between
development, raising adults' basic educational level and improving work-related
qualifications (UNDP 1993). The World Bank has already proposed promoting
work-related continuing education – "retraining of the labour force" – for young
adult school-leavers, groups with low levels of formal initial education and all
working-age adults (World Bank 1990). Furthermore, every United Nations
World Summit held this decade has had action plans on their respective agendas
calling for the active, informed participation of adults. They have also called for
different forms of basic education programmes to be set up in liaison with local
initiatives, support for projects drawing on citizens' creativity and measures to
widen access to further education. These summits include the Rio
Environmental Summit (1992), the Cairo Population Conference (1994), the
Copenhagen Summit on Social Development (1995), the Peking World
Conference on Women (1995) and the Habitat Conference held in Istanbul in
1996 (see Odora Hoppers 1996). "Adult education thus becomes more than a
right; it is a key to the twenty-first century" (Hamburg Declaration, art. 2, in:
UNESCO 1997).

1.1.3. The dynamic factors behind the rise and recognition of this general demand

This boom in the learning demand of the adult population is a response to global
socio-cultural forces. It is being fuelled by socio-economic contradictions at
work in both the North and South. Slowly but surely, social changes have built
up in the world of work, community life and private life as well as in the fields
of education and information to produce an undeniable transformation in the
learning demand of adult populations.

Everywhere today, competition and the quest for greater productivity in what are
now continental-sized economic zones have speeded up the rate of change in

modes and sites of production and stepped up the use of new technologies. This has prompted adults to demand opportunities for continuing education. The inter-generational cycle for renewing skills is now too long, compelling economic actors to turn to adult learning to raise professional and general cultural levels in the short term. It would take 20 to 30 years to significantly raise levels solely via the basic initial education of young people. Hence the increased pressure to improve the retraining and skills upgrading of the workforce and the unemployed, including foreign language learning. It would be senseless to wait for a new generation, since over 80% of the next decade's working population have already left school (Ozaki et al. 1992).

North and South, East and West, official discourses are converging around urgent demands to train the workforce, the use of education to curb unemployment, a transition to active labour-market policies, support for the independent managerial capabilities of farmers, and a demand to train thousands of peasants who are migrating to urban centres and seeking a place in the formal and informal economies.

Naturally, there are many contradictions on the road from political declarations to concrete measures, due to the employment crisis and the segmentation of labour markets, domestic and international budget restrictions, and continuing inequality in access to adult learning programmes. These policies, and the criticisms and grievances they raise, have also helped to stimulate work-related demand for learning.

The transformation and crisis of work is not the only factor increasing participation in adult learning. This is clear from the above-mentioned analysis of the 1996 and 1997 United Nations World Summit recommendations. Paradoxically, the rise in the demand for adult learning is related as much to the declining importance of work in today's society as to concerns in the world of work itself. The slow, steady reduction in the paid working week and longer life expectancy are creating new windows for learning at any age, during and after "active" life. We are looking at more than just a shorter paid working week compared with leisure time. A change of direction is also taking place. Work-related expectations are still an important gauge by which people define themselves in society (De Bandt, Dejours and Dubar 1995), but they are no longer the only one. Work is losing its predominant place as the social time that structures cultural and educational practices and social life generally. In the new "non-working time" (Gorz 1988; Sue 1994), collective action that is relatively independent of the world of work is creating new expectations, including demand for learning – in women's movements, environmental groups, associations to revitalise regional cultures, etc.

A third factor behind the sharpening increase in the demand for adult learning is the cumulative effect of the quiet but steady rise in the adult population's basic level of education. The higher a population's level of basic education and skills, the higher the rate of participation in adult learning. This trend can be seen from adult participation surveys in many developed countries (Cross 1981; Tuijnman 1991; Courtney 1992; OECD and Statistics Canada 1995; Bélanger and Valdivielso 1997) and developing countries (Psacharapoulos and Velez 1992; Sirvent 1994). Adult learning will continue to expand along with the general rise in the adult population's educational level. What is at work here are mutually reinforcing tendencies within models specific to the various cultures. The steady generalisation of initial education is generating an increase in participation in further education, which in turn is being driven by the spread of literate environments at the workplace and in local communities.

The cumulative nature of educational and cultural practices is however a double-edged sword: as advantages accumulate, a vicious cycle of exclusions and failures also sets in. The growth in adult participation in education, which is rooted partly in initial formal education, tends to have a structurally unequal impact. While learning aspirations and the need for higher skills levels prompt a wide range of responses, these develop unequally. There is a dynamic tension throughout the relationship between social demand and effective response. Indeed, this sets the underlying framework for this book.

1.2. The scope and range of responses

In every region of the world, the range of lifelong learning opportunities is increasing, albeit unevenly. There is also a proliferation of learning agencies, well beyond the acknowledged bounds of adult learning. Each analysis of the twenty-four countries covered by our international study pointed to the same trends: an explosion and fragmentation of learning activities, an increase in the number of providers, the diversification of financial sources, and an expansion of the decision-making environment where policies and strategies are defined and implemented. We will attempt to pull together these centrifugal tendencies and reconstruct the entire adult learning scene where the above-mentioned dynamics are played out.

1.2.1. The expansion and fragmentation of activities and players

The number of participants in work-related learning is increasing everywhere: in-house training, civil service and military training, agricultural extension programmes, technical training of forestry workers, admission of adults to state vocational and technical education institutions, training in non-governmental centres, such as India's polyvalent Shramik Vidyapeeths centres and the Ivory Coast's development centres, and of course training by private education firms. Sharp growth can also be seen in the many forms of distance learning, ranging from large networks to the simple but effective correspondence courses in farming conducted by branches of the African Institute for Economic and Social Development (INADES).

The field of "general" adult learning differs greatly from one country to the next. German folk high schools and social education in Japan are expanding; each year, over seven and ten million adults take part in the two countries, respectively (Nuissl 1994; Japan P 2). The same holds true for the Flemish region in Belgium (P 1). In some industrialised countries, an extensive network of state general adult learning centres has been accustomed to receiving significant public funding. Now it is the subject of debate in Australia (P 2 and 3) and would be in sharp decline in Canada (Canada 1992b) and the United Kingdom (P 5-8) were it not for some local authorities and non-governmental organisations stepping in to pick up the pieces and even become partners. In the developing countries (Darcy de Oliveira and Tandon 1994), non-governmental organisations have also picked up where governments left off in informal adult education. However, the governments of Indonesia, Thailand and Vietnam have maintained their programmes and increasingly structured them to provide flexible non-formal education more suited to local needs.

Literacy programmes and formal adult education are growing rapidly. In addition to a renewed mobilisation for adult literacy programmes, a topic covered in Chapter 10, opportunities for adults to continue post-primary and post-secondary education have generally opened up. Everywhere one looks, adults are flooding into academic and vocational secondary and post-secondary educational institutions, physical and virtual, as well as into open universities, distance-learning agencies and assisted self-learning programmes (Knox 1993; Tait 1996). Open education systems are being set up or planned in all the countries studied, both large and small. In India, more than 11% of the registered student population is enrolled in distance-learning institutions, including the Indira Gandhi National Open University, founded in 1987. Open schools were also created in India in 1989 to provide secondary-level adult education and vocational training. Also, there are the spectacular figures concerning the development of this sector in China (Dong 1996). In Namibia, the recently created Namibian College of Open Learning will handle post-literacy education, offering advanced programmes in English and helping in the further training of teachers.

In Japan in 1993, distance-learning and university extension services enrolled about 800,000 adults (CS: 12 f.). Economic pressure on Japanese universities and colleges to find replacements for their declining student populations (CS: 11) has prompted them to adapt their institutions to meet adult demand, a trend that is being reinforced by the recent shift by business towards out-of-house staff training (Okamoto 1994: 43). There is also a general sharp rise in the number of adults enrolled in part-time post-secondary educational programmes. In Quebec, colleges offering general and vocational education saw a 350% increase in their student population from 1980 to 1991 (ICEA 1994); nearly 55% of the students are over 25 years old, and 75% of those in this age group are enrolled part-time (Canada 1992b: 38).

Adult learning has not only been transformed within its conventional fields of operation, but is also tending to spread beyond its normal boundaries to become an integral part of sectorial policies. Whether in agriculture, health care, the environment, population policy or the fight against racism, almost all action plans today include a significant information-education-counselling (IEC) component.[3] In Morocco, for example, family planning policy is now based primarily on women's education programmes, often in liaison with local centres, which also have benefited from this joint effort (CS: 105 f.). The "IEC" approach has now been adopted as policy by other Moroccan ministries in the fields of health care and hygiene, environmental protection, the promotion of education for girls, etc. In Brazil (P1), the growing number of job-related accidents, now affecting more than 10% of urban workers, have led the government and the social partners to organise special training for members of local works committees. They are subsequently encouraged to offer all the personnel short sessions to promote discussion and awareness. The same trend can be seen in Italy, where a new law requires the formation of joint health and safety committees, whose members must enrol in training sessions lasting 50 to 150 hours. In Switzerland, a 1994 agricultural law (P 7) extended the concept of continuing vocational training and provided for the establishment of short courses in ecology for farmers and rural residents. Similar legislation has been adopted in Slovenia (P 1). Having recognised that the cost to clean up the environment after a disaster or even to ensure protection solely through enforcement measures is prohibitive, recent environmental protection legislation tends to flow along these active preventive lines.

Australia provides a very good example of this trend, with indirect implications for adult learning. A 1987 law on the use of tobacco, called the "Victoria Tobacco Act" (P 1), created a foundation to promote better health and stipulated that the revenue from cigarette taxes was to be used for health-care promotion and education. It is also under the banner of "health-care promotion" that the World Health Organisation has been shifting its policy to prioritise continuing

---

[3] Development agencies now use the abbreviation "IEC" to stand for these new education and counselling strategies.

education and counselling strategies and the "IEC" approach in general. These programmes appear under a variety of titles: the development and dissemination of knowledge, public communications, the promotion of daily hygiene, community involvement, safety awareness, consciousness-raising, etc.

Of the 122 adult education policy statements considered in this book, 40 could be considered "indirect policies". These statements rarely use the term "adult education" or "adult learning", but each of them contains proposals for new adult learning methods and opportunities. They are thus carrying out adult learning with little fanfare or even awareness, but often quite effectively, even though a sense of urgency in the approach to training occasionally tends to overshadow the longer-term educational objectives and a sustainable grounding in new practices. Nonetheless, these policies are injecting new resources and significant investments into the expanded field of adult learning. The new economics of adult learning has grown beyond the prevailing conception of adult education.

1.2.2. National educational scenes

Adult learning is thus changing rapidly and integrating new components that are often developing relatively independently. To better understand the general trend and the particular ways in which it is changing in different countries and regions, we will, at the risk of over-simplification, briefly outline developments in two different countries and one region: the Ivory Coast, the United Kingdom and four countries in Central and Eastern Europe.

The Ivory Coast
Adult learning in the Ivory Coast is no longer concerned primarily with literacy. In 1960, the main issues were mass education, popular education, adult courses and literacy centres. By 1994, they were further work-related training, adult education and literacy, continuing education and re-training of the labour force.

Adult learning in the Ivory Coast is now very diversified. Since 1992, the long-dormant adult literacy issue slowly has been becoming a national concern again. Whereas in Namibia the government has concentrated on the national literacy programme, leaving any action in other sectors up to civil society, with minimal state support, the Ivory Coast government has tended instead to take charge of work-related training and leave literacy up to the non-governmental organisations. In the modern sector (P 4), there is even a national regulatory budget requiring that companies invest 1.2% of total payroll in work-related adult learning. The 1991 law on Development Funds for Vocational Training (CS: 29) extends this measure to include all business sectors as well as employees experiencing difficulty. However, it has only been partially applied, and, following the crisis, the textile industry was even excluded. Private African and European firms as well as educational firms are also active in the modern sector.

The situation is different for the informal economy, but recently the Economic Commission for Africa launched a project for technical training and reorganisation, which was split into several training programmes with an accent on women and young people. This initiative was co-financed by the World Bank, through its "Project to Support the Training of the Workforce" (P 4). Work-related adult learning in the countryside has been increasingly diversified by the National Agency to Support Rural Development (ANADER), a new co-ordinating structure created in 1992. It receives aid from the UNDP, the World Bank, the International Fund for Agricultural Development (IFAD) and French co-operative funds. These education programmes are aimed at farmers, rural workers and fishery and forestry workers. The Centres for Rural Workers were also created to help the latter. Unfortunately, recession has necessitated budget cuts, while learning demand is still rising and the number of poorly educated young unemployed now tops 800,000.

The Ministry for the Family and Women's Affairs has already created 70 women's education and training institutes (IFEF) with more than 300 instructors. These provide short-term and long-term training programmes, while the Ministry of Higher Education has created the University Centre for Continuing Education, which is active in both industry and agriculture.

Up to 1980, the dominant policy in health care was remedial and prophylactic, limiting prevention to vaccination campaigns and the administration of technical measures for health protection. More recently, efforts have been made to involve the population in committees, train organisers in villages and carry out IEC-type activities. The National Health Education Service (SNES), drawing on epidemiological research by the Ministry, has also set up various nutritional education programmes and environmental sanitation training and organisation programmes. Henceforth, educational programmes are being integrated in vaccination programmes, and health education projects are being added to village water supply programmes. This is a decisive change.

Nonetheless, the economic crisis and subsequent structural adjustments that led the government to charge for all health-care services risk alienating the population just when informed participation is becoming credible and local communities are beginning to receive the public support needed to increase their capacity to assume new responsibilities.

The non-governmental organisations, including denominational groups, are playing an increasingly important role in the countryside, in urban local communities and in the informal economy. They are also attempting to make up for the sluggishness of government services in adult literacy.

Overall, the learning demand of the Ivory Coast adult population is growing and becoming more diversified. It is being met to some degree by hundreds of responses arising in an organised and disorganised fashion in industry, the countryside, health care and on behalf of women and unemployed young people. This is coming about through the "rediscovery" of the 70% of the rural population who have had no access to formal initial education and by dealing seriously with the informal economy, which has become the main means of survival. There is, however, still little official recognition of these educational responses, and they are developing in relative isolation. Moreover, dealing with the recession through the obsolete framework of passive structural adjustment programme policies continues to hinder treating adult learning as an investment and a necessary strategy for economic recovery, rather than as a consumption expense. We are using the term "obsolete framework" and the expression "continues to hinder" because the reader will undoubtedly have noticed a contradiction with portent for the future in the preceding two paragraphs. On the ground, the World Bank has begun to put aside its official reluctance concerning literacy and adult learning and become involved. It is active in the two recent big initiatives in continuing education in the Ivory Coast, that is, the "Fund To Train the Workforce" and the "National Agency to Support Rural Development", whose goals include adult learning, raising awareness, support and disseminating information. The fact that these two projects did not grow out of the educational sector and are not flying the banner of adult education or literacy simply means that the World Bank is starting to recognise the need to raise the level of adult skills in its own way, at least as concerns the economy. It is thus providing adult learning activities without being aware of it or at least without proclaiming it officially.

United Kingdom
Despite the decline in adult public education services over the last two decades, both adult community education and workforce training have been the subject of policy debates and statements in the United Kingdom since 1981. These two fields have been developing in isolation from one another, with the first growing much more rapidly than the second.

The dynamism of the British adult learning scene in the first two post-Second World War decades is well known. It featured extra-mural university and residence centre activities in the form of specific long-term and short-term programmes; the organisational and promotional role of the Workers' Educational Association (WEA) in liaison with the trade union movement; local adult education centres supported by the local authorities and monitored by Her Majesty's Inspectors for the quality of instruction; company training programmes, often organised according to economic sector; liberal education for young adults during the initial years of their careers; and the involvement of museums and libraries in the project for the democratisation of education. This flexible network of institutions and education programmes served as a reference framework for many countries.

In the 1980s, the wave of Thatcherite counter-reforms laid waste to a large part of this landscape. Some observers, obsessed by the loss of this important historical legacy, turned their gaze backwards and, seeing only what remained, feared the end of adult learning. The real situation was more complex and certainly more dynamic.

Even as the cutbacks were strangling institutionalised adult learning, two new trends emerged independently of each other. First, there was a rise in the participation of adults in general and liberal education in the Open University framework – which enrolled more than 150,000 students in 1994, 70% of whom studied while still on the job (Tait 1996) – and in the equally new network of open colleges. They also attended traditional colleges, institutes and universities that had finally decided to accept adults and provide special admissions and education schemes, including recognition of experiential learning. This is not to forget the aforementioned initiative of local authorities to offset the national cutbacks in community adult education.

Second, following the announcement of *A New Training Initiative* in 1981 and the *Towards an Adult Training Strategy* in 1983, a considerable change took place in work-related training. In-company training took off and a large apprenticeship programme for young adult school-leavers was created, which unfortunately tended to be somewhat limited to catching up and was based on a negative skills-deficit model. A network of regional and local continuing education councils, the Training and Enterprise Councils (TEC), was set up to handle financing and act as an interface between work-related training demands and responses.

British adult education and training, which now tends to be called "adult learning" to refocus attention on the learner and the act of learning, is on the rise once again, but in a different way. It is once again becoming extra-mural, but this time in the very different sense of breaking out of the institutional and semantic bounds of post-war adult education. The work-related training policies of the then Department of Education – 1982 (P 1) and two in 1988 (P 2 and 3) – were developed separately from adult education policies set by the former Department for Education and Science, such as the 1992 "Further and Higher Education Law", distance-learning initiatives, and the big corporations' training programmes. It was not until 1998 that an overall policy statement was issued. This was the year that the new Department for Education and Employment launched a nation-wide debate on its proposal, *The Learning Age* (United Kingdom 1998).

Of course, private-sector employers have hitherto tended to dominate work-related adult learning and the boards of the TECs.[4] It is also true that significant components of a pluralistic adult educational system were lost in the neo-conservative wave. Furthermore, the admission of adults to higher education as provided by the law of 1992 was so successful that a decision in 1994 tried to dampen enthusiasm for the Colleges of Further Education (CS: 11). Not surprisingly, the local authorities lost any control over the further education colleges and are now struggling to properly finance community adult learning (P 5-8). A special public fund for non-governmental organisations has been set up under the management of the National Institute for Adult and Continuing Education (NIACE). Lastly, inequalities persist. A careful analysis of surveys (Sargant 1991; OECD and Statistics Canada 1995; unpublished 1999 data of NIACE) shows that, while the overall level of participation in adult learning is rising, the involvement of less educated groups is falling.

However, the die is not yet cast. Driven by these sometimes contradictory developments, adult learning in the United Kingdom has become a weighty affair and a focus of political debate. Key social forces have become involved, not only the customary employer and employee representatives, but also women's groups and minority groups (Westwood 1991) as well as senior citizen movements. The annual mobilisation campaign by NIACE, "Adult Learning Week", has become a week-long media event covering more than 10,000 local initiatives to support adult rights to learn, ending with a special caucus in Westminster attended by all the political parties.

Adult learning in the United Kingdom has come in from the cold, driven essentially by strong social demand that has sought to break through conventional restrictions and find new responses, but also by the clamour of business for dynamic skills promotion policies. Adult learning has become a contradictory social reality. A dynamic process has again taken off. Conflicts over unequal training opportunities and the refusal to recognise differences in learning aspirations and cultural endeavours have come out into the open and are being identified. Before adult learning policies crystallise social relations, they are processes, involving dynamic social relations. Sally Westwood, referring to the British situation that we have just described, quite correctly employs the term "politics

---

[4] British law requires that private-sector employers occupy a majority of TEC board seats, with the rest held by representatives of the trades unions, local government and voluntary associations.

in formation" (Westwood 1991: 49). In December 1999, the Westminster Parliament was debating a new global adult learning policy based on the white paper *The Learning Age*.

Central and Eastern Europe
Prior to the 1989 upheavals, the Central and Eastern Europe countries all had adult education systems. These institutions are now being reformed and new programmes launched. In Lithuania and Slovenia, former adult education institutions closely linked to the old regimes have been losing their students. In Hungary and the Czech Republic, the former organisations for the popularisation of science and the cultural centres have been rejuvenated. In Hungary today, for example, they reach about a million people. The cobwebs have also been dusted off the folk high schools, and old adult education legislation has been updated.

Adult learning activities are springing up all over this swiftly changing region, without concern for whether the plethora of computer and language courses should be categorised as continuing work-related learning or socio-cultural education. A proliferation of profit-making organisations and voluntary associations has forced the various governments to adopt emergency legislation governing this sector (Czech Republic, CS: 12 f.). Financial support has been found for trade union projects and civic education projects, and measures have been adopted to regulate new commercial training firms and the activity of private foreign firms.

Here too, the sector covering programmes for the unemployed and work-related learning has been the most dynamic. In the last three years, six work-related learning centres have been created in Hungary, training over 60,000 people each year. More than 20 have been founded in Lithuania.

In this region too, the new ministries' sectorial policies are increasingly aimed at expanding citizens' capacity for action. Environmental protection, previously a government domain, is now shared. In Slovenia, the Ministry of Agriculture has earmarked funds for training small forestry landowners in this field (P 1). The ministries of health in Eastern Europe have also taken health protection measures, including in the Czech Republic (P 4 and 5), Hungary (P 5) and Slovenia (P 2). Having recognised that predominantly remedial health-care policies are problematic in the long-term, national health plans now call for setting up educational and counselling programmes.

1.2.3. The diversification of financial sources and the expansion of the decision-making environment

The expanded world of adult learning, which has so often broken through its conventional boundaries in various directions and under various names, now includes more and more people working in different networks developing in relative isolation from one another. Most of these people do not recognise each other and do not even use the same terms for what they do in common. Within this invisible, still inchoate body, it is difficult to recognise learning experiences acquired elsewhere. Given the explosive, fragmented growth in the field, both organisationally and semantically, it is hardly surprising that its financing has become diversified and its decision-making environment dispersed.

Countries still need to properly study how adults finance their continuing education and how educational agents have managed to diversify their sources of income. Our goal here is not to analyse and reconstruct the fragmented mechanisms for funding adult learning, but simply to show some of the ways in which it has grown and in which the national situations have become more complex and varied. We have only just begun to make comparative analyses of how adults finance their education in some industrialised countries (Bélanger and Tuijnman 1997; Bélanger and Bochynek 1999). In Canada and the United States, employers are the main source of financing, whereas most participants in Switzerland finance themselves. The now considerable extent of participants' own contributions could mask the significance of public investment in this field.

In all the industrialised countries, including in East European countries like Slovenia (P 4 and 6), the transition to active labour-market policies has brought about a considerable increase in state continuing education budgets in recent years. In Hungary, the Fund for Jobs, financed by contributions from employers and employees, is the main source of financing for adult work-related training. It rose from US$ 25 million in 1989 to US$ 41 million in 1993 (P 6). Just as an initial change in Swiss unemployment law in 1982 gave the unemployed a break from job-hunting to take training, the work-related adult learning offensive launched in 1989 (*Weiterbildungsoffensive*) freed up US$ 135 million for continuing work-related training and US$ 112 million to help universities open their doors to adults (CS: 172) over the following five years. Starting in 1989, Canada budgeted 15% of its unemployment insurance funds for "productive" purposes and increased its workforce training budget by 50%, allocating more than US$ 2 billion in 1994/95 (CS: 11). In the United States (CS: 176), the federal government funds work-related adult learning via more than 154 different programmes.

In 1992, the German federal and Länder ministries budgeted US$ 18 billion for adult learning, 75% of which came from the federal labour office, while business spent US$ 25 billion (Nuissl 1994: 22). In Germany as a whole, total public and private investment rose from US$ 18 billion in 1987 to US$ 48 billion in 1992. Spending by business rose fourfold (ibid.: 24). Also in 1992, the government budget for adult learning in the Flemish part of Belgium (CS: 6 f.) stood at US$ 52 million for socio-cultural education, 102 million for general education and 160 million for vocational training.

There is still relatively little data about the economics of adult education in the developing countries. An overview of activities reveals two important features. First, investment in the broad field of adult learning is on the rise. Note, for example, the huge effort made by a small country like Namibia in deciding (P1) to devote 2% of its national education budget to adult literacy programmes, an unusually high percentage compared with other countries, or the decision by a large country like India (P2) to allocate more than 6% of its federal education budget to adult literacy. Second, given the all-too-familiar impact of recession and the structural adjustment programmes (Reimers and Tiburcio 1993), the education programmes currently available to adults in any given country cannot be considered to reflect the actual demand, aspirations and need for an increase in skills. Hiding the literacy issue in the Ivory Coast (P 3) obviously did not make 70% of the rural population disappear who continue to be illiterate. The low demand for informal basic education in the Philippines is less indicative of a lack of learning aspirations than of the problems people have in expressing their genuine demand in academic formal terms that will be heard and acknowledged.

Despite continuing inequality in the way it has developed, adult learning has become an important sector, financed by adults themselves, ministries of education and labour, transnational funds and agencies, and business. In addition to the two above-mentioned ministries, other ministries becoming involved include ministries for women and the family, agriculture, social welfare, culture, health, environment, defence, transport, industry and trade, justice, etc.

1.3. Conclusion: The key social role of redefined adult learning

Adult learning everywhere is developing and reorganising in various ways.

Before examining adult learning policies, and in order to understand their significance, an analysis of adult learning must first reconsider and define its object, which, because of institutional fragmentation, is still misconstrued. Semantic exclusions must be corrected, the great variety of organised forms of lifelong learning need to be reviewed, and the different expressions of individuals' demand for greater capacity for action need to be compared with the generally unequal response.

However silent the demand for adult learning was until 1990, however under-represented it has been in official discourse, and however unequally distributed the resources to meet it may be between countries and social groups, it is undeniably growing in diversity and scale everywhere, although this is expressed differently in different contexts. Globally rising trends, despite varying rates, will continue to spur the upturn in adult learning and accelerate discussion and public debate about how to "negotiate" its development.

It is precisely because adult learning has become strategically important at work, in the community and in individuals' personal lives that it has become the subject of increasingly broad negotiations and diverse policies. It is precisely because the "society projects" that are the subject of confrontation between social actors are also becoming "learning society projects" that the debate over adult learning has intensified and come to the fore.

Redefined, adult learning is emerging as a central issue.

Chapter 2
The Process of Developing and Implementing Adult Learning Policies

The content of a policy cannot be isolated from the process of developing and implementing it. Today's adult learning policies are becoming increasingly complex due to the many different parties involved in policy-making and the wide range of problems they face.

2.1. Adult learning policies as processes

In his commentary on *The Prince*, Machiavelli's famous treatise on political science in 1532, Antonio Gramsci observed that, "in order to represent the process whereby a given collective will, directed towards a given political purpose, is formed, Machiavelli did not have recourse to long-winded arguments, or pedantic classifications of principles and criteria for a method of action. Instead, he represented this process in terms of the qualities, characteristics, duties and requirements of a concrete individual" (Gramsci 1986: 125), that is, a real individual or collective actor representing "a collective will (...) that is beginning to take concrete form" (Gramsci 1986: 129). Likewise, our decision to take account of the policy-making process is not based on purely methodological or descriptive concerns, but intends to further an understanding of the role that the collective subject of our epoch, the "New Prince", is playing or could play in adult learning policies.

The process of forging a "specific collective will" is at the heart of any policy-making, including adult learning. In this particular area, two elements in addition to the inherent distinctions and relations between process and product point to the need to identify adult learning policy with the process of forging a specific collective will. These two historic elements will inevitably influence our approach.

The first is the potential for the participating actors to change the conditions involved in setting the policy process in motion. Phillis Collins' study of policy-making trends in adult learning in the United States observed that, "when social demand (...) coincides with a historic time wherby events allow ideological space to be made, social demand explodes from many sectors besides the market-driven private sector" (CS: 182). The first element thus consists in the formation of subjective conditions to enable real historical subjects active in different sectors of social life to form a collective actor capable of expressing a general interest and intervening in political life. This obviously does not mean passively waiting for these conditions to come together, as if waiting for a comet to pass. The parties seek both to alter the policy-making process and promote the expression of new social demand. Efforts to create such subjective conditions always feature in educational activities and interventions, however microscopic. Developing a new adult learning policy thus concerns society as a whole.

Secondly, the involvement of a multitude of subjects and parties in adult learning policy-making and implementation is not a wish or a precept. It is an observation, the result of empirical observation. Consider the aforementioned contradiction between the rising social demand for adult learning and the often-observed inability of governments to serve as a benchmark and a catalyst in meeting individual and collective learning aspirations and needs. This contradiction is sharpening due to the steep rise in demand from the adult population and the simultaneous adoption of policies and strategies designed to curtail the state role through structural adjustment programmes in many Third World countries and, more generally, through the reduction and even dismantling of the welfare state itself. To maintain an acceptable level of learning provision, the new policies and strategies consequently have to rely on directly bringing in non-governmental organisations and agencies of civil society as replacements. It thus becomes increasingly inevitable that new subjects will take part in defining policies in accordance with their role.

Adopting a policy approach that treats the process of education and policy implementation as integral components has theoretical and practical consequences:
a. It helps separate questions of policy and law from the domain of the formal and absolute and restores their dimension as provisional historical products of the action of concrete subjects;
b. It prompts a view of the policy-formation process as a learning act itself, and, consequently, to the discovery of its dynamics and the observation of how subjects and social agencies consciously intervene in this respect;
c. It takes into account the type of role played by the historical subjects, especially by those with new social learning demands who are at the heart of the dynamics driving new policy-making.

From this perspective, the criterion for evaluating policy cannot be limited to analysing the purpose and type of measures adopted based on formal external, ethical or pedagogical standards. The significance of policies must first be sought in the process of the development and formation of collective actors who have expressed new learning demands and aspirations, and in the extent to which these actors are centralised, organised and disciplined (Gramsci 1986: 152).

From the dual perspective of aspirations for equal opportunity and of socio-economic necessity we can thus hypothesise different levels and patterns of participation by social actors in the process of making adult learning policy:

a. The imposition of an educational project by a socially dominant group and the consequent resistance to and rejection of these adult learning policies by other social groups;

b. The development of forms of elementary learning solidarity among adults based on the identification and defence of the learning needs and aspirations of the group concerned (social group, economic sector, etc.) and the promotion of autonomous organisation in civil society so as to reveal and respond to the concrete, specific interests of the respective milieu;

c. The demand by an organised social subject for conditions of access to different forms of adult learning that are equal to those of dominant, privileged groups;

d. The initiation of the process of developing and transforming adult learning policies by an organised social subject who attempts and, at times, is able to steer policy development in accordance with the aspirations and interests of the entire adult population, thus helping to transform the learning provision accorded to everyone.

In this typology, development can be measured by the extent to which historical subjects or actors are able to render learning policy transparent. Development is commensurate with liberation from policies that conceal real alternatives, negate adult learning demands and segment the responses to them.

2.2. The historical dimension and context of policy-making and implementation

A political analysis of the development of adult learning in contemporary society cannot be made using interpretative models that could foster the illusion of being at the cutting edge of continual progress among inhabitants anywhere in the North or South. Adult learning policies are rather a product of a social dynamic at a given moment in a precise historical context, which reflects and reinforces the state of social relations in a given society. The past, present and future jostle and vie in ever-new situations, not necessarily more advanced than the previous one.

Our policy analysis is not simply concerned with the development of adult learning organisations, changes in laws or government measures, or their capacity to promote economic growth. Otherwise, we might wind up trying to reconstruct a political process whose models and conclusions had been defined in advance. Such an approach would be justified only if we were seeking to convince the world of the superiority of models based, for example, on study circles and folk high schools or on the free market, for the purpose of exporting them.

Systems, laws, government measures and so on are just some of the structural elements of a process, the significance of which resides in the balance of power between the various collective actors who attempt to guide and govern the learning processes in a given society. The historical development of adult learning in different countries cannot be equated with or reduced to the history of the methods and technologies used to carry the policies out (paid educational leave, the opening of universities, folk high schools, continuing learning, self-aided learning, the education continuum, the recognition of experiential learning, etc.), economic history (colonialism, wars, globalisation, etc.) or scientific history (inventing the aeroplane, new sources of energy, television, computer technology, telematics, etc.). Adult learning policies obviously respond to changes in modes of production and in market organisation; they are applied using specific measures and technologies. Nonetheless, to grasp their social significance, one must go beyond indicators such as the number of hours taught, the number of participants, the different fields studied and the financial arrangements involved. The specific nature of policies demands first and foremost an analysis of policies in relation to the collective actors who support them and an assessment of their ability to express and represent the group's learning interests. This process is independent of the material wealth of a country, the adult learning model used and its technical organisation. The quality of adult learning policies is measured by the real observable possibility the subjects have to be intentionally and consciously involved in changing their material and intellectual conditions, and not merely in changes in established educational infrastructures and educational and cultural products and services.

Based on these premises, and despite a lack of systematic historical and national studies, we shall now endeavour to examine a number of case studies and assess the historical process of expressing and negotiating adult learning interests and demand. We shall consider each of the four levels of intervention noted earlier in this chapter.

2.2.1. Imposition/rejection of adult learning policies

The imposition or rejection of adult education must be viewed as a first level of concrete historical expression of the will to impose adult learning policies or to resist them. Examples can be found in the past and present of both developed and developing countries.

One of the first examples is the "refusal" of the inhabitants of the Philippines in the early colonial period, starting in 1521, to submit to education in Spanish. The people decided to evade the law by fleeing to the island's interior and, in so doing, chose not to become literate in the new language (CS: 11). Similar problems arose in the United States in 1618 when "the formal European education of indigenous people started (...) with the Henrico proposal 'as separate but equal'" (P 2: 1). Comparable problems are undoubtedly arising today in the various countries that are implementing language "standardisation" policies, enshrining one language as superior to others. In this regards, mention should be made of the turning point in the Hamburg Declaration concerning the recognition of African and indigenous languages (UNESCO 1997), and the case of the Baltic countries' programmes to restore their national languages (Lithuania, CS: 13 f.). In these cases, learning new languages clearly reflects the dominance not only of new linguistic and ethnic groups but also new social and economic groups, and serves as a tool to build new social and political identities, new states, etc. When in 1977 President Marcos of the Philippines launched his initiative for the development of distance teaching with the "Lingap ng Pangulo sa Brangay" or "How the President Cares for the Communities" programme, this ideological use of adult education immediately provoked a popular reaction (CS: 23 f.).

A decision to refuse or resist can also be observed with certain corporate work-related learning policies and programmes for the unemployed and welfare recipients, which condition allowances and even basic benefits (entitlement to social aid, etc.) on participation in adult learning programmes, thus rendering them obligatory (Canada, CS: 15; United States, P 1 and 5). The poor results achieved by the OECD countries' imposed training programmes for the unemployed are a typical example of this. They contained measures that required the subjects concerned to participate in work-related training courses, but did not take into account participants' learning projects, nor provide in return reintegration into the world of work, and thus did not succeed in motivating the unemployed (Christiansen 1995: 143). The experience should not be summed up simply as a problem of inadequate policies and the need to perfect methodology. Historically, this should be viewed as a primordial expression of passive political resistance by a social group that in the present situation is unable to express its own learning interests positively or to propose an appropriate educational programme. The group is thus resisting the implementation of arbitrarily imposed policies and refusing practices that put the unemployed "on a long-term back burner".

2.2.2. Educational solidarity among adults

The most basic forms of intervention in adult learning policy are benevolent initiatives, which have been around since the beginning of adult education in the last century and have spread to all industrial countries, from Spain to Australia, North America and Eastern Europe. This practice had its roots in the fight against poverty, but even more fundamentally represented an endeavour to meet the learning demands of the first generations of industrial workers. Episodic, fragmentary programmes and initiatives developed independently of any overall planned policy programme. These and other initiatives from community groups and the like developed to meet the interests of these new publics.

Over the last six decades, the context of world war and the subsequent mobilisation of resources have prompted the creation of basic training programmes, first for young soldiers and then for veterans. Hence the research on adult education, for example, on how "to retrain the new workforce" or to raise the productivity of the agricultural extension programme (United States, CS: 168 f.). Similar statements could be made about educational programmes to deal with urgent situations created by massive unemployment, the spread of new diseases, the onset of the information society, etc.

This model, the second level of intervention, embraces the creation by public and non-public organisations of different marginalised, isolated sub-systems of adult learning, formal and informal, general and vocational, all operating independently. Since the end of the Second World War, this model has been institutionalised in legislation and government administration, for example, in the Japanese law of 1947 (CS: 15).

These policies confirmed the role of adult learning in many sectors of social and cultural life but, at the same time, were not in themselves capable of interconnecting the different adult learning policies developing in the fields of health care, work, the environment, social security, etc. Hence the paradoxical situation has arisen where organised work-related adult learning has come to be seen as something different and separate from the response to the desire and demand for training on the part of employed workers. This is indicative of the ad-hoc, short-term and fragmented nature of this second-level intervention model.

The OECD recurrent education project in the 1970s and 1980s and the work/social participation dichotomy on which it was based created dysfunctions and met with the resistance with which we are now familiar. The proposal for a global lifelong learning project presented as a "self-directed and voluntary process", without an umbrella policy that co-ordinates the different demands and takes account of unequal social conditions, will also prove problematic and lead the OECD to more mixed (public-private) and organised strategies (OECD-CERI 1995: 217).

2.2.3. General demands and the formulation of egalitarian learning policies for adults

The third level of awareness and action by collective actors is marked by a still broader perspective and is linked to the expansion of learning demand that had not been met by the preceding fragmentary responses. The demand for equitable policies for the field of adult learning as a whole has roots in the very origins of the adult education movement, in particular its nineteenth-century populist and socialist components. More recently, it was during the movements of the late 1960s that this sentiment erupted most sharply, including internationally.

At this level, adult learning is conceived as a basic civil right for all: the right of access to all forms of existing learning possibilities and the right to participate in the relevant decision-making. What is truly new in practice is the transition from expressions of egalitarian intentions and innovative methodological practices developed in ivory towers to the realisation of political programmes, legislative and administrative measures, and substantial commitments such as the "Declaration on the Right to Learn" adopted by the Fourth International Conference on Adult Education in 1985. Adult learning policy is thus no longer identified solely with established systems and existing programmes. Greater attention is paid to mechanisms that expand or reduce access to learning and to the expression of aspirations. In this sense, a notion of the right to adult learning is being created based on both individual rights and the rights of social groups (women, the elderly, etc.). In addition, new measures are being introduced, such as the 1974 International Labour Organisation (ILO) agreement on paid educational leave.

At this new level, organisational forms exist in which policies are developed, tested, endorsed, implemented and adjusted. Organised collective actors distinct from the state have made their appearance in civil society. They work to promote and develop new learning policies for adults, and reflect and "construct" social demand and the collective will. Depending on the country, political associations, trade unions and industrial groups have up to now played this historical role, while more uncommonly specific organisations arose that expressed the learning interests of the real and potential public for adult education. It was such adult learning associations, active primarily in the English-speaking countries, that in 1972 created the International Council of Adult Education.

On the whole, the learning interests of the adult population took the form of a popular movement that is transversal and episodic, or organised in a temporary fashion (e.g., the Spanish government's new adult education policy following the fall of the Franco regime developed without the involvement of the fragmented networks of educational and cultural associations, see P 1), or represented by national institutes or federations of a multitude of different associations.

2.2.4. Steering and changing adult learning policies

The inherent logic of the egalitarian approach ultimately has steered it towards policies of change that are capable of creating equal opportunities for all to participate throughout life as well as equal starting points (Roemer 1996) and the recognition of different identities (UNESCO 1997). The institutional reaction to this aspiration can be seen in two contradictory responses: the non-refusal and even acceptance of the formal principle of equality, and the simultaneous turn to policies and financial measures that reduce expenditure on adult learning and tend to organise the general economics of adult learning on a free-market basis.

Although the Brazilian Constitution of 1988 recognised the right to basic education for adults and gave the country ten years to "eradicate illiteracy", the literacy rate is still relatively low today. The Constitution's promise seems destined to remain a dead letter. In the United States in 1989, on the occasion of an education policy summit, President Bush and the fifty state governors issued a pioneering document announcing six national education targets. Target five declared that "all Americans will be literate by the year 2000" (P 9: 2). Despite the introduction of specific legislation and policies (United States, P 1- 4), this problem has remained unsolved at the end of the second millennium. This does not mean that the solemn declarations of constitutions and political leaders should not be considered a historic achievement in terms of the recognition of the right to adult learning. Yet the fact that measures capable of effectively dealing with the problem are not being adopted and implemented, despite the acceptance and political legitimisation of the target, are signs of the inherent limits of a strategy based on the simple demand for equality through the redistribution of increasingly limited public resources.

The impact of structural adjustment programmes on informal education programmes in the developing countries is now well known and documented (Reimers and Tiburcio 1993: 29-56). When governments accept the principle of equality while simultaneously cutting the public funds required to attain it, doubts inevitably arise about the objectives themselves. In the European Union, for example, a 1994 European Commission proposal "[to] set progressive targets up to the year 2000 for the elimination of functional illiteracy, and lack of other basic skills, on the part of school-leavers" (European Commission 1994a: 25) was introduced into an official document but was never incorporated into a programme or accompanied by concrete measures.

Moreover, as the field of adult learning tends to be increasingly structured as a new market for cultural goods and services, this market is becoming a second battleground for the egalitarian approach. The rights to access and to co-manage the learning process are being posed here in new terms. Equal opportunity programmes and strategies are coming up against the inevitable demand for payment of services and the inequality of resources across different social strata. Adults who gain access to education are placed in the objective condition of being consumers, where purchasing power, economic status, sex, professional situation, neighbourhood, etc., determine whether they will succeed in this act of educational consumption or be excluded from it. Public policies, which remain sectorial, have no influence on these factors and consequently have no impact on these new processes to distribute learning opportunities. Instead of reducing inequalities, these processes heighten educational exclusion and the resulting inequalities.

The development of adult learning as an educational market has another implication for the egalitarian approach: it thwarts participation in the definition of educational programmes. With the exception of general and usually imperfect limited mechanisms to regulate short-term supply and demand, the market actually negates any opportunity for involving social groups in planning programmes and negotiating educational content. The interplay between explicit short-term demand and the supply of services determines the rise of one sector and the demise of another. The management of content has proved to be totally dependent on the capacity of educational products to win new market share. While this type of organisation may be of interest to new providers, it usually falls far short of meeting the broad, long-term aspirations of the populations, and thus social demand.

In this new context, programmes and strategies to transform educational conditions for the adult population tend to find expression outside the immediate field of learning, in individual and collective action in the various aspects of daily life: health-care actions, new demands from employees, subsistence-income generating activities, local neighbourhood life, revitalisation of regional cultures, leisure time and culture, as well as actions by women's groups, youth groups, trade unions and business groups. It is at this level that educational programmes find expression and are created and a collective will can take shape, making it possible to intervene consistently in the different spheres of overall adult learning policy: the expression of demand (individual rights, collective rights, etc.), reform of educational programmes (constitution of educational systems, reorganisation of services, etc.), and the improvement of adult learning conditions in the community and on the job (health care, employment, taxation, information, cultural infrastructures, etc.). Similarly, the Fifth International Conference on Adult Education would not have had the impact it did without repeated appeals from the various United Nations summits, which, like those made previously before other international organisations, called on the creativity and effective participation of the adult population (Odora Hoppers 1996).

2.3. The aim of adult learning policy

While the first generations of adult education policies and laws tended to be limited to setting up evening courses and public centres, adult learning policy today covers a broader field related to work, personal development, the improvement of women's living conditions, career mobility, the environment, preventive health care, etc. This broadening of the field demands a more precise definition of what it is that unifies all these educational actions and programmes.

What are the aims of adult learning policy today? What issues are involved in the policy-making process? In Chapter 1, we described the territory and problems addressed by policies. This gave a picture of the current expansion of the field of intervention and revealed bottlenecks that might be encountered in some countries at particular historical moments. However, it takes more than an inventory of the ground covered to determine the specific aim of adult learning policy. Our observations indicate that the process of developing adult learning policy has three basic aims: first, the formation of an organised political subject, second, the regulation of organised learning activities in daily life and at work and third, the appropriation/distribution of the benefits of learning.

2.3.1. Forming the organised political subject

A social actor engaged in policy-making constitutes itself as a subject, drafts a social project and develops expertise and a capacity to organise and manage. The process of forging a collective will is the product not of the action of the "Prince", but of organised individuals intervening in the broad field of adult learning. Adult learning policy develops in close liaison with the levels of awareness and organisation of the parties involved. It is in the very process of drawing up and implementing adult learning policy that the parties involved develop the skills and social roots on which the quality and results of the policy depend. The development of an educational programme is an integral part of the educational process, at all levels, including micro and macro.

Reciprocally, policy and law contribute to forming organised political subjects.

The identification of the social actors involved in the policy-making process is key to an analysis of its impact. The political actors involved are the first to benefit, in that they can enhance their capacity to manage collective learning processes. If, for example, government, business or the social partners in a given set of firms invest in adult learning based exclusively on the demands of the firms and their personnel, they may obtain the desired economic results, but run a high risk of excluding the broader demands of other social groups in civil society and coming into conflict with them.

Social actors are both subject and object of adult learning policy. Furthermore, policies that are not developed in such a way as to include all the subjects concerned will encounter obstacles in implementation and have a limited impact. Human resources development policies that neglect that active or perhaps resistant parties make up these resources are destined to crash on the rocky reality of social relations, especially in a field as closely linked to daily living conditions as adult learning.

2.3.2. The regulation of the learning process in daily life and at work

The aim of policy is to regulate the learning process. However obvious this may be, it needs to be emphasised in order to reassert the close relationship between a specific learning event, the immediate aim of the policy, and the general political situation that, whether legitimating or undermining the policy, in any case determines its context and its impact. This remark is especially pertinent at a time when adult learning policies are being developed within a spectrum that is spilling over the traditional boundaries in which the immediate structures of adult learning had been defined, whether or not work-related. Thus, for example, legislation on the management of the working week and daily living time (such as those governing paid leave and laws approved in Italy, for example, on women's "time for life") tend to determine the opportunities and moments people are able to take up learning. A similar assessment could be made of the introduction of active work policies and their associated laws that introduce new forms of labour mobility (geographical, occupational and across production sectors) and inevitably increase workers' demand for learning, as observed by Rubenson in Sweden (1994: 367 f.). The same is true of preventive health-care policies, the active rehabilitation of prisoners, etc.

Thus the aim of regulation should not be considered – as is often the case with the specific function of education policies – in terms of a simple redistribution of resources and roles and the readjustment of established power relationships or norms in the immediate field of education and training. On the contrary, in its initial stages, the policy-making process is essentially an exercise in analysis and exploration. Its initial task is to define the issues, goals, strategies and guidelines likely to help develop a social project and, to this end, to organise the provision of learning and the conditions for taking part in it.

From this viewpoint, adult learning policy is unique in that, through the management of the learning process and beyond, it creates spaces where the adults themselves potentially make decisions that more broadly affect the direction and conditions shaping their own future development, both individually and collectively. This recognition of the close relationship between the democratisation of daily life (Giddens 1992) and the intimacy of the act of learning, between the collective action of new popular movements and their educational and cultural output (Eyerman and Jamison 1991), and between broader social projects and specific educational programmes, requires that we constantly resituate policies within politics.

2.3.3. The appropriation/distribution of the benefits of learning

Organised adult learning in the contemporary sense was born and developed with the advent of "modernisation" and of industrial society. However, educational policies even existed in ancient Greece, where Solon published the first edicts on the subject. Yet it was not until the need for education was felt beyond the upper classes that general education strategies were developed and implemented, first in the form of universal schooling and basic initial education and later with the recognition of the multifaceted demand for education throughout adult life. With the modernisation and global integration of national economies, initial education and adult learning came to be viewed as closely related to the transformation of the production process.

In the final decades of the 20th century, an emphasis on the economic implications of adult learning has come to dominate the field. Paradoxically, while the military machine was said to exist for the sake of peacekeeping, education was attributed the task of increasing the competitiveness between different economic systems and growth models to strengthen a series of modernisation efforts! A study of the situation today indicates that the rapid implementation of adult learning policy is due to what could be called the "tri-partite nature of anticipated benefits". First, there is the development of a workforce who are capable of taking part in an ever-more sophisticated production process and use their skills to increase the added value of products. Second, given the contradictions inherent in all late modern advanced societies, there is the need for citizens to be able to take independent action. Third, there is the production of cultural goods and services, and the emergence of "learning societies".

This tri-partite nature of anticipated benefits is clearly present as a feature of the last generation of policies, which, with priority given to the first type of benefits, endeavoured to extend adult learning in the business world and the marketplace. The tension between these three types is in many ways the factor behind the most significant changes in the orientation of policy and legislation since the late 1970s. It has been the focus of more recent debate and discussion, as seen from the fifth International Conference on Adult Education (see the *Hamburg Declaration*, in: UNESCO 1997).

2.4. The broader mechanisms for steering and managing the process

The process of elaborating and implementing adult learning policy could also be interpreted and dealt with as a learning process. This would correspond to the path taken by the protagonists concerned in learning how to create the conditions favourable for changing, testing, checking and coming to know the specific context. This could be termed an "operational critical epistemology" (Morin 1977; Fabbri Montesano and Munari 1984). This process of learning and of reflexive action is not abstract and linear. It cannot be constrained within specific institutional procedures, nor can it be described based on a model of these procedures. Indeed, it tends to be evaluated in terms of the conflicts engendered by the diverse interests existing in a given society relative to policy objectives (the emergence of new actors, regulation of the educational process, appropriation or democratisation of the benefits of learning). This learning process will inevitably be marked by whether it is possible to formulate and legitimate educational projects that express either universal interests or the particular concerns of specific social groups. Its pace and orientation are set by the dynamics of conflicts and contradictions related to the policy objectives.

Based on this expanded vision of policy and of the actors involved and the scope of intervention, a new, more complex articulation of the policy-making process comes into view.

The formal classical model focused entirely inside institutions, with the variant of institutional openings to participation through the introduction of sites for consultation, co-ordination or co-management. This model assumes that initiatives are born in institutional sites, pass through a period of institutional verification, which may be viewed expansively, and ultimately are reflected in a directive, law or act. This model is in essence formal and linear and fails to correspond to observed practice. The process is actually much more complex, even in monarchies where policies are legitimated by royal decree, or in authoritarian socialist states where party congress or central committee resolutions form the basis for policy. Policy originates prior to any pronouncements or resolutions and it is carried on after any decrees. The problem for the analyst is thus to reveal policy's actual trajectory, which is an open question in any kind of state.

The analytical model adopted here corresponds more accurately to the actual dynamics involved in elaborating and implementing policy. It takes into account the complexity and multiplicity of decision-making mechanisms, and relates non-institutional dynamics to the formal process, over and above legal assumptions, and to its development. The model considers the initiation of the decision-making process right from the nascent forging of a collective will. It observes the actual dynamics of forming a will for change which, in the right conditions, can produce an innovation, which may then be ratified by law. This model helps to explain changes in the mechanisms of control and decision-making and gives a role to the process of policy self-regulation that will affect the social legitimacy and effectiveness of policies.

In this respect, the levels of decision-making, from local to global, have multiplied. Mechanisms to decentralise the management of adult learning are being developed in many countries. At the same time, co-ordination mechanisms are being organised and growing in relation to certain transnational authorities. In the past, the only centres of transnational co-ordination that took initiatives to develop adult learning policy were multilateral authorities with a specific mandate, e.g. UNESCO's adoption of a "Recommendation on the Development of Adult Education" in 1976, the ILO's adoption of the "Convention on Educational Leave" in 1974, the OECD's policy statement on "Recurrent Education" (OECD 1973) and the UNESCO reports on "Lifelong Education" (UNESCO 1972 and 1996). Since then, supranational authorities have proliferated, even though discussion and co-ordination are still not standard procedures in the G7 or other organisations which, like the World Bank and its affiliated regional institutions, are nonetheless playing an ever-increasing role in influencing adult learning policy. Intergovernmental institutions like the European Union have also given rise to advisory committees that examine adult learning policies and programmes prior to their approval.

As for participation in the policy-making and implementation process, the exemplary Brazilian law on workplace safety should be pointed out. It led to the creation, in every company, of committees responsible for supervising and managing safety-related problems and training. With recognition and support, this kind of co-operative, participative culture could be transferred to other problems and sectors of social and working life (Brazil, P 1). Nonetheless, there has also been a trend to create "pro-forma" committees and councils, which in practice are powerless and unable to lend any real meaning to the participatory process (Italy, P 1), and joint labour-management committees that prove incapable of carrying out their assigned tasks (Brazil, P 1).

This expanded view of the development of adult learning policy reveals a great increase in the number and diversity of protagonists involved in changing and enhancing learning provision for adults. New social subjects are acquiring genuine new policy responsibilities, as in the cases of Australia's neighbourhood houses (P 4) and the Native American peoples of the United States (P 2).

In Spain, just when laws were approved to apply general encompassing policies designed to co-ordinate interventions in adult learning, a narrow system of work-related training was created with no intrinsic link with other educational programmes (Requejo Osorio 1994). The problem does not stem from shortcomings in institutional engineering or a lack of co-ordination. It is the product of a confrontation between two types of educational programmes and the clash for hegemony over learning demands between civil society and the market.

Similar considerations are relevant to so-called deregulation policies. In the United States, for example, the situation is less one of deregulation than the introduction of new, different standards. Programmes have been subjected to more direct control by certain social actors (in particular, corporations, as in the "Job Training Partnership Act", for example; see United States, P 1). In countries subject to World Bank structural adjustment programmes, as well as in the United Kingdom, Sweden prior to 1996 and Australia, financial tools and mechanisms have been used to steer institutions and programmes towards given targets (De Tommasi, Warde and Haddad 1996).

While legislation is the main policy tool for the public management of learning activity, it is not the only tool. And while law is a potential product of policy, we also need to take into account the variety of instruments ("sources of acceptable information") that precede and follow it: official documents, committee reports, legislation presentation speeches, public consultations, adopted or rejected amendments, and minutes of parliamentary debates (Caulley 1982) not to mention the decrees, ordinances and ministerial orders associated with these laws. In this respect, there has been a new trend to introduce innovative, experimental instruments and to propose alternatives for discussion and consultation in setting policy. In many cases (Australia, Denmark, the Netherlands, Switzerland, the United Kingdom), research and pilot programmes have become integral parts of the policy-making process. Based on the results obtained, official documents are published that, when adopted by government, become instruments that influence and even guide ministerial policy, albeit without the power of law. In the cases noted, it is the general government budget act that contains expenditure items for financing the initiatives set forth in these policies. Such is, for example, the procedure followed by Australia's 1994 *Working Nation* document, which proposed new public strategies in the field of work-related learning (P 7). When these instruments, typical of an experimental phase, are translated into decisions authorising medium and long-term plans, then pilot programmes, research, orientation plans and evaluations may suffice to provide for verifiable co-management of the policy-making and implementation process.

The increasing fragmentation and diversification of the field of adult learning policy, discussed above, has proceeded to such an extent that the field can no longer be followed within the bounds of existing ministerial domains using conventional policy tools. In every country, legislation governing this sector is diffused or scattered in a plethora of laws that would be difficult to integrate. Indeed, many different efforts have been made to unify them. The Swiss *Weiterbildungsoffensive* ("continuing education campaign"), attempted, for example, to bring together all business training efforts (Switzerland, CS: 142 f.). Although this need for flexible integration has not met with a favourable legal response, it has nonetheless been expressed politically in green papers and white papers proposing a unified strategy for all policies and interventions (Finland, Ireland, Morocco, Norway, Quebec, South Africa and the United Kingdom; see Chapter 1, sect. 2) and by national (Japan and China) and regional efforts (e.g. Catalonia in Europe) to horizontally co-ordinate interventions (Bélanger 1994: 374 f.). The idea of a framework law in the field may seem seductive, but it is still premature. The field is undergoing rapid reorganisation, and the decision-making process is becoming more complex and being spread across various levels, from the local to transnational (see, for example, the *Agenda for the Future* adopted by the fifth International Conference on Adult Education in 1997, in: UNESCO 1997).

The expanding, restructuring field of adult learning will go through many more changes and attempts to knit together its disparate elements before the new general organisation of adult learning gives rise to different models with institutional legitimacy. New players and their educational programmes are increasingly being recognised, but it is still difficult to pin down these types of trends, especially since this is happening just as the roles of national authorities are being extensively redefined. For the time being, it is more useful to analyse the concrete contribution of current policies to altering the conditions underlying adult learning. These policies are clearly transition policies.

Chapter 3
The Four Functions of Transition Policies

Preliminary remarks on general learning conditions

Both in the past and today, the social function of adult learning policy tends to be one of reproduction and transmission. The theory of cultural reproduction (Bourdieu et Passeron 1977) gives a good account of the exclusion/inclusion processes that education policy tends to generate and maintain in relation to different social divisions, including social class, ethnic identity, gender, age, geographic region, etc. However, the actual dynamics of adult learning policy show that these functions are not necessarily predominant and certainly not intrinsic. Adult education cannot be reduced to the simple function of the distribution of institutionalised knowledge, nor can the function of adult learning policy be narrowed to the transmission of existing knowledge or the simple reproduction of social relations.

Addressing this matter entails circumventing simplistic scenarios of the inevitable effects of exclusion. Even more fundamentally, however, it is crucial to go beyond an analysis of the impact of these processes in order to understand how they are generated and can be influenced. In other words, what is produced and distributed (education and its contents) needs to be distinguished from the learning environment and the general learning structures and conditions that underpin the development of the learning process in different societies.

A policy and a legislative mechanism can be distinguished by the learning opportunities they make accessible to different social strata (i.e. the distributive function) and, even more importantly, by their capacity to improve conditions for ongoing learning by men and women and make it easier for them to take part in learning activities. Many factors go into creating these conditions and sustaining lifelong learning activity (physical, historical, geographical, economic, cultural, etc.). Consequently, analysing adult learning policy also requires considering its relation to changes in general individual living conditions (poverty, unemployment, disease, etc.) and assessing the impact of the different policies on the learning environments. The point is to focus on the "added value" generated by adult learning policy. We believe that the main role of adult learning policy is to take conscious action to affect the entire set of explicit and implicit rules that determine the "educational" quality of the relations established among subjects "within" specific fields of activity (agriculture, health care, work, literacy, etc.). This whole set of rules, although not necessarily consistent, regulates the elaboration, distribution and development of the learning process in daily life, at work and in the community.

The "theory of cultural transmission" put forward by Basil Bernstein (1990) is a useful contribution to the approach outlined above, in that it identifies its object as the general "learning structure", operating in all social relations and also within the field of formal and informal education.

Bernstein posits that,

"the internal nature of the learning structure is composed of three sets of rules: distribution, recontextualisation and evaluation, which are in a hierarchical relation (...) the rule of distribution being the key and the basis for the second and third rules" (Bernstein 1990: 103).

The distribution rules determine who can offer or transmit what, to whom and under which conditions. The crucial problem of distribution is equality in educational opportunity and access to opportunities and tools that promote the development of creative thinking and transformative praxis. These rules are clearly operative in both the immediate context of organised learning activities and, more importantly, in a multitude of diffuse ways in the workplace, the community and daily life.

The rules of recontextualisation structure educational discourse and integrate the teaching act into a regulatory process. "Pedagogical discourse", writes Bernstein (ibid.: 107), is based on the integration of learning into a regulatory discourse. The process of acquiring knowledge and skills is always grafted onto a regulatory discourse that guides and recontextualises it within a social order with established relations and identities. However real the transmission of a competency may be, it is an act of regulation before being an act of transmission.

This distinction between educational and training activity on one side and the regulatory discourse on the other makes it possible to more accurately define the components of the educational function of policy and legislation. It is important to clearly differentiate between the explicit themes taken up in learning and the significance of the learning process as it actually develops in the interaction between the various elements at work: the subjects, agencies, institutions, explicit learning activities, existing tools, production processes, etc. The predominant function of policies is to be distinguished less by the type of learning possibilities offered than by the characteristics of the educational relations established among the different elements involved, which determine the actual conditions of ongoing learning, facilitating or obstructing the subjects' activity and their learning and creative projects.

Bernstein identifies the rules of evaluation as the principles that regulate educational practice, its codes and methods and define what is to be transmitted over time and space. These principles specify ages and corresponding types of acquisition (initial phase, during adult life, etc.). They situate the learning process in a historical and ideological context, define the conditions for acquisition and evaluate the process (ibid.: 108).

Constructing the general learning structure and conditions and setting the rules by which they function in a society could be considered to be the unifying function of all educational policy and legislation. The main social significance of adult learning policy is how it affects the determination of the rules on the basis of which it may or may not become possible for men and women from different social strata to engage in active learning at each and every stage in their lives in relation to work, social participation and personal life.

An analysis of adult learning policy cannot therefore limit its view to the organisation, development and consolidation of adult learning programmes and structures (formal and informal) or to the "reconstruction" of educational interventions that are dispersed across a great variety of sectors (from agriculture to telecommunications). At the social level, the main feature of adult learning policy is its relationship to the general management of the process of individual and collective learning in a given society. The aim of actual adult learning policy includes, but goes well beyond, the provision of educational services. Policy concerns all the actions that modify the set of learning means and conditions in a given social formation.

This reference to the broad adult learning structure and conditions does not constitute a normative proposition; it is rather the result of an extension of the empirical observation framework needed to grasp the social significance of adult learning policies. The structures and conditions in operation today are the product of historical dynamics and contexts. They gradually grew up around goals and actions that helped create environments that favoured certain subsequent developments more than others. Relationships need to be developed between new adult learning policies and the functions that have hitherto been the main motives in the shaping of the general learning structure in different societies. These functions can be identified as follows:
1. Support in constructing a collective identity (state, nation, economic sector, market region, etc.);
2. A response to the learning demand of the economic system;
3. Support for policies fostering social cohesion;
4. The regulation of consumption.

3.1. Support in constructing a collective identity

The active participation of citizens is a dominant theme in new adult learning policy. Helping to construct a collective identity is a particular focus of attention during phases of national reconstruction and general social mobilisation based on new "social contracts". Hungary in the years immediately following the First World War clearly shows that extraordinary growth in adult learning coincides with periods of regaining national independence. This was a time of cultural mobilisation to reinforce the feeling of belonging to the Hungarian nation (CS: 2 f.). The same phenomenon can be seen in other countries in Central and Eastern Europe following the break-up of the Soviet Union, both in the attention immediately given to the national language issue and in educational programmes following national independence (Lithuania, P 1). The same is true of periods following national independence in African and Asian countries, the consolidation of a national identity in India through literacy programmes in the last decade (P 2), and the assertion of the identity of the indigenous peoples of Latin America, the Philippines (P 5) and the United States (P 2).

"The cohesion of any society is predicated on shared activities and purposes, but also on shared values, which represent different aspects of the desire to live together. (...) one purpose of education, in its many forms, is to create social links between individuals on the basis of shared references. (...) Faced with the breakdown of social ties, education has to take on the difficult task of turning diversity into a constructive contributory factor of mutual understanding between individuals and groups. Its high-est aim will then be to give everyone the means of playing an informed and active part as citizen, which is something that cannot fully be achieved except within the framework of democratic societies" (UNESCO 1996: 51 f.).

Yet this type of educational function is inevitably exposed to the dynamics and particular contradictions characterising the process of the formation and development of states. This is why, even in the framework of what are known as democratic societies, the function of political socialisation differs according to whether education is used to promote – to use Habermas' categories (Habermas 1990) – "expressive, manipulative publicity" or "a critical process of public communication". The possibility of transcending the simple level of "expressive, manipulative publicity" depends on the creation of a "public of organised individuals".

"The basic rights that guarantee a public sphere with political functions (for example, freedom of expression and opinion, freedom of association and assembly, freedom of the press, etc.) must no longer be interpreted in an exclusively negative way, but positively, as guarantees of participation"

(Habermas 1990: 330). "The development of individual freedom (...) requires a status guaranteed publicly by democratic participation (...)" (ibid.: 332).

Rights of any kind cannot be dissociated from the conditions in which they are exercised.

In a basic strategy for forming a "public of organised individuals", adult learning would be an essential component helping to turn "individuals" into "an organised public" with a social project and capable of action. It would aim to build and consolidate basic freedoms, and would thus differ profoundly from purely "expressive, manipulative" functions whereby adult education tends to be limited to an adaptive function reinforcing the status quo.

These kinds of problematics and contradictions are found particularly in adult learning policies intended to introduce and extend civil rights and citizenship rights.

Policies promoting the affirmation of civil rights, active citizenship and the equality and empowerment of women are not always related explicitly to adult learning in the traditional, limited sense. They are linked to the introduction of political rights (active and passive electoral participation, rights of association), rights at work and social security (right of association, social welfare rights and the fight against sex discrimination), educational, cultural and religious rights (economic rights, rights of access), individual rights to express different identities (linguistic, gender, etc.), "territorial" rights (to a residence, property, control over indigenous territory, etc.) and rights to the consumption of all kinds of goods and services.

The new rules introduced in this way are first and foremost the result of informal learning process gestating in the popular movements and in society in general – a process that has led to the development of new policy management capabilities. In Namibia, for example, the new adult learning policies launched by the SWAPO-formed government have roots in the liberation struggle waged against apartheid. Literacy programmes aim above all to help the people of the new state communicate and increase their social participation and productive capacity. The national literacy policy has acquired political significance and value due, among other reasons, to broad participation in the programme at every level (CS: 3). Similarly, in India during the decolonisation period from 1947 to 1964, literacy programmes were promoted "to make adult illiterates conscious of their rights and responsibilities as citizens" (CS: 78).

Secondly, the affirmation, defence and development of new rights depends on the real learning opportunities ensured by these rights (political development, with respect to work, etc.) and their capacity to strengthen the underlying collective will against the constant risk of suppression. The Philippines experience shows clearly that institutional and legislative reforms cannot be put into practice unless local actors are vigilant and there are people trained to manage the reforms. The implementation of the new decentralisation law there encountered considerable difficulty precisely because local officials and citizens did not get the opportunity to acquire the needed political skills (Philippines, CS).

Thirdly, new rights introduce new rules that, by permitting new collective subjects to affirm themselves, tend to promote the emergence of new learning demand and policy responses. Having said this, however, the recognition of the rights of new political subjects is sometimes dealt with by policies that integrate their demands and aspirations into existing rules and mechanisms. Consider, for example, recent victories in policy for the elderly in the industrialised countries. While this has led to a strong rise in learning demand among senior citizens, it has also given rise to two opposing orientations, depending on the country. One seeks to confine senior citizen demand to specialised cultural and social centres that focus on occupational therapy programmes, while the other recognises them as active subjects capable of playing a productive role at work, in education, in social activity, etc. (Bélanger 1992; EAEA 1997).

3.2. A response to the learning demand of the economic system

As emphasised in Chapter 1 (sect. 3), the expression of adult learning demand tends to be recognised essentially in relation to economic demands as an element of economic discourse. It is around this second function that the rules inspiring the general learning structure operative in contemporary industrial and post-industrial societies are defined most decisively. When forward-looking statements today assert that "the key resource will be a well-educated and highly motivated and adaptable working population" (European Commission 1994a: 12), they are simply echoing a truth recognised in the United Kingdom a century ago at the time the Mechanic Institutes were founded (CS: 152 f.). It is in regards to this inter-relationship that adult learning has acquired legitimacy as national policy in countries like the United States. Prior to 1964, it was only when faced with extreme situations such as the Great Depression, war and large migrations that the US federal government took any interest in adult literacy programmes. Since 1964 and the introduction of a basic adult education clause into the national economic opportunity act, basic adult education has been the subject of official economic policy (CS: 152 f.).

Policies responding to learning demands of the economic system have three basic sub-functions:

a. The distribution of educational opportunities to acquire the skills needed to participate in productive activity;
b. The transformation of the general learning conditions related to modes of production;
c. The creation of cultural and educational contexts favourable to economic development (strategies for economic development and for integrating actions, territorial policies, inter-systemic relations, etc.).

3.2.1. *The distribution of educational opportunities*

The elitism of adaptation policies

The most elementary model of response to learning demand involves policies to adapt the workforce to changes in the production requirements of enterprises. This model is based on three complementary policies:

1. The adaptation and upskilling of the workforce upon entry to and throughout working life, focused on standard jobs skills and the aptitudes needed for performing production tasks;
2. The continuing education of the managerial personel;
3. A system for the initial basic schooling of young people capable of providing a labour force with at least minimum qualifications, and a system for educational catch-up, for "selecting" those less-educated subjects who "merit" social promotion.

These policies introduce elitist rules into the learning systems, in that they are highly selective and hierarchical. The quality and quantity of educational provision are available according to whether one belongs to the managerial class, the skilled technicians, the majority of employees or a fourth group composed of "marginal" members, provided the latter are sufficiently socialised or "employable" to be reintegrated into the labour market. These policies also neglect the informal economy, despite its growing importance, particularly in the developing countries (Singh 1998). Finally, the system functions within hierarchical production structures that tend in turn to perform another selection based on one's membership in an economic sector and the characteristics of the firm. Small and medium-sized firms are on the fringe, whereas the services and high-tech production are generally in a favourable position compared with the primary sector.

Adaptation to changes taking place in production sets the stage for learning that evolves as a mechanism for the adjustment and adaptation of the workforce to transformations dictated by selected technology and production methods.

This is the oldest model of relations between education and the economy. It has been functioning since the dawn of industrial society and, despite certain inevitable changes, it is still found in many countries' policies. Structural adjustment programmes are imposing it in many of the developing countries (De Tommasi, Warde and Haddad 1996), which has provoked reactions, especially in Africa, where structural adjustment programmes have led to budget cuts in adult literacy programmes (Cornia, van der Hoeven and Mkandawire 1992; Mulenga 1994). In Lithuania, a similar approach advocated by the Ministry of Social Welfare a-roused strong opposition, blocking a policy decision for several months. Indeed, a number of ministries were opposed to the decision to restrict adult learning to the short-term adaptation of the workforce to the new economy and thus exclude general adult education and long-term learning (CS: 4 f.).

The elitist tendencies and characteristics of this "adaptative" policy model are related not only to its integration of the hierarchical models just discussed but also to its ideological discourse that hides the discriminatory effect of formal universal accessibility measures. As Rubenson notes,

"The basic idea informing this strategy was that everyone should have an equal right to an education, regardless of social background, sex, or place of residence. The concept is elitist in that it implicitly argues that society ought to offer higher/adult education to those who aspire to it and who are able to benefit from such education."

As regards the law passed in Sweden in 1967, he also points out that,

"The starting point for the 1967 reform was the increased demand for education on the part of those individuals psychologically inclined and socially outfitted for study (...), the so-called 'pool of talent'." (Rubenson 1994: 370).

The selective orientation of such policies is not always explicit. Laws containing fervid declarations are often passed and implemented, only to find that their allotted resources are insufficient for their stated purposes or for the problems they purport to be addressing. Hence the purpose of a law or policy cannot be deduced simply from their stated objectives. The contradiction between the goals of past earlier Coast literacy programmes and their allotted resources, and the gap between the royal declaration on literacy in Morocco and the more limited measures hitherto implemented, are typical examples of what could be found in every region. In the United Kingdom, the educational reform law in the late 1980s encouraged local authorities to respond properly to recognised demand for community and general education. However, it also undermined the potential to do so with a restrivtive interpretation of "adequate provision". Slovenia is another example of a situation where, given the need to develop unemployment policy, the inability to fully meet financial demands subverted the avowed purpose and, using the same overt discourse, led instead to a mechanism for creaming off those job-seekers with the highest level of "employability" (P 3: 8).

It is not easy for social groups who lack the resources to react and develop alternatives, to mobilise public opinion or to raise these contradictions and bring them into the open. This will only be possible when social actors are capable of responding or when strategies and policies unleash the citizenry's capacity for autonomous action and promote a civil society that is active, empowered and accustomed to taking part in solving its own problems.

The contradictions of adaptative policies

Adaptation policies correspond to systems and situations in which learning needs are or seek to be limited to immediate dysfunctions. These policies promote simple modernisation and are based on the hypothesis that development is synonymous with economic growth and the production of capital. The problem of underdevelopment is reduced to a matter of technical and structural factors of production and to the lack of financial and capital resources (Mulenga 1994: 5). The contradictions inherent in this type of policy quickly come to light. Economic actors are coming to understand that selective, short-term adaptation policies do not meet the need, which is also economic in nature, for more polyvalent competence. Hence the shift by a number of governments, multilateral agencies and social partners already in the 1970s, and especially the 1980s and 1990s, towards promoting policies that break with this model of recurrent adaptation. They considered it increasingly important to give priority to educational measures that raise the general level of qualifications broadly and thus give the workforce increased mobility, so as to be part of the new strategies for restructuring work, without losing job rights. Short-term adaptation policies are too narrow in scope to do this.

These new policies tend to be holistic, integrate an entire range of competencies. This partly explains the revival in the 1990s of discourse on lifelong learning (Bélanger and Tuijnman 1997).

The Swiss *Weiterbildungsoffensive* ("continuing education campaign") is a telling example of a government attempt to modernise policy. The *Weiterbildungsoffensive* consisted of a series of measures approved in 1989 by the Swiss federal parliament (whose authority in adult education was not evident), with multi-year funding. The initial purpose was to meet demand for new competencies for the workforce. Support was given to work-related adult learning centres, post-graduate courses and measures to promote the part-time participation of adults in diploma-oriented education, and a higher level of vocational training for the entire workforce, including women and immigrant workers. This *Weiterbildungsoffensive*, however, quickly found it difficult to mobilise the needed financial resources to meet the rising demand that it had stimulated itself (CS: 143).

The emergence of lifelong learning policies and debate on the globalisation of markets and the boom in new technology (See Chapter 1, sect. 1) need to be interpreted in this context of changing economic processes and education strategies. This is, for example, the situation in Japan with the 1990 law on lifelong learning and in the United Kingdom with the publication in 1998 of *The Learning Age*.

The main justifications for the turn to lifelong learning policy can be summarised as follows (Okamoto 1994; Nagashima, Koji and Hiroshi 1994; Japan, CS):
1. the need for broader vocational training in response to economic, social and technological change;
2. the need to transcend a rigid "diploma society" model and transfer attention from initial education (schooling, vocational training and university) to learning throughout life;
3. the need to offer educational activities that meet rising leisure-related demand by providing a cultural and educational content and orientation capable of satisfying the population's intellectual curiosity.

The aim of these policies is to build "a society in which one can freely choose various learning opportunities anytime in one's life and the outcomes of such learning are appreciated properly" (Okamoto 1994: 15). This gives rise to the development of policies, standards and services to assess and certify the competencies acquired by citizens throughout and at any time in their lives. The recognition of the acquisition of experience has thus become a key element in new adult learning policies in most industrialised countries. A similar trend can be seen in the developing countries. In China, the number of adult self-learners who consulted an accreditation board rose in 1993 to more than three million (Dong 1996).

3.2.2. The transformation of educational conditions linked to modes of production

The study of economically grounded adult leanrning policies needs to go beyond their first level of intervention: the regulation of access to organised learning. In view of Bernstein's reference to the distinction between explicit educational policies and "general structures", the process of constructing a society or general learning structure should not be confused with more explicit policies that act on adult learning services and their various subsystems. Although the set of policies that tends to manage and transform the modes of production and the set of policies that tends to define the framework and environment of citizen participation do not make explicit use of educational instruments, they do affect the determination of the adult population's general learning conditions.

To promote employment, the model of linear economic growth policy called mainly for intervention to raise demand for labour, i.e. action at the company level. The workforce would then be trained and adapted to the new requirements. To handle negative factors associated with growth (segmentation of the labour market, reduction of the workforce and – in the case of non-reintegration into the primary or secondary market – unemployment), the model provided for welfare adjustments. These policies aimed to cut costs, the unemployment rate and the duration of social welfare measures by reintegrating the unemployed into the world of production by means of encouragement, socialisation ("employability") and coercion (Canada, CS: 15; United States, CS: 176).

This model, based as it is on a one-way relationship between education and a predictable labour market and on a linear adjustment function of education, was bound to fall in crisis.

The crisis of the "economic growth policy" model is reflected most clearly in the index measuring the ratio between an economy's economic growth rate and its job-creation rate (European Commission 1994a: 45). The recent trend whereby these two rates no longer necessarily follow the same growth curve – that is, economic growth that does not generate new jobs – has had immediate consequences for the role of adult learning. When labour productivity increases as fast or faster than economic growth, "simple" continuing education policies tend to negate any possibility of creating new jobs (European Commission 1994a: 47). This has an immediate impact on the learning structure. It undermines first the right to work, and thus income, and then opportunities for organised learning and informal apprenticeships. In this situation, education as a productivity-raising tool operates to reduce employment and thus heighten inequality. In this model, education plays the role of an individual rather than a collective strategy and becomes a factor in competition among workers.

Yet these initial conclusions only hold if the active policies remain exclusively immediate labour-market management policies. However, the now-acknowledged reciprocal relationship between employment and learning, together with the dynamics of "internal" flexibility, i.e. the contribution of the working population to job creation, have called into question linear policies of continuing vocational training. Training is not simply a dependent variable. The creative tension between prescribed work and real work and between the managerial requirements of learning and the creativity of the subjects clearly shows the outmoded nature of the one-dimensional formula "education = employment". What is at stake here is recognition of the pre-existence of the subject relative to its task as prescribed by the labour process (Dejours 1993). Debate on how to increase productivity is becoming inseparable from discussion of unleashing creativity, or more precisely from discussion of systems that promote creativity for everyone in every field. The "1990s" generation of continuing education policies, despite many economistic trends, is leading paradoxically to expanded redefinitions of the concepts of production and creativity, as will be seen in the following two chapters.

3.2.3. *The creation of cultural and educational contexts in line with economic development*

Given the dispersion of learning opportunities, the polarity of demand and the fragmentation of responsibility, it is becoming increasingly urgent to develop policies dealing with all the factors and agencies involved in the field. Adult learning policies developed in response to the requirements of economic factors must also be evaluated not only in regards to the redistribution of learning opportunities and the transformation of learning conditions, but also in regard to the creation of new relations among the different educational agents. As noted in a European Union research report, "the new theories of economic and social development (...) are based on a local, participative, territorial-based bottom-up type approach" (European Commission-Human Resources Task Force 1994). It is at the local and regional levels that the reciprocal relation between employment and education can be built effectively.

The Council of Europe is promoting the same orientation in advocating the need to build local and national systems that are autonomous and complementary (Bogard 1992). The new institutional adjustments associated with adult learning policies in Africa, based on inter-ministerial co-operation and local partnerships, are indicative of these new trends.

The recognition of a plurality of educational agents has also given rise to the need for new models that integrate different functions (Bogard 1992). All this has furthered breaking down conventional boundaries and building models of partnerships and local learning systems. The multiplicity of agents contributes to the development of a local learning environment. Hence the increasing importance of territorial inter-sectoral programming. The most significant example of this is found in Japan, where the 1990 law on lifelong learning assigned regional officials the task of planning the development of lifelong learning for each local community in liaison with different ministries, local authorities and private enterprises. To develop these plans, the regional officials draw on all the resources available to the various ministries (education, labour, sports, health, etc.) and local public and private activities and organisations in every field. Similar intersectoral co-ordination efforts are to be found in Botswana, China (Guo-Dong 1994), Catalonia (Spain), and Thailand in non-formal education.

This integrative approach is also riddled with contradictions and conflicts. While the idea of developing concerted approaches to adult learning responds to the need to develop more organic continuity in educational responses and, in some cases, foster forms of resource redistribution to less privileged regions, strata or sectors, these integrative strategies could undermine learning dynamics and the dialectics of change in various ways. Systemic strategies are intended to promote unity and coherence among a variety of elements and facilitate synergies. They could, nonetheless, veer into uniformity and standardisation, unless space is made for the active participation of civil society and actors with learning demands are enabled to co-manage and control these synergistic processes.

3.3. Support for policies fostering "social cohesion"

A third function of new adult learning policies is promoting "social cohesion" in order to correct weaknesses in market mechanisms whenever these lead to "changes that are so fast that different social categories are affected unequally, spontaneously producing concentration effects and creating inequalities" (European Commission 1996: 15). Of concern here are policies closely linked to the general learning structure.

In the case of Europe, the roots of such policies can be found as far back as the Roman period (Ander Egg 1984). However, in modern times, the first use of this type of policy dates from 1883, in Prussia, with the inauguration of the "Politik von Zuckerbrot und Peitsche" (carrot-and-stick policy). After the reunification of the German Empire under Emperor William I, Chancellor Bismarck had a law enacted in accordance with the Zentralverband der Deutschen Industriellen. In response to demands for structural changes, the Chancellor and business leaders carried out reforms that held back the introduction of trade unions and their industrial demands. The policy adopted was structured around three laws: the 1883 law on health insurance, the 1885 workmen's compensation act and the 1889 law on pensions, financed jointly by the government, business and employees. "With these laws, Germany had social legislation unparalleled in any other country" (Palmade 1975: 311).

Thus originally these policies were closely linked to labour policy. Their function was to introduce "concrete" measures that recognised certain basic rights in the legislation of a liberal state. In this sense, they influenced the general learning structure, even if they did not include any direct educational measures.

These policies have become widespread since then and have undergone many changes in recent decades. The rise in unemployment and poverty and in the number of elderly and single-parent families has increased demand for social services (European Commission 1994b: 9). Social welfare spending in the European countries consequently rose to 25% to 30% of GDP in the early 1990s (ibid.: 48). This model also fell into crisis due to the "antagonistic pressures put on public spending" (ibid.: 20) by the propertied classes, who held that "support for a certain level of income cannot be the sole objective of social policy" (ibid.: 21). "Today... the role of social welfare is being re-examined in many member states to improve its effectiveness and reduce costs by increasing responsibility and selectivity" (ibid.: 16).

Similar arguments are being advanced more broadly: in the United States, where it is held that "Welfare as an entitlement is a drag on the economy" (P 9: 5), in Eastern Europe as a result of the transition to a market economy, and in the developing countries, where the World Bank has imposed huge cuts in public services, health care and education.

A new approach is being established that aims to offset market effects (loss of "social cohesion", social exclusion) rather than target their causes (the model of economic growth, social lifestyles, etc.). Actual labour policies, especially as concerns the primary market, are being dissociated from social policies. Here too a dual policy can be seen with vocational advancement and qualifications policies on one side and policies for managing the impact of restructuring on the socially "excluded" on the other. This has the effect of further fragmenting adult learning policy and creating a secondary adult learning market. Examples of this type of policy include programmes for welfare recipients and older workers in early retirement.

Compared with the Bismarckian model, the recourse to adult learning here is explicit and direct. In the United States, for example, various studies written in preparation for the year 2000 have advocated, like Robert Reich (1991), a knowledge-intensive economy while at the same time seeking to manage the ensuing inequalities and maintain a certain social cohesion. With regards to the latter, policy focuses on six points: the widening gap between the poor and the rich, the increasing exclusion of young people from the primary labour market and the modern sector in developing countries, the need to introduce more flexible conditions for newcomers (women and immigrants), the protection of employees from vulnerable social groups, the priority of qualified personnel to continuing education, and, finally, the need to co-ordinate these various public policies (United States, P 9: 2).

In this new situation, adult educators are becoming either social workers or experts in the continuing development of competency among symbolic workers. As social workers, they are asked, for example,

> "to integrate immigrants into the mainstream, assist welfare reform, break the intergenerational cycle of illiteracy, reduce recidivism, and increase employability" (ibid.).

Four different types of education policies have arisen to deal with these problems, although sometimes they are inconsistent and occasionally even in conflict:
1. Policies to provide support, financial aid and services to groups driven out of stable work, subjects in extreme need and victims of modernisation;
2. policies of adaptation to exclusion, based on reduced forms of protection and casual and temporary forms of reintegration into secondary labour markets, supported by training activity. These policies are based on acceptance of the fact that "a significant part of the excluded will never take up work again" (OECD-CERI 1995: 224);
3. "active labour policies" that use training to promote reintegration into the primary labour market, job-sharing and job creation;
4. active social policies that call for the participation of civil society, involving the following changes: from passive resistance to the rehabilitation of the handicapped; an active, productive concept of the elderly; the educational rehabilitation of prisoners; active prevention in the fields of health care and environmental protection; literacy programmes to strengthen the autonomy of the individual, etc.

Policies to empower women and strengthen involvement in associations need to be analysed precisely with regards to this alternative between integration and empowerment. The new priority given to adult literacy programmes in both the North and the South bears some relation to the ambiguity in the functions of social cohesion, since they also help to improve basic competence, as will be seen in Chapter 10. These policies are developing in a field full of glaring contradictions and sharp conflicts. Groups fighting poverty demand policies of the third type, the trade unions tend to combine policies of the third and fourth types, certain policies of the third type lead to new forms of production in the informal economy, etc.

Nevertheless, these policies, despite their ambiguities, create spaces and opportunities that give men and women the opportunity to create social and educational programmes, and encourage people to take part in adult learning activities.

3.4. Consumer policies

The orientation and regulation of consumption, which influences the general learning conditions, is a fourth major function of adult learning policy. The impact of consumer policies differs depending on whether they are:

a. Non-intervention policies (or "laissez-faire"), which tend to give free rein to the dynamics of the distribution, trade and consumption of goods and services based on market forces and mechanisms, i.e. according to individual purchasing power and producers' power to influence and stimulate consumption.
b. Active consumer policies, which tend to promote the creation of demand for specific goods using different types of tools, such as information and education programmes for potential buyers on the consumption of new products or services that still lack their own market, policies imposing the purchase and consumption of specific products, and tax policies discouraging the consumption of a product (such as tobacco). For example, the approval of a European parliament directive on new standards for electrical wiring led to a sharp increase in information and training activities concerning the new requirements and associated problems. A public training programme could even be used to create a new market by actively disseminating the basic knowledge needed to use new technology.
c. Interactive policies, which tend to give consumers the capacity to influence the modes of production and distribution and to transform the relations between them. This type of policy is especially significant from the educational viewpoint, as it tends to treat consumption both as a function of determining the quantity and quality of goods made available to individuals and as a decision-making locus, a source of power to influence the content and modes of production. Consider, for example, the capacity for action of consumer associations or the potential impact of consumer rights charters. Interaction between production and consumption has become a sine qua non for improving products and adapting them to consumer needs, as well as for policies that set quality standards.

Beyond these regulatory mechanisms, collective action can transform the social relations between producers and consumers. Due to the impact of industrial production and the "major environmental risks" it engenders (Beck 1992), interest groups are indeed organising and challenging production processes. Environmental movements are revealing the contradictions inherent in the relations of production. Business can no longer fail to respond and thus change the modes of production. A new field of expertise and a new quest for competence and "intellectual" control of the environment is thus developing in both the business world and civil society.

The dominant technocratic health-care service model is also disintegrating. The measures necessary for prevention have led patients to react and band together – each illness now tends to have "its own association". Patients' rights charters are being adopted. Medical practitioners can no longer expect to exercise unquestioned authority. Patients want to understand, to confirm the diagnosis and situate it in their particular context. Professional intervention is increasingly running up against the patient's sense of self and self-assertiveness. This situation, together with the new general structure and socio-cultural conditions, is transforming social demand for lifelong learning.

The transformation of the relationship between production and consumption also has implications for the production, distribution and use of knowledge itself. The production of knowledge is now at the core of society: "the wealth of nations is based (...) on the creation and exploitation of knowledge" (European Commission 1994a: 64). The reduction in the work week is leaving more time for the consumption of knowledge. Moreover, immaterial labour is becoming predominant even in the production of material goods and services. Technological advances are also contributing in current models to an increase in non-working time and to the development of cultural activity. We are referring here to the fact that 75% of payroll in advanced industrial economies today is allocated to "symbolic work" type functions (organisation, employee services, marketing, etc.).

This involves much more than adjusting people to the transition to "knowledge-intensive societies" and adapting people to consume more information. This linear, single-discipline, uni-directional model of production, distribution and use of knowledge is being challenged (Gibbons et al. 1994). Today's consumers are no longer prepared to sit and wait for the publication of an "independent" researcher's findings. Sites where knowledge is produced are on the increase, science is losing its "magic" aura, the end user wants to take part in the specification of scientific work and competition among different disciplines is on the rise. Patients, through AIDS victims associations and the like, are investing time and money in scientific production. The "production-consumption" duality is gradually becoming outmoded due to new modes of producing and using knowledge. The old paradigm, the recurrent adaptation of the subject to changing production and consumption, does not work any more, and this impasse is transforming learning demand.

3.5. Conclusion

The challenge facing adult learning policy is not to demand more or less production-related education or more or less consumption-related education. Nor is it to seek to reduce work-related learning to the benefit of more cultural activities or general adult education. The central issue, as shall be seen in the next two chapters, is the development of a diffuse capacity for initiative in all fields of economic, social, cultural and political participation.

These four current functions of adult learning policies are in transition toward a simultaneously global and individualised approach, which will tend to be more diversified, yet somewhat more integrated into and interrelated with the perspective of what Bernstein calls the general learning structure and conditions, and with what we think is the central issue, namely, the difficult liberation of the creative and productive forces.

Chapter 4
Shifting Perspectives 1: The Development a nd Liberation of Adults' Creative and Productive Capacities

The transformation of contemporary adult learning policies, essentially their refocus on social demand (Chapters 6 and 7) and new methods of managing learning discontinuities and continuities (Chapter 8), cannot be understood without first examining the sharpening contradiction in contemporary society between the organisation of productive activity and the producer-subject, the actors. Analysing the changing dynamics of the educational scene requires looking mainly outside the field of education, lifelong learning included.

4.1. The transformation of work and the development and liberation of the productive and creative forces

4.1.1. Economic factors behind the rise in learning demand

A crucial initial observation is that demand for adult learning tends to be recognised primarily in relation to the requirements of economic productivity and the jobs crisis. Transformations underway in economies and modes of production call for the ongoing development of the skills and capacities of adult populations, which thus acquires public importance. The previously mentioned upsurge in discourse (Chapter 1, sect. 1.2) on competition together with the need to raise skills levels and curb unemployment have encouraged the adoption of adult learning policies in many countries. A spotlight has been thrown on the need for an intra-generational rise in skills and capacities by showing that, while improvements are needed in initial schooling for young people, this traditional means of raising qualifications levels will not be able to develop the capabilities of "working" populations quickly enough. Most of those who will be adults in the next two decades have already completed their initial education. This situation, which is already well established and documented (OECD-CERI 1995), partially explains the rise of adult learning.

The need to break out of the dead-end of Taylorism in the most dynamic economic fields and to have more competent and independent staff has given rise to a real boom in learning demand in these sectors. There is a proliferation of programmes to change these enterprises into "learning organisations" (Watkins and Marsick 1993) and adapt their organisational structures to "organisational learning" (Cohen and Sproull 1995).

Until recently, this demand was most apparent in the knowledge-intensive sectors and higher occupational levels (Bélanger and Valvidielso 1997: 7), such as high-tech specialised production and the more computerised services sub-sectors such as finance, communications and information processing, i.e. areas where symbolic services are growing (Reich 1991: 171-243). In industry, the trend towards the specialisation and flexibilisation of production (Piore and Sabel 1984; Mathews 1989; Lash and Urry 1994) is threatening repetitive work systems and demanding more competence and initiative. In the service sector (Bernier 1990), the introduction of new technologies and different work arrangements is introducing more flexibility into the former Taylorist breakdown of tasks between execution and design, leading to multitask job descriptions. Job enrichment has, however, been proportional to position in the occupational hierarchy. Where these new information and relation-based environments exist, work has become more abstract, more complex and more "intellectual". It requires new abilities to manage information and an aptitude for interpersonal communication. This leads to less emphasis on the external flexibilisation of production based on breaking down activities into malleable sub-contractible units and more emphasis on internal or "dynamic" flexibility based at the micro level on expanding company learning programmes and at the macro level on active labour policies. More recently, as shall be seen in Chapter 10, learning demand has started to be expressed at all occupational levels, with special emphasis on basic adult learning, which has become a priority everywhere, in the North and in the South.

While explicit demand for work-related learning often originates with the employer or the government, trade unions have taken the initiative in certain countries. One such example is the "learning drive" launched in Germany in 1980 by the metalworkers union. Similarly, in 1987, the central Australian trade unions published a report, *Australia Reconstructed*, which opened up flexible work for negotiations in exchange for educational-leave policies that guaranteed employees the possibility of upskilling or re-qualifying (Mathews 1989). This established a close link between continuing work-related learning and the introduction of new technology. The government of Australia echoed several of these proposals in its equally well-known 1994 White Paper *Working Nation*, which states that Australia's future depends on its ability to become a "competent and clever" country (CS: 28).

In the developing countries, in addition to the jobs crisis there is the need to ensure means of subsistence and a sustainable improvement in production in farming, forestry and fishing, as has been noted in Chapter 1. The new production order not only increases demand for learning, but also tends to modify its character. In the post-Ford context, work-related learning can no longer be conceived as a recurrent updating of skills, as if each technical innovation led to new adjustments. This linear Taylorist conception of adult learning is outdated in that it reflects and maintains the culture of repetitive piecework based on narrow specialisation and a breakdown of execution and design tasks. Reflexive production cannot be based on work-related learning that fails to take into account the inevitable gap between the prescribed task and the actual task, which negates the practical intelligence the individual uses to negotiate this gap (Dejours 1993), and which aims simply to mould the producer-subject to detailed tasks set out in advance. This kind of skills updating is not cumulative and cannot last. Moreover, it simply no longer works.

New work-related demands are strengthening this new trend and broadening its impact. The overall rise in the initial education level of populations is also altering subsequent learning aspirations. The trend toward greater financial and professional independence for women is generating new types of needs for learning and retraining (ICEA 1994: 19). The 1989-1992 Women's Development Plan in the Philippines (P 4) for working women recommended special career training programmes for women dealing also with problems of sexual discrimination and exploitation. Nonetheless, this policy, which especially targeted export industries (textiles, electronics and food) where women are a majority, does not seem to have been applied often; its main effect was to reveal the extent of learning demand. Gabriella, a coalition of women's groups within which the working women's movement (KMK) has played a key role in making known the needs of these women for improved skills in difficult working conditions, offered more learning programmes than did the government agency itself.

The search to improve working life and occupational health and safety is also creating new learning needs in both the industrialised countries and the industrial zones of the developing countries, for example the Czech Republic (P 6) as part of rising trade union demand for learning to deal with the transition and its impact, Slovenia (P 2) in response to a rise in industrial accidents and the privatisation of health care, and Brazil (P 1).

The impact of the ongoing economic transition on the rising need for adult learning can also be seen in Lithuania (P 5), with the restructuring of agriculture into family micro-enterprises, and in Vietnam (CS: 11 f.). In the latter country, a Communist Party congress in 1993 recognised the urgent need to remedy a situation where only 11% of workers had any technical training, a problem that is worsening due to the rise of the private sector and the difficult transition of many workers to new production sites.

New trade union officials in Central Europe, the members of joint work committees in Brazil, the delegates on committees of local working women's groups in the Philippines, and co-operation leaders in the Ivory Coast are all demanding learning opportunities to take part more effectively in new representation and bargaining mechanisms.

Economic globalisation is acting as a catalyst in every country: competition in expanding markets is exerting additional pressure that is accelerating changes in the modes of production and is revealing both the need and people's aspirations for a higher general level of skills and capacities. Hence, one of the limited number of institutional structures created by the North American Free Trade Agreement (NAFTA) was an office to assist small and medium-sized enterprises in work-related learning and literacy programmes in the workplace. An exchange network involving community colleges and some universities was also established to this end. The European Commission and most of its member states adopted a similar, but much stronger programme. The EC initiated an active work-related learning policy and proposed the development of a "learning society" to meet the challenge of economic globalisation (European Commission 1996). Similar policy statements in the Pacific region and Scandinavia have already been noted in Chapter 1.

A few remarks are necessary in regards to what may seem to be a rosy picture of the trend in work qualifications. First, this is not a matter of an inevitable, widespread rise in skills requirements, but very much a trend that is already dominant in certain leading sectors and seems indicative of future developments. Second, this observation does not negate the existence of converse situations where the introduction of new technology tends to lower skills levels (Braverman 1974; Aronowitz and DiFazzio 1994). Third, this rise in learning demand is definitely linked to the jobs crisis and thus to the segmentation of the labour market and the structurally uneven general situation of adult learning today.

4.1.2. Non-work economies

While economic change tends to demand a rise in individuals' productive capacities in certain sectors and at certain levels, this has its price – the non-work economy. Analysis of a trend underlying the rise in learning demand cannot ignore victims of "rationalisation policies" who have lost their jobs due to corporate restructuring (Reich 1991: 91). The decline of work, that is, non-work economies, is the flip side of the learning enterprise (Rifkin 1995). Layoffs have been massive. In *The Jobless Future, Sci-tech and the Dogma of Work*, Aronowitz and DiFazzio (1994: 322) point out that the number of jobs in the United States fell by 66% in steel and 33% in car manufacturing from 1970 to 1990. Economic growth has not been able to absorb the number of workers made redundant. Nonetheless, most discourse on adult learning and jobs continues to project a utopia without unemployment, a dream of full employment achievable within the current work structure. In Australia, for example, at a time when unemployment was at 10%, the main discourse promoting lifelong learning (P 7) was still based on a virtually un-nuanced assertion of the twin dogmas of full employment combined with renewed steady economic growth.

Yet the accelerated transformation of production and the predominant mode of managing the comparative benefits of labour markets is leading to a national, regional and international division of labour, and consequently to imbalanced developments in lifelong learning.

An analysis of changes in the paradigm of adult learning policy must take account of two key contradictory facts: first, a transition to reflexive production, which is offering new possibilities, thus leading to positive growth in the adult learning scene; and second, economic segmentation that, in the words of Lash (Lash and Urry 1994: 130 f.), is creating an "underclass" comprising a third of the population, those who could be called "reflexivity losers". The economic growth in services that, until recently, enabled other industrial societies to absorb the shock of drastic cuts in primary sector jobs is having no impact now that services are becoming high-tech. This dilemma can be seen in Spain, where unemployment has topped 20%. Similar trends of varying extents can be seen in Brazil, India, Mexico (Aronowitz and DiFazzio 1994: 337-342) and Central Europe. In this last region, the collapse of old industries has been devastating, such as in Hungary, where the official unemployment rate is over 13% and where 25% of the population now lives below the poverty line, and in the Czech Republic, where even nurses are leaving their underpaid jobs behind to take their chances in the new labour market.

In Brazil, jobs are being created mainly in the middle and upper levels of the occupational pyramid, whereas there are more and more victims of unemploy-programmes for the unemployed are much more likely to play a latent role of calming discontent rather than to provide genuine work qualifications. In the Philippines, it is not only work that is being relocated, but also workers. Trends here are literally reversed as highly qualified personnel are leaving the country that financed their education[1] to go to the developed economies (mainly North America), while the country is also exporting a large amount of low-paid flexible labour. The 700,000 Filipino contract workers abroad are one of the main sources of hard currency inflows. Due to the lack of access to proper programmes, the workers tend to do their best to learn the linguistic and other skills needed on their own in an essentially invisible autodidactic learning process.

---

[1] The Philippines is one of the leading exporters of medical personnel to the First World (CS: 117).

4.1.3. The ignored economies

An economy is not limited to production based on wage-labour alone. Production in urban environments outside the "modern" sector (ILO 1991: 42-45) as well as unpaid crafts and agricultural activities are also part of today's national economies. The informal economy thus plays a role in all societies, and takes on increasing importance as a means of survival wherever the formal economies are in difficulty or undergoing rapid transition (Singh 1998). In 1985, 50% of the urban Ivory Coast population earned most of its income from this "employer of last resort" (ILO 1991: 42). Recent studies in the industrialised countries have shown that the benefits people obtain from "social redistribution", including both goods and services (provided by the unpaid labour of family, friends, community associations, etc.), exceed the basic income obtained from waged labour. In France, income from "self-production" reached a level of 56% to 60% of gross domestic product (Sue 1994: 74), a large share of which was produced by voluntary groups. It is no coincidence that one of the strategies proposed by the European Commission to reduce unemployment involves drawing on "new job pools" in welfare, ecology, education and culture. The operation envisaged here aims to transform into paid work what had previously been provided to people in the form of the unpaid labour of family members or voluntary groups – even if this is kept within the limits of the social economy (UNESCO 1996: 25). This sheds light on just how important for social groups it is to be able to use policy to determine the goals of individual and collective "self-production" activity, especially when this constructs identity and becomes production of the self or the creation of a "many-sided self".

Adult learning policy has only recently, and still gingerly, taken account of the demands of the informal economy. Adult learning programmes and policies tend to be limited to the formal economy of large, medium and small "modern" enterprises, even though they only constitute a part and sometimes even a minority of the economy as a whole. Likewise, policy ignores the millions of independent women producers and traders and thousands of micro-enterprises.

Yet here too innovative trends abound, including, for example, the popular micro-banks initiated in Asia and now expanding into other regions, community corporations and small production co-operatives, and even the informal tourist services of Central Europe. In 1992, having acknowledged that more than 40% of national production derived from the informal economy, Ecuador adopted a policy of "training the population who are economically active in the informal rural and urban sectors" (P 2). In 1990 in Brazil (P 3), the national career training service (SENAC) modified its policy to take account of persistent unemployment. It has expanded its work with neighbourhood community associations to promote the creation of micro-projects. These efforts to develop a social or "solidarity" economy in response to the failure of the modern economy to create jobs is also helping to undermine old paradigms. The sociologist Claus Offe has written a book on the emergence of production circles and trade co-ops that produce goods and services outside monetary circuits, based on a barter economy (Offe and Heinze 1992). On their own, of course, these micro-strategies can only be a partial alternative. However, given the fundamental crisis in jobs and full employment, these centres of innovation, thriving amidst broader movements that question the way work is organised today, present stimulating utopias. They expose a key contradiction: given their current structure and orientation, the formal economies cannot ensure full employment and above all cannot bring into play the productive energy and potential activity of all those who seek to work and take part in the economy (Offe and Heinze 1992: 216).

The fact that change is possible can be seen in new labour policies that take into account the structural crisis in employment (Aronowitz and DiFazzio 1994: 342 f.; De Bandt, Dejours and Dubar 1995: 195 f.; Rifkin 1995: V), in the rise of nation-wide talks between the social partners linking employment and training, in calls for new solidarity (UNESCO 1996), and in the recent appearance of special measures to correct educational exclusion, in Sweden in 1997 and in the United Kingdom in early 1999.

The change in the paradigm of adult learning policy is very real and goes far beyond the formal economy.

4.2. The productive forces and social and cultural production

A society's production is made up of more than just its economic production. The "production-producer subject" tension at the heart of debate on work-related lifelong learning can be seen in other fields as well. A fixation on the activity of policymakers in the field of adult learning tends to conceal the no-less real process of the extension of this contradiction (production-producer subject) beyond the economic sector, the informal economy included. Focusing demand for greater competencies on the world of work alone is simply becoming anachronistic.

Challenges facing contemporary societies, wherever they may be, cannot be confronted without relying on the increased capacity and participation of citizens. There is no solution to the geometric increase in health care costs without new health care promotion policies and prevention and education strategies. There is no solution to rising criminality while the number of prisons continues to grow and there are no active policies to rehabilitate inmates (Sutton 1992) and develop the human resources of poor communities. Environmental risks cannot be dealt with unless people are increasingly enabled to take action themselves and to garner information from a variety of sources.

These challenges cannot be viewed and treated as problems to be dispensed with by quick fixes by experts and professionals or legal restrictions or compulsory "vaccinations". They demand the action of groups and individuals, and hence an increase in the diffuse capacity for initiative.

It is no more possible in the social realm than in economics to await the arrival of a new generation, that is, the time needed to renew the knowledge and capacities of the adult population based simply on initial schooling. This kind of intragenerational process would take at least twenty-five years, but the need to empower citizens and enhance their capacities is too pressing. More than 80% of the next decade's civil society has already left school. Enhancing social and cultural creativity and developing people's potential for action is now an inevitable and urgent need.

Delegates at the International Conference on Adult Education in July 1997 referred to these conclusions, which were reiterated at the various summits organised by the United Nations between 1990 and 1997, as they demanded a more sweeping perspective and the active participation of people across all sectors of activities to meet today's challenges (see the *Agenda for the Future*, in: UNESCO 1997, para. 12).

Such is the social demand that, however silent today, is nonetheless implicit in the actions and changes under way in health and the environment, daily life, demographics and the "extra-parliamentary" revitalisation of politics. It is the driving contradiction between the development of the productive forces and the transformation of modes of production in health care and the environment, and between the gridlock of simple modernity and the potential of individual and collective actors. Perhaps now the need for a more all-encompassing redefinition of production is clearer, not only for the heuristic needs of researchers, but above all practically, in order to understand the implications of the way that learning policy for adults, who often do not even know the proper name of what they are doing, is rising and spilling over conventional boundaries. The trend toward "knowledge-intensive" production involves more than merely economic production.

With the crisis in the welfare state and the changing role of the state in the social arena, individuals and local communities are being called on to assume new responsibilities. The redefinition of citizenship and the "social contract", linking rights and responsibilities (Roche 1992: 229-246), clearly indicates that the dominant discourse on duty, in contrast to the neo-conservatives' limited definition in recent decades, requires in return that the social conditions underpinning social participation are secured. Yet here is the crux of the problem: are we witnessing the withdrawal of the state or a transformation of its role to ensure not only industrial rebirth, but also the impetus needed for active participation, in short, to a transition to different models of a "participatory" welfare state?

Democracy demands specifically political competencies to evaluate policies and to debate proposals (ICEA 1994: 22-24) and the development of an extra-parliamentary right of reply in a new culture of citizenship. This is evident everywhere. In Slovenia (CS: 11), the demise of a system in which the state managed everything created new demands on both citizens and officials in the new government. The folk high schools in Hungary (P 1) have rediscovered their pre-1949 objectives of educating citizens and have developed a guide (P 2) for this purpose. The transition to a pluralistic democracy in Lithuania (CS: 10) is demanding new competencies from citizens – the capacities to obtain and process different sources of information, to master the rudiments of parliamentary procedure, even in non-governmental organisations activities, and to draw up written recommendations and reports. In post-apartheid Namibia, participation, previously suppressed, is now growing. Literacy programmes use local organisations or establish Scandinavian-style study circles to enable local communities to identify their problems and develop solutions (CS: 16). In the Philippines (P 1), the 1991 law on local government has opened the door to new forms of participation (local referendums, popular consultations, right to take part in deliberative assemblies) and provides for the concomitant training needs of elected representatives and citizens.

The same situation exists at the supranational and international level. In the European Union, for example, all the partners at the second European Conference on Adult Education in Dresden recognised the importance of continuing education "for the political and social participation that European integration demands of Europe's citizens" (Germany 1994). The global is civil too.

An acute treatment crisis is widespread in health care, reaching extreme levels in African countries like the Ivory Coast, where popular services have virtually collapsed. Health care policies adopted over the past ten years in Latin America, Australia, the United States, Italy and Central Europe have reduced or at best set limits on high-tech medical treatment, and all of them include a new "health care promotion and training" component. These educational programmes target firstly personnel and secondly the public, in various forms, depending on the country – public conferences, workshops and discussion groups, consultation and home visits, the integration of "health and hygiene" modules in literacy programmes, training for members of local volunteer committees, etc. In the United States, the main argument used in the adoption of AIDS legislation (P 6) is that the transition from welfare to learnfare is the best means of ensuring the viability of social investment. The World Health Organisation has made this kind of educational re-orientation an official policy plank; it thus became a partner in the Hamburg Conference, where it organised a round table. The objective of "Health Care for All" has been reflected in various programmes and initiatives, including education and the promotion of health care, the promotion of environmental health, family planning and projects promoting women's health, public health information, promoting healthy lifestyles, educating local communities in water hygiene, etc.

Following the shift in environmental affairs recommended by the "Brundtland Commission" in 1987, *Agenda 21*, adopted by the 1992 Rio Conference, strongly promoted a shift to participatory approaches. This is based on general awareness-raising involving all social forces and requiring the development of competencies at every level to analyse problems and of capacities to intervene. In June 1994, the Ecuadorian government adopted an environmental action plan (P 3 and 4), in which educational work and the participation of organisations from civil society were to play a key role. According to the terms of a 1994 government decree (P 4), the vulnerability of the ecosystem calls for popular involvement and an extension of responsibility to include all Ecuador's people. The case of the management of Slovenia's forests is also noteworthy. The suppression of state controls first led, from 1990 to 1994, to a devastating wave of tree-felling by farmers and other small owners, who were poorly prepared for this new responsibility. Then, in 1994 (P 1), a training programme was set up for these 300,000 new guardians of "public interest" goods. Protecting the forests demands learnfare policies (United States, P 8).

Rapid demographic growth calls for women's training and advisory services, such as those operating in Morocco (P 1 and 3). In India (P 1), it has encouraged a change in outlook and the announcement of new decentralised people-oriented policies. It led the International Conference on Population and Development in Cairo in September 1994 to propose a series of measures focusing on women's rights to information and advice, the expansion of small-group training and public education programmes.

4.2.1. The eye-opening case of ageing populations

The trend towards an expanded view of productivity is evident everywhere, but the contradictions involved are particularly striking when considering the dynamics of ageing populations. The planet's elderly population is growing fast. From 1985 to 2010, the number of people aged 65 and over will have grown from 155 million to 325 million in the developing countries and from 131 million to 188 million in the developed countries (UN 1987: 43). However, what is of concern here is that this demographic trend has prompted a series of reassessments: the reconstruction of residual representations of ageing, a challenge to the linear "education-work-retirement" model, a critique of one-sided analyses of the sharp rise in the costs of ageing, and a re-examination of the notion of production in relation to retirement (Bélanger 1992). The new gerontology has abandoned pathological, one-dimensional definitions of ageing and seeks rather to identify and expand individuals' "reserve" capacities, their potential for development, cognitive abilities, aerobic and muscular performance – in short, their capacity for self-determination. This active reconstruction of the extended lifespan and of this population group's potential is taking place just as employment opportunities for the elderly are becoming rare and the serene prospect of retirement is becoming less certain. The massive displacement of older workers from the workforce and their hunt for odd jobs to survive is clouding the transition from career to retirement. Life cycles are both intermingling and differentiating (Guillemard 1983; Walker 1996). The trajectory of a continuous career leading through an orderly transition to secure retirement is no longer the rule and today even smacks of privilege. Since the 1970s, a series of factors (see below, Chapter 5 on reflexive modernisation) have been undermining this model. The consequences are grave for many workers of both sexes: exclusion from career paths where education and work alternate to meet the greater need for skills and flexibility or, quite simply, forced retirement and permanent unemployment (David 1990). But such an outcome is not necessary. Other scenarios are possible. Part of the ageing crisis is bound up with work-sharing among social classes, including age groups, as discussed previously.

Furthermore, the idea of old age as "a time of being socially useless" no longer holds (Guillemard 1980). In addition to contributing in the form of part-time and even full-time work, seniors also take part in activities outside the formal economy such as crafts, the bartering of goods and services, small-scale agricultural production and intra-generational mutual aid (Tornstam 1989: 63; Egidi 1990: 30). Similar considerations pertain to the recognition of the socio-economic contributions of senior citizens as to the unpaid labour of women looking after children – they tend to be ignored so as not to pay them or recognise them in cost-benefit calculations. Senior citizens also take countless initiatives and collective actions in response to the new challenges facing civil society at local, national and international levels. Expanding the notion of productive activity must not stop with the field of economics, but should also encompass the social arena, cultural expression and creativity. The refusal to acknowledge potential contributions in the later stages of life steers policies on ageing, including on adult learning, into a dead-end where only the rationalisation and rationing of spending count (Guillemard 1983). Yet planning for the future and diving into projects are no longer the exclusive prerogatives of the young. We are re-discovering that "mental health relies on being allowed to hope" (Dejours 1993). The dependence versus development conflict also rages in regard to the elderly.

By trying to deny the productivity of this age group (Moody 1993) and their capacity to learn new competencies (Schuller 1996) and help others to do so as well (EAEA 1995), and by treating this population as a passive force, the golden years risk being stripped of their existential reality. The democratisation of intimacy (Giddens 1992) is an ongoing, ageless transformation. Passive policies that focus on costs calculated using actuarial tables rather than on comparative benefits discourage investment in this sector. They strip ageing of any positive meaning, disregard individual people and rob them of this active period of their life. Certain African cultures searching to understand the meaning of ageing provide food for thought here (Diop 1989: 101).

Furthermore, seniors who have remained active and lead an active community life with new values and projects will not settle for a flawed definition of their generation for long. The protagonists of the world of work and new groupings are positioning and repositioning themselves in relation to the question of ageing. Senior citizens' actions can take the form of pressure groups to change policy (Bengtson, Rosenthal and Burton 1990) or be extensions of the activity of trade unions and community groups to obtain decent, independent living conditions (David 1990: 116). Perhaps collective actions and new social movements will emerge and give a new meaning to this "new age".

It is against this background, which varies from one country to another, that the demand of senior citizens for adult learning and empowerment is taking shape and being transformed and that the vision of education becomes not only lifelong but also intergenerational.

4.2.2. The ambiguous question of free time

The crisis in work is also a crisis brought about by its own implosion and the challenges created by new spaces outside the world of work. Given extended life expectancy and the fact that work today offers individuals and society new spaces for development, productive activity that has hitherto been limited to the confines of the world of wage labour can now find expression in a multitude of new forms. Naturally these expressions differ with the context, but overall there is more involved here than the marginalisation of working time or even the rise of a "leisure society", as was proclaimed in the 1970s. Above all, we are witnessing the transformation of wage labour and the rise of productive time outside the labour market, where productivity can now blossom in a broader sense and where the management of time has escaped the grip of industrial managers.

Earlier retirement, longer life expectancy and a shorter working week are increasing the amount of "free time" to the extent that it is beginning to exceed the total length of "paid" working time in post-industrial society (Sue 1994). Demand for adult learning that is not related to "paid" production is increasing and will continue to increase in the same proportions.

Nonetheless, the notion of free time in discourse on lifelong learning is often limited to the question of a quantitative increase in available time. Yet free time is not a neutral resource whose simple expansion automatically represents progress or emancipation. A basic question needs to be raised about the quality of free time or, more specifically, the freedom to make independent use of the increasing amount of non-working time over a lifetime. A gain in time outside work does not automatically imply, as André Gorz (1982) would have liked, "using time freely". The question of whether the time being freed is genuinely free was raised by T.W. Adorno (Adorno 1991: 162-170). He observed that, despite appearances, the more fundamental conflict was not between work and free time, but between the consumption engaged in during free time and the autonomy of the individual in a free democratic society. Adorno concluded that the consumption of "free time" tends to be regulated by the culture industry and is exercised in a functional continuity between work and free time.

Recent surveys of the incredible number of hours senior citizens watch television, particularly women in North America, indicate the need to more closely study the impact of the leading "leisure industries" and the new social conditioning being created in order to better understand the conditions that could make an increase in free time a factor promoting development and cultural democracy. "To spend all one's time watching television," Adorno wrote, "one needs a great deal of free time and little freedom" (Adorno 1991: 48).

Since the somewhat one-directional analysis of Adorno (see Bernstein's introduction to Adorno 1991: 8-18), media sociology has produced more dialectical studies of the relations between the media and various social groups, revealing autonomous spaces where resistance and alternatives corresponding to the real aspirations of these groups can grow. Reality is more dialectical. The ability of the culture industry to control cultural inclinations is limited, since it meets resistance and even has to face contradictions within the industry itself. As it seeks to occupy and structure these spaces, the culture industry comes up against the relatively autonomous feedback of various identity groups, competition from popular movements and the growing trend of individuals to want to manage their own time, to negotiate their life stories and to explore alternatives as they develop their life paths. The general organisation and economics of adult learning must be analysed in relation to these dynamics.

The problem is posed differently in the rapidly developing countries and the less economically developed countries than in post-industrial society. Specific research is necessary to understand these different dynamics. In the developing countries and in those parts of developed countries facing a jobs crisis, non-work, far from being free time, essentially represents a period of forced unemployment. This prompts survival tactics, seeking work in the informal economy to increase income to offset inadequate wages and pensions eroded by inflation. Our previous discussion of ignored economies has already noted the unrecognised learning demand arising in rural communities, urban neighbourhood associations and women's groups.

Sustainable development is impossible without the active involvement of the adult population and their creative energy, which gives development its very meaning.

Chapter 5
Shifting Perspectives 2: Productivity and Creativity. Rediscovering the Actor

The new requirement of productivity is ambiguous, as it simultaneously imparts new meanings and undermines old ones. To grasp the significance of these contradictions, we first need to recover the full scope and significance of production and to rediscover the subject who produces. Producing means taking an active part in production, working with others and developing one's capacity. It also involves influencing manufacturing and distribution modes and processes, by raising questions and proposing changes, and thus transforming practical know-how. Producing also means producing meaning, producing change, producing *oneself* – the subject too is expressed in his or her production (De Bandt, Dejours and Dubar 1995: 7 and 99-120). This expanded view of production leads to taking into account all fields of activity, not only the formal and informal economy, but also health care, the environment, political life and personal life.

The productive forces thus encompass not only technology and skills, but also the appropriation by the producer-subjects of this know-how in practice and consequently their capacity to act. It is this last active meaning that will be considered here, as we focus on the actor in production, the subject, as part of the workforce and more broadly. The open dynamics involved here, this space in the contradiction of still relative determinations, imbues adult learning with political significance. To say that social conditions influence action implies neither absolute determinism nor an automatic, intrinsic functionalism.

This redefinition of productive activity becomes all the more significant in today's transition to "reflexive" production methods that call for the more active and interactive involvement of the subject, particularly in the context noted above of changes in active policies in health care, environmental protection, etc. Before returning to these changes, which lead to the rediscovery of the actor, another ambiguity between productivity and productivism needs to be resolved.

5.1. Productivity and productivism

The criticism of productivism as economic growth as an end in itself could, if we are not careful, prompt a rejection of the very notion of productivity (Giddens 1994a: 178 and 247). Yet a society that rejects productivism because of its inherent risks and short-term outlook should not really forgo either the production of goods and services or carrying this out "productively" so as to achieve its goals! Production must be dissociated from the ideology of productivism and economicism (Giddens 1994a: 248).

Moreover, an increase in productive efficiency has liberating potential due to the concomitant reduction of working hours and the improvement of production conditions (Cuvillier 1984). It is not instrumental rationality that is in question, but an instrumentality that has been fetishised and cut off from its ends. Instrumentalism severs productivity from its relationship to the actor and its broader implications in all fields of activity. The world is not a giant factory.The critique of productivism does not mean abandoning the notion of productivity, but rather asking "why produce?", "for whom?"and "for what?" and re-establishing productivity as a requirement for better attaining a society's chosen goals, which also need to be reflected in the very ways production is organised. It means not allowing productivity to be approached exclusively from the angle that the one-dimensional discourse on economic competitiveness would impose. This leads us to reconstruct a synthetic vision of the producer and citizen[1], and a dialectical view of productive and creative activity.

A contradiction thus becomes evident: while expressions of economic demand for higher workforce skills and capacities are soaring, recognition of the producer subjects is difficult to obtain and sometimes completely opposed.

The dynamics involved here differ by country and region. The search for productivity is currently leading economies of the centre to concentrate on technology-intensive production on their own territory and to outsource labour-intensive production to regions with lower labour costs and poorer working conditions. However, as the countries receiving the relocated production are integrated into the new international division of labour and profit from these investments, they also seek to develop production and the export of goods with higher added value. This two-pronged trend is stimulating demand for continuing education, especially in countries endeavouring to attain a larger share of knowledge-intensive production and a better balance between export-oriented production and endogenous production.

The Frankfurt school has shown that the omnipresent contradictions between the productive forces and modes of production develop differently in different societies and, through the interaction of the existing social forces, lead to different scenarios (Held 1980: 271 f.). Indeed, while these contradictions have a specifically international character – market globalisation; a new international division of labour; a shift in production from the centre to peripheral zones with

---

[1] See the still relevant introduction by Jean-Paul Sartre to the first issue of *Les Temps Modernes* in 1945 (Sartre 1945).

lower labour costs; the export of the workforce (Philippines, CS: 117) –, national situations are far from the same. Different modernisation scenarios exist. Conflicts over development paths and international shifts in production sites also have implications for adult learning policy. And such dynamics goes beyond the historic field of social relations in the wage ecoonomy (Jay 1973: 57).

Demands to participate in development expressed by many popular movements and local community groups in the Philippines (CS: 117-124), in discussions of health care policy by women's groups in India (P 1), in the environmental movement in Ecuador (P 3 and 4), and in self-managed micro-projects in Morocco (P 5) all contain a learning demand linked either to vocational training or agricultural extension, environmental education, literacy and post-literacy programmes or the transformation of relations between universities and the local community.

The producer, as we have said, is a subject. He or she reacts to production, observes the problems involved and has to deal with them. In short, "knowledge-intensive" production tends to develop environments that, although obviously "knowledge-intensive", are above all "actor-intensive". Reflexive production leads to the gradual freeing of the actor (Lash and Urry 1994: 119). It requires the individual to be able to acquire and apply knowledge and expertise, and, wherever necessary, to change practical methods. It demands an aptitude for handling written information and communications and an ability to make use of collective knowledge and build on the experience acquired by members of a work team. The reflexive modernisation sociologists, including Ulrich Beck, Anthony Giddens and Scott Lash (Beck 1992; Giddens 1994; Beck, Giddens and Lash 1994), provide a more in-depth understanding of these contradictions and the significance of this gradual freeing (*Freisetzung*) of the actor from the grip of the social structures.

5.2. A new historical moment

We are reaching a turning point in modernisation. A general feeling of malaise and disorientation is pervading the end of the 20th century. These last one hundred years, which began with unshakeable faith in scientific progress and industrial growth, are winding up amidst uncertainty about the future, but also, via the questioning of the role of production, with the rediscovery of human resources, that is in ordinary language, the actors themselves.

We are witnessing a genuine societal transformation under the cumulative, expanding impact of unplanned change. Growth scenarios are no longer predictable and are losing all credibility. Economic globalisation is shattering long-established employer-trade union compromises on which economic upturns used to rely. The very idea of steady progress is being challenged, as are both the free-market and socialist models of growth, due both to their results and the recognition of the plurality of civilisations (Wallerstein 1996). Techno-industrial centres are generating environmental hazards that they are unable to control and that eventually call into question the very economic models on which they are based (Beck 1992). These hazards, combined with new diseases, are also undermining any serene prospects for the continuing improvement of health-care conditions. "Sexing the self" (Probyn 1993) – women are pluralising cultural models based on sexual orientation and membership and an alternative reconstruction of the division of domestic labour and reproduction. The general rise in the educational level of adults is proceeding silently in every country. Representative democracy is no longer able to legitimately fulfil its role of substituting for the active participation of citizens. In a word, "all that is solid melts into air."[2]

Linear industrial modernisation is giving way to reflexive modernisation. The infallibility of economic and scientific dogmas is succumbing to discourse that focuses more on possibilities than on functional adaptation. Scientific absolutes are being challenged; popular customs and beliefs and non-institutional health practices are no longer rejected out-of-hand as occult and mystical, as they were in post-1948 Hungary (P 5) and elsewhere.[3]

Prescribed models and customary linear pathways are being questioned at many levels, leading to greater individualisation. Faced with a rising number of increasingly fragmented models and reference points, individuals have no choice but to constantly negotiate and hew their own personal paths. Men and women who have lost their previous landmarks and now face a multitude of unexpected crossroads are no longer living out the life stories expected of them. A key characteristic of reflexive societies is precisely this individualisation, where the pathways taken in life are hacked out on the basis of the probabilities and observations of the different scenarios outlined in one's working and living environments (Beck and Beck-Gernsheim 1994).

---

[2] We refer here to the title of the marvellous book by Marshall Berman (1982). His analysis of literary developments in the 19th and 20th century forecast this crisis of modernity and the post-modernist dead-end. By examining three contemporary authors' initial apprehensions and "literary intuitions" about this period of the first industrial revolution (and the first traumas of modernisation), he was able to anticipate the similar heuristic context today and the possibilities of new dialectics in the emerging crises of late modernity.

[3] The post-war Hungarian government even banned from public libraries publications on alternative health remedies and natural herbal treatments, which were very popular before the Second World War (P 5).

These "risk" and "reflexive" societies demand in return a variety of production sites, the constant checking of knowledge and information, as well as a new concept of public service by the media and by knowledge banks. In addition, they require space and opportunity for changes in pathways, and the right to be different and to err. "Reflexive society" demands a high level of communications abilities from its citizens, polyvalent qualifications from the producers, new active consumption patterns (see Chapter 3, sect. 3.4) and support for synergies among the diverse phases of adult learning throughout life.

A new historical *momentum* is being created, where the diffuse capacity for initiative and the fuller development of the productive and creative forces take on new importance. In this fresh environment, where the subject is being rediscovered, competent participation demanded and spaces opened up by the ambiguities and reflexivities penetrating every field of activity, it is no more inevitable that productivity will be subverted by productivism than it is that the emancipation of the subject will be guaranteed by the reflexive context. It is not only the experts but also the "secular" population that is being obliged to put its brains to work, to continually interpret new knowledge, technical information and expertise, to test these through a daily routine of trial-and-error, and to make the best possible decisions (Beck, Giddens and Lash 1994: 6 f.). "Safe" technical solutions are giving way to a reflexive citizenry. In a world of intense social reflexivity, democratisation and democracy require the recognition, reinforcement and renewal of citizenship, that is, citizens who are themselves reflexive (Giddens 1994:7-10). Of course, the structural inequalities of a now more reflexive modernisation continue to have an impact. Furthermore, modernisation is more reflexive in some social and economic sectors than in others. Yet a new dynamic is being born, where the emancipation or empowerment of all the actors, already an essential condition for a reflexive society, is also becoming a key challenge and goal, and will certainly be the subject of debates and struggles to come.

This is why, far from opposing the advocacy by economic agencies of adult learning to raise productivity and the skills and insights of producers, some innovative collective actions are making full use of the contradictory nature of this still selective and one-dimensional movement. In Australia, Italy, Namibia, the Philippines and Quebec, this legitimate albeit still limited programme for the development of human potential is being taken at its word and pushed even further by demands that it be made available to everyone in every sector of life.

5.3. The policy response: the real but difficult and unequal liberation of the creative and productive forces

Although demand to develop human potential and increase competencies is leading to the adoption of new policies and programmes, these responses differ greatly in the world of work and other areas.

5.3.1. Adult learning and economic productivity

Developing and freeing productive and creative capacities obviously depends not only on education itself, but more fundamentally on the broader learning structure discussed in Chapter 3. Continuing work-related training is, however, becoming a concrete demand everywhere.

Chapters 3, 7, 9 and 10 of this book analyse the actual functions of policies implemented in the 24 countries studied. Here we want to emphasise the strengths and limitations of current policies in relation to social demand.

Bear in mind the upsurge in work-related adult learning activities over the past decade. Continuing training has become a major component of work practices and policies. The overall level of public and private investment in work-related adult learning is now considerable, even when excluding individual financial contributions which, in Canada and Switzerland, for example, are as large as those of business. It is worth reiterating the figures given in Chapter 1: the combined annual contribution of business and government comes to about US$ 50 billion in Germany and approximately US$ 200 billion in the United States. In terms of the US government's share, the greatest growth has been in literacy and basic education programmes for young adults and welfare recipients. New active labour market policies have freed up significant sums by using unemployment insurance funds for educational purposes. In Canada, this policy led to about US$ 1.5 billion of additional investment in adult learning in the 1994-1995 financial year. Finally, much of the expansion of adult learning provision is due to post-secondary educational institutions opening their doors to adults and getting "full-time equivalent allocations", including further education colleges in the United Kingdom, community colleges in Canada, and universities, private educational centres and systems of continuing open education.

Adult learning budgets are also on the rise in Eastern Europe and the developing countries. Employment and training budgets to finance continuing education have been established in Brazil (P 6), Hungary (P 6), Lithuania (P 6), the Ivory Coast (P 4) and also in South Africa in 1999. European Commission programmes provide major financial support for work-related adult learning in the form of structural funds in Mediterranean EU countries and restructuring areas in other member states, the "Phare" and "Tempus" programmes in East European countries (Slovenia P4; the Czech Republic P 6 and 7) and, more recently, the European Training Foundation. Governments are generally budgeting more funds for work-related adult learning. In Hungary, a 1993 law on work-related learning provided for various measures, including educational leave and an annual budget of US$ 40 million to educate 70,000 people; the World Bank has provided additional funds in the form of credits (P 6). The agricultural act adopted by Lithuania in 1991 and the 1992 implementing decrees established a budget for adult learning programmes that involved 13,000 new farmers in 1993.

As has already been mentioned, more than 5% of India's federal education budget is currently spent on adult literacy programmes. In Namibia (P 1), the figure is 2%, which already greatly exceeds the international average. International assistance for continuing education is also growing. The Asian Development Bank has been financing adult literacy programmes in the Philippines since 1993 (P 7: 3). In Ecuador, the World Bank provides loans for basic adult education (P 1) and works with the Inter-American Bank, the United Nations Development Programme (UNDP) and bilateral co-operation (P 2) to support work-related adult learning. In Morocco, agricultural training programmes (P 5) receive aid from the United Nations Population Fund (UNFPA), which works with UNESCO and Unicef to aid the national literacy programme as well (P 4). In the Ivory Coast, the United Nations Economic Commission, the UNDP and the World Bank are beginning to financially assist the training of farmers (P 2) and adult literacy programmes (P 3), the latter in co-operation with Unicef, UNESCO and the UNFPA. Work-related adult learning in the country is assisted by the ILO and bilateral aid.

Nonetheless, the authors of the 20 country studies emphasise that government proclamations and the multiple expressions of demand have not necessarily led to a corresponding level of investment in and expansion of adult learning opportunities. In Canada, extra funds from the unemployment insurance budget have been used as a reason to reduce job planning programme budgets by more than 25%, i.e. over US$ 350 million. In Slovenia, although a 1990 labour relations law opened the door to work-related learning and educational leave, in practice the economic crisis has led to a reduction of the overall number of participants (P 4). In Brazil, a lack of funds is paralysing the implementation of legislative innovations in occupational health and safety (P 1). In India, major investment in literacy does not seem to have been followed up or accompanied by a corresponding commitment to post-literacy programmes and work-related adult learning in the formal and informal economies, despite the development of open learning systems and the efforts of certain organisations such as the Shramik Vidyapeeths centres. In the Philippines, an analysis of seven different policies produced the same conclusion: funds are lacking to implement policies developed during the opening created by the Marcos dictatorship's fall, and financial decentralisation is tending to favour the wealthiest urban areas. In the Ivory Coast, despite the aforementioned new programmes in less organised sectors, the priority given to the modern sectors is being undermined by the crisis and is leading the government to relieve business of its financial responsibilities for work-related learning (P 4).

The country studies and the surveys mentioned above indicate that the structure of work-related adult learning today reflects the segmentation of labour markets: investment in organised learning is concentrated essentially in the modern sectors, in large corporations (even though jobs are created mainly in small and medium-sized enterprises; see United States, CS: 173 f.), in the upper rungs of the occupational hierarchy and in the formal economy. Most corporate financial support goes to male employees (Bélanger and Valdivielso 1997: 16). Claude Dubar (1991: 179-195) earlier observed this same trend in France, noting that the dualisation of the labour market is reflected in a dualisation of intervention models in work-related education. Big corporations have integrated education and training measures, while government programmes for vulnerable groups engage in their socialisation to marginality.

Lifelong learning has emerged at the moment when lifelong jobs are disappearing. The erosion of job stability and the fall in job duration are transforming corporate training policies, which are becoming less oriented towards training staff who may well not remain in the company. In Japan (CS: 42-44), this has led to a trend to shift work-related learning from business to universities, which are better able to offer qualifications recognised by all employers.

Only extensive organisational changes, work-sharing and a reconceptualisation of the relationships between the formal and informal economies can offset the latent exclusionary impacts associated, in the current context of jobless economic growth, with current training policies for the unemployed.

5.3.2. Adult learning and social and cultural productivity

The development of skills and knowledge does not stop in the workplace. There is rising demand to liberate people's creative potential outside the world of work. The response has been uneven and taken different forms. There is firstly the strategic concern of adult literacy which, in addition to helping raise the general level of basic competency, has also become an important vehicle that sectoral ministries have used in educational measures to bolster their policies on health care, population growth, environmental and other areas. We will return to this in Chapter 10. A large volume of activity centres on general and socio-cultural adult learning. This takes place in local community centres, libraries and non-governmental organisations, and is also provided by distance-learning organisations, continuing education services and post-secondary educational institution extension courses. In Japan, social education (the term for general adult learning there) is provided to about 12 million adults per year (CS: 8). In Germany, about 10 million people were already involved with the folk high schools in 1991 (Nuissl 1994). Despite being undermined by budget cuts, similar trends can be seen in Australia, Canada, Spain, Finland, Italy and the United Kingdom. In Eastern Europe, the centres established under the former regimes have collapsed and been replaced by newly created or revitalised folk high schools and by new initiatives from local authorities, various voluntary groups and private education centres, especially in the fields of language and information technology. A variety of subjects are on offer: culture, health care, environmental protection, new technology, second languages, etc.

Moreover, despite government efforts to justify cutbacks in this sector by deriding it as "socio-cultural leisure activity", resistance and protest movements have arisen, especially in Australia, Canada and the United Kingdom. Likewise, in Japan there have been efforts to counter the integration of social education (CS: 28-31 and 46). Advocacy reports in this field in Australia (CS: 21-25), Canada (ICAE 1994) and the United Kingdom (P 5- 8) rediscovered ways in which adult learning contributes to the community, by empowering women, strengthening male-female relationships in the family, improving health conditions, mastering new technology in daily life, taking up environmental matters, creating space for inter-personal dialogue about tolerance and lifestyles, learning second languages and teaching immigrants the first language, and helping senior citizens become more independent.

The use of adult learning in sectoral interventions (health care, environmental protection, population policy, etc.) constitutes an entirely new field for adult learning. Significant funds are being invested, including for education in family planning in Morocco (P 1) and India (P 1) with the aid of the UNFPA and Unicef and, in India, with loans from the World Bank and support from bilateral co-operation; in promoting health measures in all countries, including Australia, the Czech Republic (P 4 and 5), Hungary (P 5), Italy (P 6), the Ivory Coast (P 1), Slovenia (P 2), and the United States (P 5), with help from WHO, Unicef and the European Development Fund; and in environmental protection, as in Ecuador, which receives support from the Inter-American Development Bank, the World Bank, the UNDP and bilateral aid. Although these funds may be ensconced in various sectoral programmes, they diversify and expand the economic base of adult learning.

The modalities of these new interventions nonetheless raise questions about their quality and educational productivity, that is, the possibility for learners to grasp the knowledge transmitted and the potential for autonomous action thus acquired so as to ensure sustainable development. Information-education-counselling (IEC) programmes for adult populations in the fields of health care and environmental protection represent a culturally significant qualitative turning point, including in the advanced industrial countries.[4] They also pose a challenge. Information campaigns and vertical public communications can reach populations and help change daily practices. However, their impact will remain limited if they do not do more to empower individuals and enable them to integrate learning acquisition, and if they are not based on local cultural dynamics and do not encourage local committees and groups to take charge of their problems and redefine them according to their specific contexts. There is a dilemma here. Broad "IEC" programmes can reach their targeted publics and help a certain number of people adopt recommended practices in health care, family planning, etc. However, the impact might well not last beyond the educational campaigns.

The introduction of a national population policy in India in 1994 (CS: 89-91 and P 1) provoked broad discussion and debate that, while acknowledging the policy's strong points, was also fearful of a narrow educational campaign limited to birth control. While the Indian national programme will help change individual practices and may advance the debate about the links between demographic growth and improving the quality of life and access to education, it was reluctant to base itself on an active civil society favourable to the reflexive appropriation of messages and make room for discussion of the feminisation of poverty and the meaning of the public transformation of intimacy – in short, at fully freeing up cultural potential.

"IEC" policies are a good example of current contradictory trends. They target adult populations, link up with them in their daily environment, nourish learning aspirations and create space for more significant changes. They would have much greater impact, however, if they also enabled populations to interact to acquire new information and extrapolate their learning to new fields and contexts, that is, to participate more actively and become more competent. New one-way "IEC"-type preventive strategies are running up against popular resistance, such as in non-governmental women's centres in Morocco, where women want to replace short individual informational visits with meetings allowing top-down information to be discussed and compared with experience and local aspirations. Educational policy concerning population planning in Morocco (P 3) generally tends to be expressed in deductive, vertical actions. Nonetheless, the

---

[4] Consider, for example, the cultural impact of the 1994 American policy on the prevention of sexually transmissible diseases through decentralised programmes, with subsidies for information, counselling and education (P 6).

resistance, challenges and innovations that it provokes in the women's centres, and the laborious forging of reciprocity in knowledge relationships, gives a sense of what the future of adult learning policy could look like.

5.4. The diffusion of the capacity for intiative

The number of men and women who want to carry on learning is rising rapidly everywhere, and adult learning aspirations as well as the demand put on all citizens to enhance their competency is spreading well beyond conventional boundaries. Yet not only is demand increasing, its nature is changing, leading social agents to redesign learning programmes. The broad gamut of adult learning policies is increasingly being unshackled from linear conceptions of skills updating and the adaptive socialisation typical of "simple modernisation", and is taking a new direction: the difficult liberation of the productive and creative capacities of actors, all actors, in every field. We have sought to discover the significance of these changes by analysing the contradictory relations between, on the one hand, the transformation of economic, social, political and cultural production and, on the other hand, the limited recognition of the autonomy of actors and the unequal development of their capacity for action.

We conclude on two facets to this change in paradigm: first, the micro-synergistic effect of enhancing the capacity of actors and the impact of this on policy macro-synergies, then, simply but crucially, the "return of the actor."

5.4.1. The synergistic effect of enhancing the capacity of actors to act in different sectors

Without becoming so enamoured of the *knowledge-intensive* economy that we forget the massive layoffs on which it has often been built, it must be recognised that it does represent a step forward. The emphasis on competence, however segmented, leads to and forms part of a broader dynamic involving the knowledgeable participation of populations and the autonomy and creativity of actors, not only in the formal sector of the economy, but also beyond the boundaries of the economy itself.

It is increasingly clear that development of the potential for action and communication is cumulative. The acquired capacities to think, create and produce fuse over time and transcend spheres of activity and disciplinary boundaries. Adult learning policies, often confined to technical adaptation and focused on short-term adjustments, cannot prevent tasks from being defined ever more sweepingly. Long-term investment does not become pointless just because business is showing less interest in long-term investment to train a more mobile workforce. As in Japan, the same objective is being pursued through other mechanisms, in particular the steady turn to educational institutions. Nor will the tendency of health care ministries to focus on the conditions of existing health care practice (and in any case epidemiological research is helping broaden their vision) halt the empowerment of *patients*, which is also being bolstered by prevention measures.

This premise of the accumulation of learning acquisition and the synergy between components of the ever-more fragmented world of adult learning is central to changing the dynamics of adult learning policy. This is likely to lead to a new generation of legislation and programmes, which have already started to take shape in recent policies. Paradoxically, it is the chaotic development and proliferation of learning opportunities that may now make possible, not a centripetal return to the bosom of some ministry of adult learning planning, but new post-traditional multi-sectoral ways to realise these potential synergies.

Dysfunctions associated with still highly institutionalised cleavages (general vs vocational education, productive training of the workforce vs socio-cultural leisure activity, occupational therapy for senior citizens, curative vs preventive practices, etc.) are indicative of future trends. The European region, drawing on its cultural roots, has pushed this contradiction to the extreme by identifying general education with Socrates and vocational training with the artist, architect and humanist scholar Leonardo da Vinci. If these labels seem inappropriate, it is not merely because administrative jargon cheapens the image of these two historical figures, but above all because they themselves would reject these divisions and instead seek diverse expressions of creativity in every field.

The growing recognition of the synergistic effects of learning acquisition in any field on an individual's subsequent educational biography leads to re-examining the current compartmentalisation of policies in order to unleash the full potential of the diverse processes involved in developing and liberating capacities for action. It also leads to seeing the converse effect of this cumulative process as tragic, that is, the "negative synergies" whereby the starting thrust for initial education has been insufficient and inequalities are subsequently reproduced throughout life – unless, obviously, policies change!

5.4.2.   The return of the actor

The dynamics of contemporary reflexive society make possible a better understanding of the current proliferation of adult learning policies. The point is simple, but decisive: there is no production without actors. Although today this stands out most visibly in the economy, it is being seen in an increasing number of other fields, sharpening and transforming the dynamics of adult learning policies. It is key to their significance – there can be no productivity without first raising the economic, social, political and cultural productivity of the actors. Indeed, there is a clear aspiration and a pressing necessity everywhere for the active, general social participation of adult populations. That is why enhancing adult populations' capacities for initiative is increasingly the subject of policies and interventions, even if this trend is highly uneven and counteracted in various ways.

For the moment this dynamic tends to be dealt with in discourse on competitiveness and productivity, but this too is contradictory. It is simply one trend within a more complex interaction of relations. Spurred on by the acknowledged deadlocks in the world of work and in the new fields of environmental protection, health promotion and the emancipation of minority groups, collective actions and government proposals are revealing the significance and full extent of the growing demand to unleash the productive and creative forces.

It is "the return of the actor" (Touraine 1988), the producer subject, the citizen and collective action; it is the rediscovery of action that requires the reinforcement of the capacity for action and the autonomy of the subjects.

The tendency to refocus adult learning policy on "social demand" is a key change indicative of these new trends.

Chapter 6
The Expression and Management of Social Demand

The problem of developing policies to influence the possibilities for expressing learning demand is being posed all the more forcefully at a time when the "classic educational model" no longer corresponds to reality. The policies generated by this conventional model are based on a stereotype of learning demand that is no longer dominant in the world today. Its contents and "moments of learning" (see Neugarten, cited by Schuller 1995: 29) are predetermined by standard programmes and conform to a life model broken down into predetermined stages in which education – or at least the bulk of it – is concentrated in childhood and youth and in a few other rare but predictable moments of adulthood. In this model, the only function of policy is to regulate flows into and out of the education system.

6.1. Transition to a policy for the synergistic expression of demand

The rising social demand for diversified learning throughout life and the desynchronisation of life paths (see Chapter 4) are rendering the established policies obsolete and opening up possibilities for new policies. Previous policies were limited to offering responses to demand that was known and voiced. They tended to reproduce the inequities of initial education. Hence the emergence of policies whose application precedes that of educational provision, policies that affect not only the expression of immediate demand, but also the context and living conditions in which it arises.

The need for such policies was already explicitly stated in a report (in August 1984) by the National Council on Educational Reform instituted by the Japanese government, which recommended the transition
"from a theory of lifelong education that was based on a supply-side approach to education, to a demand-side concept of a 'learning society' in which anyone can voluntarily learn whatever he or she wishes to learn according to the learning needs at various stages of life" (CS: 22).

The same orientation also seems to be taking root in India, where the need is being felt for a shift from "target-oriented" policies to "people-oriented" policies (CS: 81). Another concrete example of this is the failure of family planning policies that attempt to use education simply as a "quick-fix" tool (the dissemination of birth control techniques through information campaigns, etc.). Their poor results stem from the failure to involve men and women in a process of identifying and taking charge of the problem and collectively finding possibilities for a solution, including new roles in family and social life. This shortcoming also plagued irrigation programmes implemented in the Ivory Coast (CS: 53 f.; P 2). Initially, the construction of artesian wells in various villages was supported simply by providing technical courses to train local personnel to repair faulty pumps. However, these policies did not allow for communicating and negotiating local demands, and clearly did not foresee that the arrival of the wells would, for instance, rob women of the opportunity to meet and socialise at the traditional watering hole, however far from the village. Nor did they foresee that this gift from on high would be fairly useless if information were not provided about why well water is preferable from a sanitary viewpoint.

Choosing a policy for the synergistic expression of social demand does not mean attempting to regulate supply and demand. This new alternative is not simply about managing a market. It aims to enable all those with a particular interest in learning to express their aspirations and to define and better control their own learning projects. It thus generates activity and measures
-   that influence the identification and expression of learning needs and thus accord the individual or collective actor the opportunity and ability to become involved in defining their own programmes and legitimating the demand expressed;
-   that create more favourable conditions, remove cultural barriers and open access to all social strata, while also providing for individual efforts;
-   that affect the concrete conditions that foster or impede the expression and intellectual development of all subjects, that is, major factors, whether temporal (by helping the subjects to manage time devoted to learning), spatial (measures facilitating geographic mobility), motivational (by building links between organised learning and life goals) and managerial (by involving the public in the management and control of actions).

These new policies for the expression of demand give material substance to declarations on the right to learn.

6.1.1. Adult learning as the project, right and responsibility of the learner

For a long time, the concept of the right to adult education did not go much beyond statements of principle in constitutional charters. "Obligation" is more central to the traditional (school) model of policy based on educational provision than is "right". It is up to people to take the opportunity of available offers. Some legal systems refuse to allow those who have not completed a certain number of years of study to exercise some professions, and yet neither guarantee these people the right to resume their studies at any time nor recognise learning acquired on the job.

With the introduction of policies for the expression of social demand for learning, the problem of an individual's right to adult learning is posed anew. Indeed, if the distribution rules and roles of different subjects are not defined, the expression of demand will once again be subject entirely to the unwritten rules of social reproduction and the prevailing balance of power in society and the educational market.

The measures adopted by various laws and policies refer not only to basic rights (individual and collective), but also to the right to benefit from specific measures to guarantee access (subsidies, educational leave, etc.).

A recent trend, albeit secondary, is worth noting here because of its particular impact. Some organisations tend to avoid the concept of right or saddle it with caveats, preferring instead the notion of a "learning contract" as expressed in the subject's assumption of "responsibilities" and the "free choice" of the individual adult learner. Thus the approach proposed by the OECD Centre for Educational Research and Innovation holds that:

> "the adult learner is distinctive in a number of ways. The most obvious is that he or she is a voluntary learner, rather than somebody who has been forced to attend school by legal and/or parental pressure (...) a free-willed consumer of education and training" (OECD-CERI 1995: 204).

The same philosophy can be found in Japan, where, for instance, a 1990 report by a government-mandated commission in charge of developing strategy for a new national law on lifelong learning stated that:

> "Lifelong learning should be based on the individual's spontaneous willingness to pursue quality in life and vocational ability, as well as to enrich the self. (...) Lifelong learning should continue throughout life, and should include such measures and contents as are seen fit by the individual" (CS: 26).

The common characteristic of these two documents is that they refer to an abstract subject whose learning process depends basically on their individual will and assumption of responsibility. However, individual responsibility and will cannot be cut off from the concrete conditions, including the learning contents, that go into determining them. To be expressed and put into practice, individual will and responsibility must transcend these contexts. The two documents refer to an individual in isolation from their social context. They neglect the relationship between the individual and collective dimensions of assuming responsibility for learning projects and expressing them. They ignore not only the possibilities that collective actors have to define learning projects but also the barriers and limits they encounter. The two documents thus fail to take into account the restrictive processes engaged in by business, government, the market and educational agents at work and in daily life. They also neglect the need to find new and different ways to transform and awaken an individual's will and sense of responsibility with regard to the learning process.

"Laissez-faire" policies tend to reintroduce old forms of exclusion. In contrast, policies for the expression of social demand generate measures to involve the individual and collective subjects in such a way that they themselves are able, through learning, to instigate processes to change the conditions that have hindered or blocked the intellectual development of all citizens. These measures thus affect concrete historical subjects, actors and their emerging projects, as well as the learning conditions that they aim to transform, in a way that promotes the formation of individual and collective projects that transcend these conditions.

6.1.2. The power of the learner and the power of transformation: investors and beneficiaries

A policy promoting the expression and synergy of demand does not entail simply managing the same types of educational interventions in a different way. It involves allocating resources before, during and after organised learning activities.

A series of studies to determine the main vectors through which recession and structural adjustment measures influence educational programmes and policies in the developing countries show that the following "indicators" have a decisive impact on the possibilities for expressing educational demand:

1. Household income and spending: while demand is relatively independent of living standards, this is not true of access to services and thus of concrete participation.
2. Public budgets and education spending: government cutbacks affecting first and foremost non-recurrent, non-contractual and non-payroll spending have a particularly negative impact on the effectiveness of adult education services and tend to increase disparities between cities and outlying areas, high income and low income strata, etc.
3. The level and distribution of employment and unemployment rates: the situation and level of employment influences the expression of demand and concrete participation, including the exclusion of older workers.
4. Business profitability and taxes: vocational training financed by business taxes, such as in France, the Ivory Coast, Nigeria and Zimbabwe, makes it possible in profitable sectors to offset government cutbacks (Mulenga 1994: 42 f.).

Although the financial cost of each operation and the impact of financial and economic measures can be evaluated, not everything is calculable in cash. Linking adult learning to the business policies of both private and public companies inevitably favours those with the means to control and generate learning opportunities. Robert Reich clearly explains what the developed countries gain from making this close link. He starts with the observation that "either we win or they win" and then proposes "symbolic analytic" work, i.e. work with a high knowledge content, and its global export as the strategic key to ensuring the greatest gains and prosperity to countries capable of sustaining this programme (Reich 1991: 306-312). This kind of strategy, however, runs the risk of dividing the countries of the world into learning exporters and importers and offers the latter only a future of dependence, as losers.

An active policy promoting the expression of demand takes into account financial factors and the balance of power in a society without accepting that these should be determinant. The need to rely on the world's imagination and intelligence is too widely accepted to remain dominated by laissez-faire market forces. An "organised self-educating society" (Gramsci 1986) can be built under diverse conditions. Its growth does not necessarily depend on the purchasing power of its members; there is no inherent prerequisite (first wealth and an acceptable living standard, and only then lifelong learning). Sequential and hierarchical systems of needs are the empirically baseless ideological arguments of an unequal international system of lifelong learning.

A policy for the expression of demand rejects economic determinism and makes it possible for actors to organise independently to overcome obstacles to intellectual development. Such a policy focuses on civil society and on the capacity of people to transform their problems into resources based on their independent capacity to develop new forms of community life and to adopt new roles. Schuller's observation is fitting:

> "I would argue that we need a clearer public understanding of the relationship between rights and responsibilities if the notion of citizenship is to be taken beyond that of the individual consumer (...). The volume of voluntary or unpaid activity in domestic, social and cultural settings is extraordinarily high, but largely unrecognised. In one sense, it occurs to me, such activities are the essence of citizenship. The socialising role of adult education in this sense is one which enables people to contribute actively, at whatever level, to the society in which they live" (Schuller 1993: 10).

At a time when the importance of education in the production process and thus in workforce skills is being recognised and when education is itself becoming a negotiable service, the question of the cost of the entire educational process and how it is distributed is raised in more explicit terms. The use of learning opportunities, in terms of the use of educational services and of the process of development of individual learning paths, is becoming an explicit and integral part of the new adult learning policies and the general organisation of adult learning. The beneficiary is no longer simply the immediate consumer of educational programmes. The real beneficiary is anyone with an interest in "what individuals can do as result of their training" (Australia, P 7: 3).

Policies to aid demand financially (by means of grants, paid educational leave, etc.) thus need to be analysed and discussed not only as policies to finance cultural "consumption" services and products, but also as payment to the learners to increase their productive capacities. In the case of the unemployed, the same explanation and justification holds for financing learning and providing allowances pro rata to the time spent in education, provided at least that the goal is labour force reintegration and the fulfilment of their right to work. Immediate payment for participation in adult education amounts to an investment aimed at reducing long-term dependence so as to reduce social welfare spending and increase tax revenue.

Despite the growing recognition that learning is a productive resource that has an impact on general productivity, government and business are attempting to reduce the costs they underwrite and shift them to the different parties involved, including individuals and families, associations and local authorities. In Australia, for example, the cutback in the state role and the introduction of customer-focused learning demand policies has resulted in a situation "generally centred on the needs of business" (CS: 20). This has not led to the disappearance of monopolies, but instead to the appearance of a new, more or less latent educational conflict. It is also introducing some forms of hegemony, which tend to pass on costs to the individuals and thus increase inequality.

6.1.3. The growth in learning demand and state policy

In more than one country, it is claimed that the state is no longer capable of assuming all the costs required to meet recently recognised new learning demand. Consider the example of Canada, where in 1985 the Quebec government adopted an "open budget" policy, with no pre-defined cap on the government budget for ensuring access to secondary education for all adults who want it. In just a few years, this measure doubled the number of those enrolled in secondary-level literacy and education programmes. However, due to the rise in demand and the cost of education, the ministry has begun to cut back the "open budget" by introducing limits on acceptable spending (CS: 8). The same phenomenon could be seen in the United Kingdom in the early 1990s. An increase in learning demand induced the central government to limit the power of local education authorities to provide "adequate provision" (CS: 158).

Other ministries also face this challenge of diversifying financial sources and adopting long-term investment policies. New adult learning policies are based on a redistribution of educational expenditure according to the diverse goals to be met. Economic policies are thus being developed from an inter-ministerial and inter-sectorial perspective.

The Swedish participatory welfare state

Rubenson's description (1994) of the historical development of adult learning policy in Sweden provides a useful comparative basis for identifying the problems and contradictions in this field. At the time of the 1967 reform, the Swedish parliament created a Department of Adult Education as part of the National Education Council, granted new powers to local authorities in the field and demanded that television broadcasting take on board the needs of adult education. This reform bore fruit, as the law brought about an increase in explicit demand for adult education by those who already desired it and were capable of benefiting from it, i.e. members of the pool of talent and the nation's intellectual reserve.

Sweden's 1975 reform went even further and adopted certain measures such as social benefits for adult learners and subsidies for affirmative outreach measures to stimulate learning demand among disadvantaged strata. The new policy differed from its predecessor by endeavouring to remove obstacles to participation, in particular time and cost factors. Swedish policy in 1974 reflected the economic optimism of the decade and relied on an increase in government employment to extend the right to adult learning to all.

A change in policy in 1976 saw a gradual freezing of funds due, among other factors, to a crisis in government finance and a change in political objectives. While the social-democrats sought to promote a change in working conditions, the conservatives emphasised the role of individuals and their ability to change their living conditions.

In the 1980s, attention focused on the learning needs of the workforce. The policy challenge then was to decide how to meet rising demand for adult learning in a situation that precluded any increase in public spending. A decision was taken to authorise government institutions to enter the market and sell their learning services. Thus began the purchase of services and the entry of business into the educational system.

In the 1990s, the Swedish government was faced with a continuing public finance crisis, a constant rise in informal learning demand for services in the state-managed sector, and the establishment of a parallel continuing education system managed by business and independent of any real government control. Legislation in 1991 induced a radical break with the 1967 arrangements. The state renounced its role as principal educational agent and called on associations to take charge of informal adult education. In co-operation with the adult education movement, it set up an ad-hoc office, the National Council of Non-Formal Adult Education, with public financing of about US$ 250 million (Rubenson 1994: 378; Sweden 1995 and 1996). Yet it did not take away any powers previously granted to local authorities. Nor did any of the new measures make any substantial reference to the new, business-run continuing education system, which consequently continued to develop independently, with the trade unions exercising a sort of negotiated control (Rubenson 1994: 369-381). Somewhat later, in September 1996, the Swedish Ministry of Education and Science adopted a national programme for formal adult education. This enabled some 100,000 adults to complete their secondary education each year, at an annual public cost of US$ 800 million. Based on its participatory welfare-state approach, the Swedish adult learning policy also drew on the local authorities and the informal education network, and involved all the social partners (Sohlmann 1998a and 1998b).

6.2. The strategic policy objective: Liberating subjects' capacity for initiative

6.2.1. An emerging response

The statement that "learning systems cannot indefinitely meet sharp growth in demand" (UNESCO 1996: 176) does not justify adopting policies for small, gradual incremental shifts, much less abandoning strategies for equality. Widespread confusion would result if the entire lifelong-learning scene were identified too closely with formal "education systems" alone. We believe that the dynamics set in motion around the world by the different social actors are opening up windows for establishing conditions to promote the ongoing intellectual development of all citizens.

The crisis in the conventional model of adult education policy does not necessarily nullify the possibility of using public policy to acknowledge the collective interest. The old, still operative model set policy the task of defining and managing educational measures specific to clearly defined social groups. This was done by creating specialised sub-systems based on the type of education offered (literacy, university, work-related learning, informal education: culture, health care, sports, etc.) and the type of social group and period of life (education for youth, job-seekers, young married couples, workers, the retired, etc.). These measures were not necessarily co-ordinated. Programmes included one or more different sub-systems, depending on the needs and resources of the state. The reason it is in crisis, however, is not simply that the "state-educator" model is economically unfeasible. Its more basic limitation is educational. This model focuses only on the immediate dimension of learning. It is not suited to looking at education's contingent dimensions, to the multidimensional extensive life-paths that are actually involved. It is a system model that functions based on access to educational activities and not on the learning life-paths of its subjects. It fails to take into account either changes in learning environments or the relationships between individual and collective histories and the concrete conditions of life and work.

Several governments are already developing new orientations that take into account the growth in learning demand in all its spatial and temporal dimensions. These "open" policies, though not without their birth pangs, aim to "liberate subjects' capacity for initiative".

To understand the concrete nature of this change, it is worth considering the rich policy experience of sub-Saharan Africa, where an evaluation of the limits of agricultural development policy has raised questions, not so much about policy structure or extent as about the lack "of a policy to transfer responsibility and power to the farmers" (Ivory Coast, CS: 53). The issue here is not whether it is necessary to provide technical training, but of combining the acquisition of skills with a spirit of initiative and active participation in development (CS: 52). In the current model, whenever the state or any public or private educational agent withdraws, everything fades away. Policy is not grounded in a strategy for activating social demand and hence a strong recognition of demand and the co-management or direct management by the subjects themselves of projects. The evaluation of the Ivory Coast's agricultural development programmes rightfully concludes that organising the farmers at every level, in particular in the field of basic education, training, production, marketing, processing, management and finance, is the only way to genuinely enable them to take control of their economic and social activity.

A similar tendency can be seen in developments in work-related learning policy in Japan since 1993. Here, the emphasis is not on the collective actor but on raising "self-development... which would bring companies new vitality and contribute to reinforcing the basis of prosperity, not to speak of developing the workers' abilities." (CS: 39) Subsequently, Japan has also taken additional steps to promote forms of organised social life considered essential to self-development (ibid.).

The trend to emphasise the active role of the subject in the management of the learning process can be seen in many other countries' policies. The Council of Ministers of the Nordic countries – a body composed of ministers from Denmark, Finland, Iceland, Norway and Sweden – reached similar conclusions in its important report on adult learning. Speaking about the barren prospects for creating good learning environments, it held that "all education and learning should be structured so that it reinforces the learner's capacity for taking initiatives, his or her self-confidence and sense of his/her own worth" (Nordic Council 1995: 15). The Dutch government's three-year social policy plan, inspired by the principle of enabling individuals to become active, independent citizens, expressed a similar view (Netherlands 1994).

Also noteworthy in this regard is the Tribally Controlled Community College Endowment Program — established by legislation in 1978 and updated in 1983 – by means of which United States law acknowledged the right of Native American peoples to create independent learning institutes (P 2). Reference could also be made to the Vista programme, which was part of Lyndon Johnson's "War on Poverty", which was updated in 1993 by the National and Community Services Trust Act. The latter programme aimed to encourage social groups to take part in participatory forms of learning and solve their own problems.

6.2.2. The development of a society with the capacity for initiative

As we delve into the factors driving change in current policies, we also need to point out their contradictory nature. They can lead, and have led, to strategies that take "diffuse initiative" to mean convenient, low-cost arrangements for the most vulnerable, who are abandoned to their fate by so-called self-development and unsupported self-learning policies.

The goal of a "society with widespread initiative" prefigures a new model of the participatory welfare state, based on active learning policies and the participation of each individual and collective actor, and not on abandoning subjects to "laissez-faire" policies. Making the citizen the primary agent in the process of change entails not only developing each individual's human potential, but more especially freeing learning resources that are currently suppressed and woefully under-utilised in society and at work. Intelligence and learning opportunities are wasted in a variety of ways: from the many people left with no opportunity to learn to read and write, through the unemployment of millions of skilled people, to the reluctance to create environments that stimulate curiosity, imagination and active participation.

A learning strategy for a society based on the diffuse capacity for initiative focuses on changing existing conditions by unleashing individuals and organisations. It deals with existing contradictions by relying on the intellectual development of the subjects. It cannot therefore be reduced merely to self-directed learning policies. Instead of a view essentially based on the individual and competition, a perspective is needed that combines autonomy with interdependence and interconnectedness as the vital complements to any genuine autonomy (Caffarella 1993). Brookfield believes that

"the most complete form of self-directed learning (...) combines critical reflection about the contingent aspects of reality, the exploration of alternative perspectives and systems of signs, and a change in individual and social conditions" (Brookfield 1985: 58 f.),

thus entailing corrective and supportive public measures.

6.2.3. The acknowledgement and refusal of repression

It is not sufficient simply to consider the historic and collective conditions and modes that make it possible to liberate these creative capacities. It is also necessary to examine practices and policies at work and in daily life that tend to repress or deform the subject, and which permit external social agents to appropriate the interest and sociality of individuals (De Sanctis 1975). To break free from such educational coercion, a theoretical and policy approach is needed that can translate demands into action programmes that affect all learning factors.

Suchodolski was well aware of this problem when he examined the "learning city". He concluded that:

"It is not education that will determine how the essence of a man is formed, but the new man in the whole of his being who will stimulate and steer education" (Suchodolski 1993 : 49).

He added:
"We need to find a way of life that nurtures the blossoming of creativity in every field, in the arts and sciences as well as social life" (ibid.: 113).

6.2.4. Policies that negate and absorb the capacity for initiative

A policy for changing adult learning conditions must aim above all to do away with measures that undermine, absorb or even destroy subjects' capacity for initiative, well before their learning demand can even be fully expressed. No examination of adult learning policy can dispense with an analysis of policies that repress the expression of demand. First among these are "educational exclusion" policies. This refers to short-term policies that have been implemented to respond to an urgent situation and, in so doing, have over-simplified the situation and lack the means to effectively handle the full extent of the problem addressed. This leads to the production of new exclusions. Some literacy programmes provide good examples of limited measures that are not commensurate with the extent of the problem (Morocco CS: 98 f.; P 4) and thus cannot meet the egalitarian goals of official proclamations. The same holds for certain policies whose appearance is "delusive", in the sense that they define a right or an obligation but do not set aside the resources needed or establish multi-year programmes capable of serving the entire targeted social group. Their starting point is thus the presupposition that not everyone will demand access to organised adult learning. They use adult education programmes as a new selective tool to absorb people, in a manner of speaking, in accordance with a "filtering theory" that views adult learning as a way to effect an initial triage for access to the labour market. Recent developments in the United Kingdom can be viewed through this same lens. Despite having noticed that the prevalence of a work-based approach led to a high drop-out rate in certain social strata, it took a long time before necessary corrective measures were taken (CS: 156f). An analysis of the 1988 Reform Act in the United States, which established the Aid for Families with Dependent Children (AFDC) programme, provides similar corroboration. This programme enables its participants to define their own plans for "employability" based, among other factors, on access to work-related learning so as to promote their entry into the world of work and foster their economic independence. Nonetheless, "persons who have volunteered for educational benefits and who have employability plans approved are still waiting for training" (United States P 5: 10).

Secondly, there are policies that could be defined as "policies stigmatising social groups". Such policies tend to absorbe or negate people's capacity for initiative. They define their target groups in terms of shortcomings, as "deprived" subjects who need to be offered partial compensation, but who are refused measures that could affect the factors creating or reproducing these inequalities. This type of policy, typical of mainstream literacy practices during the past decades (see Chapter 10, sect. 2.1), can also be found in certain European Union programmes which, without really undertaking to fulfil the EU commitment to eliminate "basic illiteracy and the lack of other basic skills on the part of school-leavers by the Year 2000" (European Commission 1994b: 25), proclaimed the goal of fighting poverty and youth unemployment. In the United States, the Job Training Partnership Act defined unemployment as an individual problem related to a lack of skills, resulting in a policy that offered only "immediate prerequisites" (P 1).

A policy adopted by India in the late 1980s is significant in this regard. It is a particularly illustrative example of the conflicts of interest that lead to stigmatising social groups. The problem was posed in policy terms as follows: since the Indian economy's performance had given rise to poverty, the country needed to rely on the middle class, the 10% of the population who produce new entrepreneurs. This led to investing in the education of members of the middle class and improving the quality of post-secondary education so as to ensure a skilled workforce for the modern sector of the national economy. This programme exacerbated educational differences between entrepreneurs and wage earners in the modern sector on the one side and all the rest of the population on the other, expanding the ranks of those deemed "illiterate" (CS: 75-79). A non-selective policy of basic education was set up later, with the creation of the National Literacy Mission.

Thirdly, we need to consider the negative impact of policies that undermine people's right to express themselves and communicate using new media and new technology. The establishment of distance education and the introduction of new technologies in current programmes are necessary, but can only partly address this issue. The underlying problem is that there are few international indications of any trend to defend the public's right to communication and expression outside the private sphere. The Tabor Charter proposed by the International Federation of Film Societies in 1987 remarkably encapsulates the public's aspirations when it declares in its first point:

"Everyone has the freedom of expression, to receive the expressions of others, and to reply. Defending the public's rights means taking action so that all human beings have the full concrete possibility to communicate. There is no humanisation without communication" (IFFS 1987).

The ice has begun to be broken. Nonetheless, the possibilities for free access to communications and audio-visual and "virtual" expression within non-government networks and community-based media groups, occasionally with the support of public grants, show that other orientations are possible. They are incubators of the changes demanded. However, this active presence, combined with chaotic ferment that is creating a thousand alternatives and local resistance to monolithic discourse, obviously cannot in itself overturn relationships and democratise the new technologies and media. The democratisation of cultural activities requires both the emergence of alternatives ("counter-practices") and the reform of the large institutions.

Fourthly, it is worth noting policies that are absorbing the capacity for civil society's initiative by passing on the human and physical costs of learning activity to individuals and to unpaid labour in the voluntary sector. Australia's experience is noteworthy in this regard, as non-governmental education organisations have been asked to play the role of educational agents in the national continuing work-related education system (CS: 20). This has prompted some local organisations and associations to abandon their formal role and act as "semi-private providers of government programs" (CS: 21), thus modifying their nature and role.

6.3. Conclusion

We are at a turning point in the development of adult learning policy. Both "supply-side dogma", which imposes time, pace, content, structure, modalities, individual paths, results, and evaluation methods, and "laissez-faire" demand policies, which give the appearance of imposing nothing, actually repress the expression of social demand and reinforce existing inequalities. These approaches are outdated. While claiming to uphold the right to lifelong learning, they negate this right in fact and hinder the required participatory development process. These policies have become obsolete because they cannot meet the mounting learning demand associated with contemporary society's increasingly felt need to enhance people's capacity for initiative.

Chapter 7
Policies and Measures Promoting the Expression and Synergy of Learning Demand

Policies and measures to promote the expression and synergy of learning demand and adult education arise out of the broad accumulation of diverse political choices, occasionally even contradictory ones. In this respect, two different approaches can be distinguished. The first focuses more on individual rights to educational services, while the second concentrates more on social factors that influence individual learning paths. These reflect two different ways of interpreting demand policy. The first, rooted in the realisation of basic educational rights, aims at promoting the participation of adults in organised learning. The second is based on the decision-making processes that precede learning activities and encourage different publics to express, mobilise and negotiate social learning demand.

Certain institutional policies already reflect the first trend. In Hungary, a legislative bill was enacted in 1994 (P 1) that focused on the general right to self-expression, a state guarantee of support to each individual, the right to organise independent associations, the decentralisation of decision-making power, the defence of local and national cultures and the defence of immigrants.

The general approach in Japan reflects the second tendency. A 1992 report declares that,

> "people should be able to freely choose from a range of learning opportunities and that the nation should strive towards becoming a lifelong learning society. (...) The major tasks needing immediate action were summarised in the following four points: the promotion of recurrent education for working adults, the promotion and support of volunteer activities, the enrichment of young people's activities outside of school, the enrichment of up-to-date learning opportunities" (CS: 29).

Accessibility policies essentially treat the subject as a participant in a programme, a learner, whereas policies that give more play to the voices of actors take into account living and working environments and aim especially to create more favourable situations for the emergence and realisation of learning projects endogenous to these environments. The distinction suggested, which is sometimes hard to detect in practice, should help highlight the currently significant dissociation between immediate strategies for accessibility and considerations of the diffuse but decisive impact of social relations, and between these two factors and the concrete negation of adults' rights to learning.

Policies to promote access currently receive the most political and legislative support. While no one wants to underestimate the necessity for accessibility policies, focusing too narrowly on access to educational services runs the risk, to use Freire's expression, of falling into the dominant logic of "banking education" (Freire 1972: 56), which dispenses the knowledge held by specialised institutions.

Indeed, these two types of policies are actually complementary and in our opinion inseparable. New demand policies indeed seek to combine in different ways policies for access to learning services and policies for creating new learning environments to help subjects develop their initiative.

Demand-side access policies can thus be differentiated based on whether they aim to ensure a greater use of existing educational opportunities or strengthen the subjects' defence of their learning interests. Demand policies act on living, working and educational situations themselves. In each of these three contexts they affect the institutional, situational and psychological factors influencing participation or non-participation (Cross 1981; Rubenson and Xu 1997). With this kind of matrix in mind, we propose analysing the main measures associated with these policies: firstly, accessibility measures, and secondly, policies that enhance the diffuse capacity for initiative.

7.1. Accessibility policies and measures

One of the main features of outreach policies to ensure participation in existing educational activities is their impact on everyday life and working hours.

7.1.1. Time-release measures

Participation in the various forms of adult learning requires, first, freeing up time for this purpose and, simultaneously, challenging the seemingly neutral breakdown of time earmarked for education, work, and consumption with respect to subjects' actual or desired life rhythms. These changes clearly reflect the times and are triggered by a two-sided dynamic: besides the obvious demand associated with economic growth and production in a broad sense, the desire and need for a higher quality of everyday life is being expressed increasingly strongly by different social groups. The situation is less and less one of "hyper-participation" in work or household tasks, but rather openness to involvement in new socio-cultural and educational opportunities. Moreover, this quest to re-structure working hours and everyday life can help meet the challenge of growing structural unemployment:

"The paramount problem today is increasing demand for new servic (...) insufficient demand currently constitutes (...) the bottleneck that is preventing a substantial resumption of employment levels (...). The consumer's lack of time is a factor blocking or braking the full development of demand for services. From this viewpoint, a policy on social time that seeks to reduce working hours and increase the time available for the consumption of services is now an important part of an overall strategy to create new jobs" (Paci 1995: 1).

The two dimensions of learning demand – that is, increased work-related qualifications and socio-cultural aspirations – merely appear to be in conflict. The need to develop professional competency can offer new possibilities for socio-cultural education, and vice versa. The point is certainly not to hinder job creation and increased economic productivity, but to use this opportunity to extend, expand and reaffirm the right to self- and co-management of free time.

A breakdown of the main measures to free up time (based on the three aspects of work, everyday life and learning environments) will help flesh out our proposal.

Work:
1. Shorter working hours, i.e. reduced daily, weekly or annual work timetables; restrictions on holding two jobs and overtime; and sharing that now precious resource, regular salaried work.

2. Work-training contracts for young job seekers that require employers to authorise study leave and individuals to devote part of their free time to training. This dual system is typical of the German-speaking countries and the Netherlands.

3. Paid educational leave for employees, the costs of which are shared between the company, the government and the participants themselves. As has already been mentioned, this measure first took root internationally in the 1970s. On 5 June 1974, the 59th session of the International Labour Office General Assembly approved Convention No. 140. Article 1 of this convention declares the right of workers to a specified length of adequately paid educational leave during working hours. This convention has been applied in various ways by the 23 countries that had ratified it by 1992 (Federighi 1990; Paul 1991; Schütze 1996). The arrangements for paid educational leave tend to make such leave more suitable to big corporations and the primary labour market. It is nonetheless worth noting that in France, for example, although employer-paid training tends to favour employees in big corporations, individual educational leave (CIF) is also apportioned in accordance with company size. Following the 1990 training credit law, CIF costs are paid out of funds collected from businesses combined with government aid (Centre INFFO 1990). With the exception of

Germany, France and Sweden, educational leave policies tend to favour work-related training demanded by the employer.

4. Forms of "job rotation" that provide for salaried employees on generally lengthy educational leave to be replaced for this period of time by employees on short-term contracts specially trained to occupy the vacated posts. This measure was introduced in Denmark by the new law on paid educational leave (EAEA 1995). However, it was already in operation in agriculture in the Netherlands in the 1980s (EBEA 1985). In Sweden, employees aged 25 to 55 who have worked at least five years

"are eligible for a training credit if the local partners concerned agree that the employer takes on a long-term unemployed person to replace the applicant for education. If the latter wishes to continue their studies at the end of the year, they can obtain the assistance offered to regular students" (Sweden 1996; Sohlmann 1998a).

5. The increasing introduction of training clauses into collective bargaining agreements between employers and trade unions extends educational opportunities and introduces co-management measures into this new field of industrial relations (Ozaki et al. 1992; Canada, CS). In practice, however, there is more support for this in some countries than in others, especially in Northern Europe (Sweden and Germany) and Canada as compared with the United States and the United Kingdom. If employers continue to expand continuing education budgets and trade unions continue to introduce educational clauses into collective bargaining agreements, these bargaining agreements will gradually eclipse paid educational leave policies (Schütze 1996: 309).

6. The compulsory nature of training for certain social groups (the unemployed and those threatened with unemployment), i.e. the granting of forms of minimum payment guaranteed by the state provided that the recipient takes part in educational activity. These kinds of active labour market policies are now common in all the industrialised countries and are spreading to countries in transition, as can be seen in Hungary (P 6), Lithuania (P 6) and Slovenia (P 6).

7. The arrangement of forms of part-time work at the end of professional careers to extend the time older employees can remain professionally active, while enabling them to spend their non-working time in social and educational activities. This is one of the measures contained in the "Delors Commission" Report recommendations on "chosen time" (UNESCO 1996: 115).

8. In certain cases, such as Lithuania, language standardisation programmes have introduced the requirement that certain professions (doctors, judges, civil servants, managers, etc.) learn the new national language.

9. Educational leave tailored to farming. In Lithuania, a law to reinstate private property in agriculture provides that "farmers who take part in basic or more advanced agricultural training programmes of a maximum length of 48 days per year shall be granted financial assistance equivalent to the minimum wage" in order to finance a temporary replacement (CS; P 5: 4). Similar policies have been in place in other countries for several decades.

10. In response to the problem that educational leave has always been restricted to the formal economy, a number of international adult education and women's networks have launched a movement called "one hour a day for learning". This campaign was ratified by the Fifth International Conference on Adult Education (see *The Hamburg Declaration*, para. 26, in: UNESCO 1997; Swiss Commission for UNESCO 1998).

Everyday life:
1. The reduction of unpaid working time in everyday life, for example, by changing the public opening hours of government offices, the introduction of new technologies for the remote consultation and use of various services, etc. (Paci 1995).

2. The extension of study grants and assistance to individuals of any age. These resources are not limited to those adults enrolled in formal education.

3. The development of strategies to help manage the expression of individual learning demand is prompting the introduction of educational "vouchers" distributed to certain categories of citizens (Schwartz 1972; United Kingdom 1998). Although this approach is interesting in that it corresponds to a strategy for the more equal redistribution of resources, its implementation is running up against major discriminatory tendencies concerning the participation of different publics in socio-cultural activities (see Bélanger and Bochynek 1999, chapter 4).

Learning environments:
1. Flexible times and periods of entry into and exit from formal adult educational activities and, where education is interrupted, the possibility to still obtain "credits" that can be used later when study is taken up again.

2. The recognition and certification of knowledge acquired outside formal networks, a measure by which authorised institutes and sometimes even companies can certify the knowledge actually possessed by individuals who so request (Serres 1992; Péarker, Leplatre and Ward 1994; Belisle 1997). This measure has its roots in the demands of salaried employees and trade unions trying to gain recognition of skills acquired on the job and in the demands of women's groups seeking to compensate for inequities in occupational hiring and promotion and

in access to education. Such measures have been officially introduced into formal education systems (in Europe, the best-known examples include France, Germany, Ireland, Slovenia and the United Kingdom). These new models for evaluating and certifying knowledge are essential supplements to individualised forms of learning, where the educational programme is designed and implemented based on specific subjects and can take different paths, including as concerns the level of results.

7.1.2. Financial support

The reduction of educational costs or exemption from payment is the second main aspect of outreach policies. The impact of cost on access opportunities varies with income. Recent studies in several post-industrial societies have shown that this factor is a considerable obstacle (ASTAT 1996; Rubenson and Xu 1997). The following are some of the corresponding measures:

Work:
1. Credit facilities and the tax deductibility of educational activity costs for individuals and/or companies. In Canada, for example, this takes the form of refundable tax credits (CS: 9).

2. Allowances or wages granted by employers when a certificate is obtained. In France, large corporations have adopted an educational plan and budget that covers 100% of the expenses of company-sponsored programmes and pays for part of training undertaken at the employee's initiative, either directly or from the mutual funds for individual educational leave (CIF). Legislation in France, the Ivory Coast and Quebec imposes a tax of 1.5% to 2% of total payroll, a sum that the company can recover if it spends this on officially recognised training activities. South Africa adopted a similar scheme in 1998 to create a Labour Skills Development Fund scheduled to be set up in 1999. In Slovenia (P 3), companies can receive subsidies if they take steps to raise the qualifications of employees threatened with unemployment. In Australia, for example, according to statements in *Working Nation*, the government co-finances a training wage when the employer provides officially recognised training (P 7: 6).

3. The introduction of credits solely for work-related learning. This might include measures like the Smartcard, a form of training credit introduced in the United Kingdom following the White Paper *Employment in the 1990s* (P 3) and managed by the Training and Enterprise Councils.

4. The granting of financial assistance to undereducated adults, such as the special programme adopted by Sweden in 1996 and supplemented in 1997, which

grants 100,000 scholarships each year to those returning to full-time studies for a period of twelve to twenty months.

Everyday life:
1. The right to the free use of certain services. The right of adults to free access to basic, primary and secondary education, i.e. right up to the end of the "compulsory" level of education, is being increasingly recognised (see, for example, Burkina Faso, Canada, Namibia, Portugal and Spain). The transition to active labour market policies includes the right to basic education, work-related training and career guidance and placement services, as provided in the United States, for example, by the Job Training Partnership Act (P 1).

2. Learning credits entitling citizens to a sum of hours to be used in learning activity or, more generally, the right to attend certain types of activities or institutes. In Namibia, for example, people aged 15 to 44 with literacy problems can enrol in national basic education programmes for three years. The same programme also gives communities and villages the right to request literacy programmes and guarantees a response within two months of any request (P 1: 5). In sub-Saharan Africa, basic education instructors are paid in kind (food, etc.). In Australia, for example, in the field of teaching foreign languages to immigrants, the law provides for special courses of at least 510 hours and finances schools to the tune of US$ 300 for every student who has completed their studies. The report to UNESCO by the International Commission on Education in the 21st Century, chaired by Jacques Delors, again advanced the proposal – already made by G. Rhen (Sweden 1995: 75) – to establish a "time-credit" for education. The idea is to grant every young person the right to a certain number of years of education (UNESCO 1996: 28 and 193 f.). This arrangement involves setting up a "chosen time bank" responsible for monitoring the various individual educational portfolios and keeping precise accounts, given that everyone has the opportunity to increase the time in their account if they save time in previous years. This proposal by the Chair of the Commission was ratified in 1997 by the fifth International Conference on Adult Education (see the *Agenda for the Future*, para. 49, in: UNESCO 1997).

3. The introduction of various forms of tax deduction or individual loans to cover educational costs. European Union programmes posit the hypothesis of introducing types of "tax relief or financial assistance through loans for individuals paying for their training" (European Commission 1994b: 25). This type of measure has been implemented in many countries.

Learning environments:
Measures to encourage the development of adult learning institutions based on the number and type of participants recruited. In Australia, for example, "the

government provides financial support of Aus$ 1,000 per trainee to companies to encourage the recruitment of new participants" (P 7: 6).

Mention should be made here of the recent movement, which originated in the United Kingdom and has now spread worldwide, to hold an annual week to promote adult education.[1] The aim is to promote the participation of men and women in different types of adult learning and to mobilise all employers and employee representatives for this purpose.

The subsequent development of this project in the form of a "United Nations Adult Learners' Week" was adopted in a resolution by the Fifth International Conference on Adult Education, which enunciated several aspects of a policy for the expression of learning demand:

> "We commit ourselves to creating conditions for the expression of people's demand for learning: (a) by adopting legislation and other appropriate means recognising the right to learn of all adults, proposing an enlarged vision of adult learning and facilitating co-ordination between agencies; (b) by facilitating the expression of the learning demand of people within their own culture and language; (c) by creating public information and counselling services and developing methods for the recognition of experiential and prior learning; (d) by developing strategies to extend the benefits of adult learning to those currently excluded and to help adults make informed choices concerning the learning routes best suited to their aspirations; (e) by promoting a culture of learning through the 'one hour a day for learning' movement; (f) by underlining the importance of observing (...) International Literacy Day (8 September) (...) and promoting adult learning by developing a United Nations Week of Adult Learning." (*Agenda for the Future* para. 17, in: UNESCO 1997).

7.2. Policies promoting the collective action of different publics

7.2.1. The defence of adults' learning interests

The concept of defending individuals' interests in learning and the adoption of mechanisms needed to secure their rights have been utterly absent from existing legislation. Nonetheless, in the 1970s, educational conflicts of interest in some countries started to reach the courts based on labour, constitutional and private

---

[1] The following countries organised a week like this in 1998 or 1999: Australia, Belgium (Flanders), Benin, Botswana, China, Estonia, Finland, Germany, Jamaica, New Zealand, Norway, the Netherlands, the Philippines, Portugal, Slovenia, South Africa, Switzerland and the United Kingdom. In November 1999, the 30th Annual Conference of UNESCO unanimously adopted a resolution recognising the "International Adult Learners' Week".

law. This was a new move in that citizens were previously the ones usually brought before the bar for failing to respect certain legal obligations. Today, it is the citizens who are bringing proceedings for damages caused by the failures of institutions, companies and even the educational system itself.

This spontaneous movement, which is still in its infancy, is of great political significance. It expresses people's desire to evaluate and control the direction and orientation of their learning biographies. Underlying this movement is the growing importance in people's lives of prolonged initial schooling, followed by continuing education, and the influence of these successive environments on their quality of life.

The direction and impact of paths imposed or guided by political, economic, educational and cultural agencies do not necessarily correspond to the life projects and intellectual development of individuals and communities. This observation points to the deforming power of certain continuing education models and their ability to cause "educational harm" to an individual. This notion of harm in education, which is similar to the harm caused by poor working conditions, has always been undermined by the fetishism of the educational object and by the perennial interpretation of the concept of harm in material terms.

It is actually possible to suffer harm that threatens not only an individual's physical integrity, but also their learning potential and character, whether at work, in a training centre or in private life. Adult learning policy must become more transparent in this regard. Contemporary society must become capable of detecting and transforming every situation that prevents people from developing their potential and leads to educational damage. The process of uncovering educational harm and encapsulating it in legal and policy formulations that underpin methods of detecting, guiding, controlling, transforming, repairing and compensating can lead to the systematic development of new rules capable of raising the level of learning for all. If no action is taken to lessen educational harm and eliminate its causes, adult learning policies will be doomed. An element crucial to their success will have been neglected. Greater knowledge cannot be demanded of all citizens while negative factors are neglected that block the pursuit of learning biographies, at least so long as they are left undetected and unrepaired.

7.2.2. Policies to promote creativity

As shown in Chapters 4 and 5, it is crucial and not at all utopian to assign adult learning policy the function of promoting creative potential. In 1994, the Commonwealth of Australia published a policy programme entitled *Creative Nation* (P 6). This document deals mainly with government guidelines firstly on cultural policy in an inevitably multicultural society with a view to promoting artistic and cultural groups, including the Aborigines, and secondly on policy to raise national productivity.

A policy on creativity requires new relations to be established between the public and the cultural infrastructure. Implicit to improving the quality of life is a public that knows how to become involved in the aesthetic realm of existence, including work, and in a "pedagogy of environments" (Orefice 1978). Improving the quality of life means more than changing physical living conditions; it also requires improving and bringing to life people's cultural environment. The crisis plaguing the cultural world is rooted in the domination of opportunities for artistic expression and communication and in the "laissez-faire" commercialisation of cultural life.

Yet this crisis is also opening up new prospects. Some cultural infrastructures may well largely conform to the image and appearance of the bourgeois public for whom the first libraries, theatres, art collections, etc., were created, and thus take on as their main task conserving and disseminating the culture of the dominant social groups. However, reality is more complex. The entire educational and cultural system needs our attention,

"not so much as (...) the product of 'established facts', i.e. 'things in themselves', but because, considered in isolation and in their entirety, these are the many different concrete forms and levels of modes of perception, thinking, evaluation, and the common action of members of a social group. They thus represent the response to certain 'cultural models'" (Orefice 1978: 41 f.).

Educational and cultural infrastructures can indeed be considered to be the expression of social relations, which are in part pre-determined, but which are also sites of social transformation. These changes open up new prospects for educational-cultural relations and enable educational action to function no longer as

"an instrument of cultural assertion or even domination, but as a means to change the dominant cultures. It follows that it is culture (and conceptions of culture) that are at the service of people's learning processes. Conversely, education is not at the service of one or more cultures" (De Sanctis 1988: 55).

Otherwise,

"adult learning would be nothing more than the didactic figurehead of the power of a minority who control the majority, to which we belong" (ibid.: 58).

Of course it would not be appropriate here to reproduce a certain ethnological assumption whereby "people must solve their problems themselves, in accordance with their cultures (...) glorified as perfect visions of the world" (ibid.: 60). If we were to take this direction, we would end up promoting protection and conservation policies rather than conversation, confrontation, communication, dialogue and mutual transformation policies.

A policy for the expression of learning demand entails the adoption of guidelines and measures that promote public collective action to alter the learning environments dominating the heart of cultural infrastructures, and thus make the transition from archaeology to praxis. The big question is whether to apply a policy in each type of infrastructure for the expression and handling of social demand, that is, to promote the public's participation in restructuring institutions based on the aspirations and uses specific to the new publics.

This can be seen concretely in new public service policy, as reflected by the Danish law on public libraries (Denmark 1999). Measures to introduce forms of social management and to train every level of the public to be able to manage the infrastructures and use them in accordance with their problems are applied to cultural infrastructures, both large and small. This Scandinavian policy aims to ensure a sound link between action programmes and the problems existing in the territory concerned. This requires taking into account the socio-cultural conditions (reading levels, residence, working hours, etc.) of the public living in the given territory. It also lays down spending targets for different budget purchases, based on the various public strata for which they are intended, so as to guarantee a fixed proportional allocation for new publics.

In this context, it is important to extend the concept of cultural creativity to include capacity for innovation in education itself. Two basic fields can be determined here for the application of policies designed to express and handle citizens' learning demand.

The first draws on people's possibilities and capacities for taking charge of organised learning processes. The first fundamental factor in the development of the process of identifying the public as a subject capable of handling organised learning processes in line with the dynamics of the changes to be made consists of the act of joining with others to find a solution to common problems, managing the organisation of collective relations, handling them with a will and intentionality inspired by egalitarian relations, and seeking new prospects by means of collective work and discussion.

The second involves the public's possibilities and capacities to handle the process of changing the agents that determine the current general learning environment. This entails the ability to draw up educational strategies, programming plans and educational conversion projects for all the bodies that condition peo-

111

ple's learning, both at work and in everyday life: from the workplace through public institutions to a range of infrastructures and services and even the daily relationship with television and radio.

7.2.3. Policies to promote the development of forms of organised social life

Policies to promote the development of forms of organised social life constitute both a major tool and the ultimate goal of adult learning policies. Beyond the purely educational field, forms of organised social life represent ways in which active citizen participation and the education of collective actors capable of guiding social dynamics are either promoted or held back.

"Adult education thus becomes more than a right; it is a key to the twenty-first century. It is both a consequence of active citizenship and a condition for full participation in society. It is a powerful concept for fostering ecologically sustainable development, for promoting democracy, justice, gender equity, and scientific, social and economic development, and for building a world in which violent conflict is replaced by dialogue and a culture of peace based on justice." (*Hamburg Declaration* para. 2, in: UNESCO 1997).

These forms of organised social life tie in with the process of setting up an identified education "public" as a collective actor. They are essential for enabling and promoting the participation of citizens in political life. Habermas expresses this well:

"The constitution and definition (...) of a pre-state private sphere and a public sphere with political functions that plays the role of mediator between society and the state take on new values (...) because of a system of convergent standards whereby state and society mutually interpenetrate, thus giving birth to an intermediary sphere of semi-public relations ordered on the basis of social right, which has its source in the state; that which cannot be guaranteed indirectly by means of this definition now requires positive protection: participation in social services and institutes in the political sphere" (Habermas 1990: 350).

Habermas notes further that, "the intermediary sphere of semi-public relations" can be rounded out to guarantee private interest and that
"this competition of organised private interests leads to (...) a 'refeudalisation' of society whenever (...) social forces assume political roles (...) Opposed to this real trend towards the weakening of the public sphere, understood as a principle, is the functional metamorphosis of basic rights that is taking place in the social state (...): state bodies extend the public sphere's normative power to organisations that operate with reference to the state. As

this process goes on, a public of organised individuals replaces the now altered public of individuals who maintain personal interrelations. In the current situation, only these actors can participate effectively in a process of public communications via the channels of internal parties and associations and on the basis of public communications that are now active and effective, using the network of relations that these organisations have with the state and among themselves" (ibid.: 351).

Forms of organised social life as a whole are a collective subject in whose bosom the evolution of state functions is itself determined. This is made clearer by listing all the forms of organised social life: the family (the most elementary form), work, consumption, and other categories of social life. The process of creating a collective identity within each of these frameworks is the object of policy and also, of course, of attempts at control, one purpose of which is the "refeudalisation" of the state and society.

It is, secondly, necessary to examine the typically educational function of community life as a means and site of the production and appropriation of knowledge. Community life not only expresses the "narrative knowledge" of "the people" (Westwood 1991), but also provides immediate and concrete opportunities for acquiring other forms of knowledge.

"There is recognition today of a pluralism of knowledge and of ways to learn and express this knowledge that does not always come under the realm of scientific rationality (...). Today, more is being learned through action" (Sue 1995: 73).

This is clear in work with a high technological component and is especially true of the educational dimension of community life, where learning and transforming the conditions of everyday life and work are constantly subject to collective assessment through action.

Adult learning policies to promote the development of community life mainly act on this second element. A clear example can be found in Japan where, in 1992, the Lifelong Learning Council stated in a document on "measures to promote further education" that

"it is desirable that people grapple with lifelong learning, not only for self improvement, or vocational advancement for themselves, but also to increase social contribution or teaching others, etc. (...) Volunteer activities are not only related closely to lifelong learning but also to social problems in society. Therefore these activities are important for the development of a rich and active society and the construction of a lifelong learning society" (Japan, CS: 2 f.).

Nonetheless, what qualifies policy as befitting a democratic state is not the legitimisation or negation of the role of community movements. Policies qualify more on the basis of the role they play in creating a community culture and promoting conditions that foster its concrete development in social life. The primary terrain for policy intervention consists of modifying conditions that tend to destroy the development of community life.

> "Authoritarian pedagogies do not promote an opening towards community life in school or at home. False models of community life transmitted by school and local authorities may often be more dangerous, because they pass on a model of community life with no real decision-making power for young people, and they are subject to control that, while obscured, is always present" (Gelpi 1990: 45).

If these institutional pedagogies are reinforced by "false models of identification in community practices" imposed on young people by consumption, and by brutal and violent forms of submission forced on young people at work, generally unpaid, and in private life, it is understandable that "young people find it more difficult to create and build associations themselves" (ibid.).

Moreover, we need to examine the real function that policies attribute to community associations, that is, the conditions of development that they tend to prefigure for the future of the voluntary movement in adult learning.

For this purpose, it is useful to take note of a typology of functions developed from research by the European Association for the Education of Adults in twelve European countries (EAEA 1995) into the functions of voluntary associations in the field of adult learning. These functions are not mutually exclusive, but take careful account of a diversity of approaches. They can be distinguished according to whether they tend to promote in community life a function:

of complementarity, i.e. completing action undertaken by other systems managed by major agents, such as the state and business. They comprise a logic that uses community movements as a low-cost replacement or supplementary resource for any public action. Another of their goals is to increase the impact of public or private policy, while avoiding undertaking medium and long-term commitments. The reintroduction of voluntary action into the healthcare system (Hungary, P 5) and poverty action programmes (United States, P 5) often plays this type of role;

of support, that is, as a pool of human and material resources to be used when needed by entirely incorporating these resources into policies designed to meet various priorities decided outside community life. This phenomenon can be generated directly with regards to voluntary associations, but also via the creation of para-state associations. In Switzerland, for example, a special apparatus was created to deal with the problem of unemployment, and the task of managing action was given to a para-state organisation made up of employer and employee representatives. Action is taken by relying on centres and resources in the voluntary association sector (Switzerland, CS: 135 f.). The same holds true in Canada (CS: 14 f.). Certain distortions arise when pseudo non-governmental organisations are created for this purpose, financed by national authorities as a low-cost solution or by outside agencies (e.g. international co-operation agencies) to take national action while evading the control of the national authorities. Observers of the African literacy scene could provide a thousand such examples;

of anticipation, that is, impetus given by community groups to propose and experiment with responses to social problems in education well before they have been formalised in institutional programmes. In this sense, the world of adult learning and especially associations and community groups have been assigned the task of expressing the new social demand, developing original responses and then transferring these innovative learning activities to other agencies and institutions. In these cases, policy is normally limited to defining the general objectives to be attained (find responses to an influx of immigrants – as was the case in Italy upon the arrival of Albanian citizens – or other emergencies), to make certain resources available and to let the state carry out any subsequent action;

of the autonomous and alternative handling of educational responses to problems where the state, business and various agents lack the policy or will to intervene. This illustrates the antagonistic role played by associations: to bring about a change, to propose alternative views and practices, to transform existing learning conditions. This role is essential to social dynamics and fundamental to learning dynamics. By playing this alternative role of establishing counter-practices or organising resistance, which often, albeit not inevitably, entails conflict, the associations transform the conditions that gave rise to the learning demand. These cases can vary widely: from the situation in the Philippines where many adult education associations and non-governmental organisations are appearing that refused until very recently any form of co-operation with the government (CS: 118), to situations where official policy recognises the right of associations to opposition but nevertheless promotes measures to support them (Belgium, P 1; Italy, P 8). This same approach is found in policies of assistance to non-governmental organisations based on respect for the autonomy and pluralism of these organisations and their learning activities. This is the case in Scandinavia and Germany (the folk high schools), in Quebec, where policy supports voluntary local education organisations and, more recently, in England, where a federative association (NIACE) manages public funds to that end.

7.2.4. Support measures for community life

Support measures implemented by legislation (in particular, the legislation studied in Belgium, Italy and Japan) can be classed in a summary list according to whether they are intended to promote participation in community life, the availability of basic services or the financing of voluntary associations. A range of approaches is used: flexitime and educational leave, support measures by the social partners, replacement of military service by participation in community work, and provision of basic services. Other measures include providing space for social activities, making cultural infrastructures available for activities, providing access to the activity site (prisons, hospitals, etc.), research services, the training of facilitators and the introduction of "voluntary action" as a study discipline in schools, decentralised information and documentation services, specialised multimedia centres and resource centres, etc. These support measures are complementary to essential financial assistance, and can be implemented in various ways: basic funding of operations, financing of learning activities and projects, tax deductions for contributions to voluntary associations and tax exemptions on the economic activities of voluntary associations.

The "study circle" model so widespread in Denmark, Finland, Norway and Sweden is the first historical (and still existing) example of a policy promoting a culture of voluntary associations. This model is based on adopting a policy entitling all citizens who create a study circle made up of a certain number of participants to access to state-provided experts chosen for their ability to help the group explore its learning needs and interests in more detail. A "study circle" normally operates in keeping with the following principles laid down by law (Blid 1990):

1. The principle of equality and democracy: the activity is based on the concept of equality among circle members (generally never more than 12), one of whom is chosen as leader.
2. The principle of liberation, relying on the experience and knowledge of the participants in a way that strengthens and liberates their intellectual resources.
3. The principle of co-operation, with activity based on joint efforts in management and organisation in all activities.
4. The principle of the liberty and right to define the circle's learning goals, with no educational authority having the power to influence or guide the circle's study plans.
5. The principle of continuity and planning, such that the participants themselves decide on the time and pace of their learning activities and organise themselves accordingly.
6. The principle of active participation, by virtue of which all participants assume responsibilities for all aspects of the circle's activities.

7. The principle of availability of study material, such that each study circle is equipped with the teaching material needed for its activity.
8. The principle of transformational action, such that study is not aimed merely at passive learning out of context, but at action and change.

In education as in all means of communication, the medium is the message. Educational and cultural democracy is thus measured in concrete terms and real spaces that enable creative potential to blossom. This is why the central questions are the appropriation by different social groups of the educational issues, the restructuring of the role of the state, and civil society's ability to monitor these processes and deal with their impact.

Chapter 8
Learning Continuities and Discontinuities

Preliminary remark

Before introducing this chapter on the continuities and discontinuities in adult learning, a preliminary remark is necessary. Without genuine learning opportunities and policies to develop educational responses, policies promoting the expression of demand have little impact. Co-ordination and liaison work cannot be successful without a lasting consolidation of diverse educational services. Ad-hoc interventions do not enable subjects to consistently accumulate skills and learning and do not promote the endogenous development of communities. They are thus merely dead-end expedients. Any effort to secure continuity between different educational actions, build bridgeheads between them and support adults as they pursue their learning pathways would be futile without strategies to continuously structure new forms of adult learning and thus ensure ongoing learning possibilities. This fact, however obvious, must not be forgotten.

The history of adult learning policy abounds in cases where different socio-economic subsystems use educational resources simply to address essentially ecological, nutritional and occupational problems without any continuity or "sustained structuring".

This "logic of short-term priorities" is typical of a phase in the history of policy-making during which adult learning is envisaged and used as a supplementary measure to deal with other higher priority problems. It is often common practice in adult learning, with the promotion of specific initiatives and ad-hoc programmes to deal with various emergencies. These situations often involve goals that have strong legitimacy (expressed in a wide variety of measures) and lead to the adoption of emergency solutions that draw on all society's resources, including adult learning.

The hypothesis or promise in this type of venture is that, by first addressing emergency situations, sustainable responses that guarantee the population's learning and cultural demand can subsequently be developed. The problem is that hopes are more often than not thwarted. Adult learning never becomes a priority. Together with people's creative potential, it is used in the most diverse ways only to be sacrificed subsequently to "raison d'Etat", i.e. to the interests of the privileged.

In Greece, for example, general adult education policy was developed in a period when a rural exodus was being encouraged and the modern nation-state was being formed. There was strong but temporary demand for civil servants, which was met by training a sufficient number of urbanised citizens who had received appropriate initial education (CS: 2 f.). Policy implementation was limited to this period and to specific social groups, and ceased as soon as this initial demand had been met.

Brazil (P 1, 2 and 4) and the Ivory Coast (P 1-3) provide other examples where adult education was linked to environmental, agricultural and AIDS emergencies. In these situations, special programmes and even new infrastructures were created to absorb the shock of the environmental, food or AIDS crisis. The problem being addressed was given absolute priority, while no effort was made to tackle the problem's source, i.e. the failure of subjects to take part in eliminating the causes. Policy intervention merely provides information and raises awareness. It utterly fails to give the people affected any opportunity to act as transforming subjects to deal with all the factors at work.

The current ambiguity and inadequacy of this type of strategy stems from the fact that a historical assessment of the results of these interventions seems to be inspired more by a "tolerance threshold theory" than by getting to the roots of the problems addressed. The "logic of short-term priorities" tends to delay intervention until problems have exceeded the threshold of safety and social tolerance. Intervention only occurs once the problem (poverty or unemployment, for example) becomes a social danger. Otherwise, i.e. below the tolerance threshold, the problem is considered to be under control and thus acceptable. An ad-hoc intervention or campaign consequently becomes a micro-system in which cooperation among the actors and the integration of different aspects of social life becomes difficult, as does the transformation of the factors that made the campaign necessary in the first place.

What is most difficult here is the transition from an emergency sector-based logic to longer-term educational policies that ensure the normality and durability of different learning practices and paths and promote synergy among the different forms of educational participation. It is clear that any society must make short-term decisions about which component of adult learning to prioritise in order to react to emergencies arising in a society at a particular moment. However, these emergency decisions do not conflict with making a strategic choice of a general policy to develop each individual's creative potential. Furthermore, these functional priorities can succeed only if they are based on properly organising and networking a variety of well-grounded opportunities for lifelong learning. As stated in the *Hamburg Declaration*[1], lifelong learning must

---

[1] "Adult education is both a consequence of active citizenship and a condition for full participation in society. It is a powerful concept for fostering ecologically sustainable development and promoting democracy, justice, gender equity, and scientific, social and

be viewed as essential for addressing different crisis situations rather than simply as a supplementary resource. Only then will choosing priorities make any sense.

The real problem is that, in a logic of priorities that assigns an ancillary role both to adult learning and to "the genuine enlightened participation of all sorts of men and women" (*Agenda for the Future* para. 1, in: UNESCO 1997), the priorities themselves suffer. Responses to emergencies are always partial and temporary, with results far from those promised, since they do not have a structural, lasting impact on the roots of the crisis, as numerous examples attest.

In Morocco, for example, family planning policy (P 1) has taken the form of campaigns that have failed to produce widespread, long-lasting results due to a lack of the kind of substantial, protracted involvement in the educational and social fields needed to empower the men and women concerned. In addition, the programme was sector based and cut off from socio-economic and cultural changes (P 1: 12). In India, policies were based on a logic that focussed on hygiene and sanitation programmes. Adult learning intervention was used essentially to inform and communicate, train facilitators and produce didactic material. This approach had the merit of extending beyond a technical intervention concentrating on the adoption of contraception and sterilisation measures. However, it did not produce the results expected partly because it lacked an aspect of organised learning that would have helped men and women "discuss" their situations and habits, take part in change and thus become involved in practically modifying their conditions of life at home and at work (India, P 1: 10).

Agricultural development programmes in the Ivory Coast have not really taken off due, among other reasons, to a lack of basic education opportunities (P 2: 24 f.). In 1976, the Ivory Coast Ministry of Women's Affairs (CS: 47) was established to inform and educate women. Yet this initiative also had limited results because it was not linked to policies promoting the integration and accumulation of competencies and did not make it possible to link the many existing programmes and cultural and educational agencies.

In Lithuania, language training programmes tend to fail when there is no stable organisation promoting learning opportunities and no possibility to develop continuity and the accumulation of competencies by relying on and using the learning required in emergencies. Furthermore, the Lithuanian government's language standardisation programme to replace Russian with the national language

---

economic development (...) Adult learning and education for children and adolescents (...) are necessary elements of a new vision of education in which learning becomes truly lifelong. The perspective of learning throughout life commands such complimentarity and continuity." (UNESCO 1997: para. 2 and 4)

has not been able to meet demand through ad-hoc interventions, and the government has been forced to gradually extend the deadline set for the adoption of the national language in institutional and business life (P 1).

The limits of the "emergency operation" model can also be seen in the Swiss campaign, the *Weiterbildungsoffensive* ("continuing education campaign"). Two years after the campaign was launched, the federal government decided to prioritise curbing unemployment. Without the necessary learning resources, changing the goal did not have the desired effect (CS: 142 f.).

In short, all the measures mentioned in this chapter to promote the continuity of learning pathways would be ineffective without the "sustained development" of different forms of adult learning.

Having said this, let us now return to the subject of this chapter: the continuities and discontinuities in adult learning.

Introduction

Continuity in learning means above all pursuing the learning process over time. From this point of view, the importance of adult learning policy is to ensure that, after initial education[2], adults have the opportunity to participate throughout their lives in different forms of learning. We thus speak of "lifelong learning". However, in addition to temporal continuity, there is also the matter of cultural continuity, or discontinuity. This involves in particular the reproduction of initial educational inequalities and the perpetuation of relationships of pedagogical dependency and of the dominant cultural orientation engendered by schooling

---

[2] Initial education, as opposed to adult education, refers to the first phase of uninterrupted organised learning carried out by young people, prior to their "adult" life, either at school or in special informal basic education programmes. This includes pre-school programmes and primary education, but is increasingly extensive at secondary level and, for the more privileged, well beyond that. Subsequent education and learning take diverse educational forms throughout adult life. From the temporal viewpoint of continuing education, immediate changes in national learning scenes correspond to transformations in relations between initial education, adult learning and learning environments. Educational reality is obviously more complex. The phases intermingle and transitions between initial education, adult life and the extension of learning into retirement are growing more complicated, especially since starting a career and leaving the world of work are being knocked out of synchronisation by the jobs crisis. Finally, and fortunately, increasing opportunities for informal self-directed learning are clouding the picture even further. Nonetheless, to understand changes in education in the sense of lifelong learning, it is helpful to refer to these three specific components and to study how the relationships among them are changing (see Bélanger 1994).

(Bourdieu and Passeron 1979). We will return to this ambiguity in continuing education discourse and policies at the end of this chapter.

Paradoxically, it is impossible to develop continuity in lifelong educational pathways without "stepping back from" initial education, and thus without a certain rupture with the school model of initial learning. The specific nature of adult living and learning conditions, the diversity of their individual and collective programmes, and even the discontinuity of educational biographies after leaving initial education have to be recognised. This demands the adoption of specific policies on the expression of demand, as discussed in previous chapters, and also policies to promote general continuity between the various educational services and the transformation both of adults' immediate learning conditions and the cultural context in which they operate.

8.1. Policies on the spatial continuity of educational programmes and services

The most well-known learning continuity policies focus on developing various educational services offered to adults, establishing links between these programmes and addressing the rigid compartmentalisation of different types of educational provision.

8.1.1. Policies to develop educational services

One way in which adult learning policies ensure lifelong learning continuity is to guarantee a given population a basic minimum of different educational programmes. This is the approach in Germany, where regional legislation passed in the 1970s, but still in force (and dating from more recently in the new *Länder*), guarantees a minimum number of places and a specific volume of course hours available each year in local neighbourhoods. The hours and places are calculated on a per capita basis. Thus, in theory every adult has the opportunity to participate every four years in a "general" education programme of their choosing (Germany, CS: 22-28). More than 20% of the country's adult population, i.e. more than 10 million individuals, make use of this right every year. Japan takes the same approach with "social education" (CS: 15 f.). All Nordic countries offer adults similar opportunities for general or socio-cultural learning in folk high schools and study circles. Hungary does the same in its folk high schools and cultural centres, as do the English-speaking countries in community adult education programmes provided by the local authorities. In Quebec, a limited programme of popular education in public primary and secondary education networks provides minimum services in this field.

The vast public basic education and adult literacy programmes in India and Namibia, the more limited programmes in this area in Brazil, Ecuador, Morocco and the Philippines, and the new co-operation set up among ministries and non-governmental organisations in this field in West Africa (for example in Senegal) represent an important expansion of adult learning opportunities.

Policies are also being adopted in China, Vietnam, Brazil and all the industrialised countries to extend adult access to the formal education system, or more precisely primary, secondary and higher education establishments. These include adult literacy and advanced basic education courses leading to secondary teaching certificates and the opening of post-secondary institutions to adults (more flexible course schedules, the adaptation of current programmes, more flexible admissions standards than those designed for young people moving directly from one level to another, and changes in teaching and learning conditions). In China in 1990, 38 million people took part in formal adult education leading to a primary or secondary level certificate, while about 2 million adults were enrolled in university level programmes (Dong 1996: 770). Some distance education programmes and correspondence courses are now offered everywhere, and open universities are expanding (ibid.).

In the field of work-related adult learning, vocational training centres and institutions are being opened to adults. Businesses, especially large corporations, are offering in-house training programmes to their personnel. Secondary education establishments are opening continuing education centres with the support of human resources development ministries (see the Japanese law, "The Human Resources Development Promotion Law", Japan 1985). In China, again in 1990, 110 million adults took part in company training programmes, i.e. three times more than in 1986, when 32.4 million were enrolled (Dong 1996: 770). Some countries have created "training funds", often financed by a special tax calculated on the basis of total payroll, along the lines of the now familiar French model. This last measure, where educational activities are defined precisely enough to avoid mis-spending, helps make up for low participation rates whenever the company has been slow to invest, i.e. in certain economic sectors and for small and medium-sized enterprises. In Denmark, the "rotation" policy helps regular employees take extended educational leave by temporarily leaving their positions to unemployed people (Ant 1997: 4).

Legislation in Australia, Finland and Japan even requires that members of certain professions, such as doctors and accountants, take continuing education and refresher courses to maintain the right to practice.

In addition to company training assistance, policies have also been implemented to promote the increasing role of non-governmental organisations in adult learning. These include the public financing of non-governmental adult education systems, such as the networks of study circles and folk high schools in the North European countries and the German folk high schools; international public financing (i.e. through co-operation agencies) of an increasing number of non-governmental literacy programmes in Africa and popular education programmes in Latin America, the Caribbean and Asia; national finance programmes to be applied for annually by a variety of popular education associations as in Belgium, France, Hungary and Quebec; and finally, and often as a supplement to the above-mentioned policies, tax exemptions for non-profit-making educational organisations (Bélanger and Bochynek 1999).

Current policies to develop educational services inevitably have to make choices about the content of learning to be made available to the adult population of a given territory. Some policies help by expanding capacities in certain sectors, while others, it should be emphasised, are characterised by imbalances. This is the case with the Quebec government's 1988 policy, which drastically reduced socio-cultural educational programmes, i.e. non-formal popular education, from public adult education services. In contrast, in 1992, the Lifelong Learning Council of Japan (Okamoto 1994: 53) proposed making social education a priority and consequently recommended changes in financing. It proposed giving top priority to programmes on the environment, healthcare, new technology, ageing, etc. Literacy programmes are favoured in some countries, but elsewhere, such as in the Ivory Coast, there was hesitation until 1999. The agencies in charge of structural adjustment programmes support continuing education in Africa, Latin America and Asia, but mainly within the framework of economic modernisation programmes. This list, which could easily be extended, underscores the ambiguity and diversity of educational provision policies as well as their capacity to stimulate change.

8.1.2. Links between educational programmes and services

As adult learning grows rapidly, it often happens that relations and communications are not established among the various educational agents, whether work-related or socio-cultural, public or private. Learners find themselves faced with a forest of educational providers who are often not even aware of each other's existence. Several countries have started adopting "learning demand policies" in an effort to ensure continuity in learning pathways amidst the diverse educational possibilities (see Chapters 6 and 7). This is usually done without imposing the standardisation of educational institutions and curricula; such a policy, while typical of initial formal education, would be impossible in adult education.

One appropriate measure of continuity is the availability of public information on educational opportunities in a region or locality. This can take the form of regularly published, widely disseminated catalogues, local "one-stop" information outlets, 24-hour telephone "help-line" services, learning cafés and co-ordinated information campaigns like the "national week for adult learners".

As regards linking programmes and all their possible interconnections, there is an increasing number of complementary efforts to develop more flexible arrangements for bridging and making transitions between educational programmes and for mutual recognition of accreditation among institutions. The adoption of special admissions standards for adults, for instance, facilitates access. These innovations were first introduced by open learning systems in a number of countries and are now being adopted by school, college and university networks. These institutions are also beginning to allow promotions from one level to another within professional channels, which was formerly restricted to those holding general academic diplomas.

This decompartmentalisation can be seen at all educational levels. In Vietnam, for example, new policies (P 1) allow adults who have successfully completed an initial stage of general or work-related informal education to transfer to formal programmes offered by regular institutions. The adaptation of accreditation schemes to adult learning conditions and the establishment of mechanisms for the recognition, certification and equivalence of experimental learning is another measure that helps learners make the transition from one educational programme to another. A variety of innovations (CEFA 1982: 350-354) have been tried in different countries to assist in the transfer of qualifactions and certifications, including the introduction in French-speaking countries of a system of "capitalizable units" (Franchi 1999), the creation in South Africa of a national council on the accreditation of qualifications, the South African Qualification Authority (Issacs 1997), and the introduction in the United States of "continuing education units" or "credits", to name but three examples. Inspired by the North American experience (Paquet 1987), more and more post-secondary institutions are also beginning to grant stage certificates for programmes that give a BA after six to nine years of parttime study.

The accreditation of educational organisations for tax exemption, a new practice especially in Central Europe (the Hungarian law on this dates from only 1997; see the Law CLVI on public interest organisations), is or soon will be widespread. Nonetheless, this does not give learners any guarantee of quality or outside recognition of the learning acquired. The accreditation or introduction of "quality labels" for various continuing education institutions, as demanded by the Swiss Federation of Adult Education (FSEA 1998) for example, is more complicated and more uncommon. The goal is, to use the current expression in the United Kingdom, to aim simultaneously for flexible and high-quality educational services while respecting the specific nature of adult learning conditions and pressing demands for the acquisition of competencies and taking into account individuals' diverse projects and aspirations (United Kingdom 1997: 14).

Another strategy to promote continuity was proposed long ago, but never got off the drawing board. This was to revise the duration and content of initial vocational educational programmes to concentrate initial education on basic skills and then intensify recurrent education throughout the professional career. The crisis caused by the all too short duration of initial teacher education in Africa, for example, could be handled by offering educational opportunities throughout the professional career, in connection with work experience.

8.1.3. Continuity and discontinuity between general and work-related education

No policy on educational continuity can avoid re-examining the often-rigid compartmentalisation of general education and vocational training. This division between work-related education and "general" education endeavours to maintain divisions in reality that, at least in adult learning, are increasingly untenable. This is not a matter of recognising or negating technical skills requirements, or accepting or refusing the need for basic education. It is a case of understanding that a number of convergent factors are making the borders between the two fields increasingly permeable.

This new phenomenon primarily reflects transformations in the mode of production. New production methods are moving away from the Taylorist system and require a broader range of competencies, as can be seen in Brazil, Japan, Europe and North America. An ILO study in this field in the industrial and developing countries (Ozaki et al. 1992) showed the same trend towards increasingly polyvalent job qualifications for employees. After a period of hesitation, trade unions are now trying to negotiate measures with a broader vision of the skills required (Bernier 1990; Meghnagi 1995).

For example, a study of a large state-of-the-art metalworking company (Doray 1989) found that a new work culture is emerging in this knowledge-intensive production sector. There is a growing gap between job descriptions and the jobs actually performed, leaving more room for worker initiative. Jobs are becoming multi-skilled, and the collective knowledge of teams is increasingly important.

In Italy, job qualifications are also beginning to focus on the acquisition of broad skills, "linking technical know-how and social experience, general education and vocational training, the disciplines taught and the concrete situations lived"

(Meghnagi 1995: 339). Taking into account the impact of work environments and the crucial role of accumulated collective and individual experience and knowledge, educational content is becoming more flexible while the process by which subjects integrate their experience and knowledge is becoming more systematic. Work competence is based only in part on knowledge and know-how acquired in specific technical training programmes. This professional competence is, moreover, "an element of a person's cultural wealth" that may well be employed outside work too.

In these new working arrangements, where the volume of organised learning activities is growing fast, the initial goal is obviously for company personnel to master the techniques required for production. However, some companies are also beginning to introduce new technology in tandem with educational programmes that accord with the expertise already acquired by individuals, while also taking into account their views and analyses. Certain organisations are already developing work-related training based on the subjects' capacity for expression, in connection with their practices and modes of communication (Doray 1989: 75). There is a trend to take explicit account of the experience and know-how already acquired, to rely on individual potential for development, to expand work-teams' scope for initiative, and to seek out methods of participatory management. Taylorist education and training and the compartmentalisation of tasks tend to be rejected. This trend, while strong in the most modern sectors, is also increasingly characteristic of all work-related learning at all skills levels (Schwartz, cited in Meghnagi 1995: 346). The importance of raising the general level of basic education is being increasingly acknowledged by employers and economic ministries (OECD and Statistics Canada 1995).

Furthermore, vocational training agencies, such as TAFE in Australia (CS; P 7), and corporate training departments in the industrialised countries are increasingly offering basic education and literacy programmes, language study, communications courses and creativity workshops. Large Japanese, British (CS: 164) and German corporations are taking steps to encourage their personnel to continue their education, almost regardless of its content and immediate relevance.

The purpose of developing multi-skilled education that unlocks initiative is obviously to enhance production efficiency and quality. Yet this approach, although still not dominant, will have a definite impact in other areas of life where the subject is active. It is already beginning to challenge the existing dichotomy between general education and vocational training. This trend, which is both an indicator and a driving force for the whole of adult learning, is nonetheless far from widespread. Where this approach has been implemented, this was done unequally between economic sectors and different occupational levels.

127

The country studies on Australia, Brazil, Germany, Morocco and the Philippines all reveal definite discrimination in favour of men in work-related education. Studies in the industrial countries on participation in adult learning also point to a sex-based distinction, with male participants tending to receive more financial support for learning (Valdivielso 1997). The country studies also show a gradual variation in educational content and duration in relation to occupational level and labour market position. There is a hierarchy of educational content favouring creative learning and the mastery of new technology that corresponds to the occupational hierarchy, especially in large corporations.

This duality between work-related education and other types of education is handled differently, based on the country and economic sector. Even though outmoded, it lives on, because, as can be seen in some of the industrialised countries (Canada, Switzerland and the United Kingdom), it favours a certain type of learning demand for education. Nonetheless, while this hardening of the vocational education versus general education duality has hitherto helped legitimate the priority given to business, it is becoming dysfunctional even from an economic viewpoint. It is causing reaction and retaliation, as in Switzerland and England, not only from regional and local authorities and the voluntary sector, but also from an increasing number of economic actors.

The separation of educational content is also losing its relevance in the urban and rural sectors of the informal economy, where community and economic needs closely intersect. The vocational training offered to the workforce in these sectors includes an increasing number of elements of basic education.

Conversely, demand for non-employment-related learning increasingly includes technical and other work-related educational content. In Ecuador (P 2), the basic educational content offered by the Ministry of Education is increasingly intermingled with elements of technical training requested by vocational training services to meet participants' varied interests. The voluntary sector and local community groups, with their diverse interests, are also beginning to break with this dualist model. Literacy programmes in Morocco and Vietnam increasingly include first-level vocational training. Literacy activities in India and popular education programmes for women in the Philippines provide training in microenterprise management and the organisation of income-generating activity.

General adult education centres in Australia and Germany are also scheduling an increasing number of new technology and business management courses. One of the justifications in the 1991 Australian report on general adult learning, *Come In Cinderella* (Australia 1991), for maintaining investment in this field was the indirect contribution of community education to economic growth, based on the higher general level of competencies and the promotion of a culture of lifelong learning. The same argument was made in Germany (Eurydice 1993) for maintaining investment in the two sectors of adult education and continuing education (*Erwachsenenbildung* and *Weiterbildung*).

The dysfunctional nature of the dichotomies inherited from certain school systems, on which a great deal of adult learning policy is still based, can be seen in the personal details of subjects' learning biographies. The mutual interaction and accumulation of vocational and general learning, both formal and experiential, is evident. What an individual learns on the job can also be used off the job, and vice versa. Learners today, through their involvement in various learning processes in community life, private life and at work, cannot help but draw links and, on whatever few occasions arise, integrate the knowledge acquired and make it their own.

8.2. The continuity of learning biographies

Until recently, adult learning policy aimed above all at developing and managing the provision of adult learning services. In this regard, it attempted to co-ordinate educational programmes and activities. What is changing now is the very logic of seeking continuity based on a prescribed arrangement and sequence of curricula, i.e. the model typical of initial formal education. The goal is no longer to simplify and "academically" plan the inevitable diversification of learning opportunities in adulthood. This is impossible! The aim is rather to support subjects as they follow their unique paths through adulthood, choosing from among the many possibilities and combining them in their own idiosyncratic ways.

These kinds of individual continuities and learning pathways cannot be assured without establishing certain preliminary conditions, the most important of which is the right to learning throughout life.

8.2.1. Ensuring adults the right to continue to learn

As emphasised in Chapters 2 (sect. 2.3) and 6 (sect. 1.1), the recognition of the right to learn and an end to age limits on formal education access policies constitute the two legal mainstays adopted to promote the continuation of education beyond initial schooling. The recognition of this right is often accompanied by policies requiring public authorities and business to provide a minimum of educational services and the conditions needed for participation. In 1988, Brazil guaranteed adults the right to education in Article 208 of its constitution (CS: 13). In 1982, a board of enquiry in Quebec (CEFA 1982: 73 and 96) recommended the recognition of "the right of adults to education, without regard to sex, age or profession". The board stated that, "each individual, regardless of their age or material circumstances, has the right to be able to undertake the learning needed for the critical and independent realisation of their potential, in every sphere of human life". Law 107 of the Quebec Parliament recognised this right in 1989. This legislation and the free provision of education that it stipulates helped raised the number of adults participating in primary and secondary levels of education from 102,000 in 1980 to 236,000 in 1991 (ICEA 1994: 37). Also in 1989, the Hungarian Parliament adopted a constitution that included the right to education for all. Similarly, in Spain, chapter 3 of the organic act of 1990 (P 1) guaranteed adults free access to a basic education. In both cases, as already noted, the popularity of the measures, reflected in participation rates, was so great that the authorities subsequently decided to put a ceiling on the number of available places.

All other general education, literacy and informal basic education policies reported in this study (see Appendix I) set out priorities and, unless adjustment policies dry up their budgets, will help broaden the opportunities for adults to continue their education. However, none of these policies guarantee adults the right to education as recommended by UNESCO in its 1976 recommendation (UNESCO 1976) and in the *Hamburg Declaration*[3].

Certain policies, far from reasserting this right, even introduce age restrictions, officially excluding people over the age of 35 in India (P 1) and Vietnam (CS: 3) and over the age of 45 in Morocco (P 4), even though some flexibility seems to be allowed in practice. Unwritten but effective rules also deny older men and women workers participation in vocational training programmes. This general trend is confirmed by participation data (Schuller 1996: 196-198), which show people with the lowest qualification levels particularly penalised.

The older programmes which have no special outreach measures or measures to deal with adult learning conditions tend to reproduce initial schooling inequalities and only recruit adults who already have a high level of education (Rubenson and Xu 1997). Rectifying this tendency, which has been confirmed

---

[3] "Adult education thus becomes more than a right; it is a key to the twenty-first century (...) It is essential that the recognition to the right to education throughout life should be accompanied by measures to create the conditions required to exercise this right. The challenges of the twenty-first century cannot be met by governments, organisations or institutions alone; the energy, imagination and genius of people and their full, free and vigorous participation in every aspect of life are also needed. (...) To that end, we will forge extended alliances to mobilise and share resources in order to make adult learning a joy, a tool, a right and a shared responsibility" (UNESCO 1997: para. 2, 9, and 27). See also the *Agenda for the Future* (UNESCO 1997: para. 24 and following) also adopted in Hamburg in July 1997.

countless times by participation studies, is one of the cornerstones for the development of adult learning policy, i.e. correcting inequities in access and the unequal development of learning spaces. In Chapters 3 and 7, we described how policies can reduce the burden of inequality by means of positive measures to help adults overcome institutional, financial and cultural barriers, as well as the adoption of new information-education-counselling policies that reach the public at large and, given a minimum level of interactive communication and trained local facilitators (see Morocco, P 1), help lead to new learning projects. In Chapter 10 we take up the other component of these strategies, literacy policies.

8.2.2. Promoting the continuity of learning biographies

The growing number of different opportunities and places to learn poses a big challenge to individuals. The numerous learning activities developed independently by different educational agents are experienced or "suffered" by the individual subject who has to learn to deal with them. The inevitable fragmentation of adult learning provision does not merely pose the mechanical question of the recognition of diverse learning acquisition, a subject we return to later. The more basic question is the unity of the learner subject. The individual must be able to make the links, take on board the various learning experiences, and constantly reshape their own personality.

This helps clarify the demand that is the foundation for the above-mentioned new policies, which provide for the creation of information and consultation services for individuals. From the viewpoint of the subject and the temporal and spatial continuity of learning pathways, the development of this transversal role of adult learning policy is crucial.

The reconstitution of learning biographies (Dominice 1990; Alheit 1994; Pineau 1994; Bron 1998) clarifies this educational dialectic in another way. There is obviously a range of learning types and places and above all the discontinuous nature of continuing education. Unexpected events, moments of crisis and choices that become possible at different moments in life are all strategic opportunities for learning. Adults at these points find themselves faced with substantially different practices and orientations. While some actions seek to support the subject's search for autonomy, others offer learners repetitive approaches and short-term adjustment. The long random transitions by young people (Alheit 1994) from initial schooling to regular employment in the formal economy, and the long roads of sometimes more than 15 years trudged by young Africans before finding a steady position in the trades and livelihoods of the informal economy, discourage and disrupt these pathways (ILO 1991: 44). The massive layoffs of older workers denied any opportunity for career mobility and education quite simply deprive them of the resources and conditions needed to continue their educational lives (Guillemard 1995).

The way that societies treat these transitions in private and working life is a revealing indicator of the type of continuing education emerging today. These new, often ambiguous spaces created by the desynchronisation of life cycles and by the dialectical nature of learning biographies in contemporary society are becoming critical points of analysis and major benchmarks in the handling of continuities and discontinuities. They call into question the theory of "human capital" and one-dimensional talk of "return on investments", which ignore the costs of failing to help raise the competency and productivity of all citizens, both in developing and developed countries.

The well-known Club of Rome report, *No Limits to Learning* (Club of Rome 1979), already gave central place to the argument that only active learning continuing over time and space would enable contemporary society to solve the problems it faces.

However, in addition to the shattering of types, times and places of learning, a more deep-going and significant process of diversification is taking place among responses to demand. This involves the plurality of programmes' cultural orientation and, despite predominantly adaptive approaches, the spaces thus created that make room for difference.

Complementary approaches exist, centred more on the learners than on the organisation of educational provision and involving the organisation of information and orientation services and the recognition of experiential learning. Reference, guidance and support centres are more uncommon, yet crucial. They enable individuals to evaluate their situation, explore possible pathways and concretise their learning programme. They also enable groups and companies to analyse their needs and develop and negotiate suitable programmes. These proposals have been tested in the Nordic countries and Quebec, where broad implementation studies are underway (Nordic Council 1995; Quebec 1998: 28 f.).

Mention should be made of some significant innovations in the adult learning scene in the United Kingdom. First, there is the expansion of public/private information-consultation-orientation services throughout the country (CS: 156 f.; P 3) by means of the network of Training and Enterprise Councils, even though these latter were until recently under the exclusive control of employers and were limited to work-related education. In addition, polyvalent reference centres for adult learning are being developed in certain localities (P 5-7). More recently, in the wake of *The Learning Age* (United Kingdom 1998), there have been proposals to transform the Councils into adult orientation centres and networks.

The purpose of these one-stop centres or services would be to identify a region's learning resources, determine learning demand, inform adults about opportunities to pursue their learning and provide them with reference and guidance services (Kayembe 1988). This approach is evolving in North America, Asia and Europe, as seen in the previous chapter.

More importantly, services are starting to emerge to recognise learning acquired outside formal education, i.e. learning acquired formally and informally for the purpose of accreditation or access to formal programmes. Policies for the recognition of general and specialised competencies acquired in various ways by adults and the introduction of a personal educational passport is becoming a normal part of the new panoply of adult learning policies in Australia (Benton 1992), Canada, Europe and the United States. Reference has already been made to the practice of recognising experiential learning acquired on and off the job (see above, sect. 1.3). Yet there are also efforts, such as proposed in the new Quebec policy (Quebec 1998: 30-39), to establish links between the different systems recognising extra-curricula learning. Nonetheless, informal learning is not going to be accredited without resistance from certain organised professional bodies, such as the medical and paramedical professions excluded from the obligations of the 1992 French law and its related 1993 and 1994 decrees on the recognition of experiential learning (Centre INFFO 1992 and 1994).

8.2.3. Financial support policies for learners

Policies have been developed to promote the participation of certain groups, often in liaison with business and local authorities. They allocate financial aid in the form of educational leave, vouchers, job-sharing measures, reimbursement of educational costs, loans and grants for adult full-time and part-time students, tax exemptions, childcare services and, in the informal economy, subsidies and contributions in kind to participating small-town and village groups (for a review of such measures in the European region, see Bélanger and Bochynek 1999). These measures are crucial to the more equitable participation of all social groups and to ensuring that self-financing does not lead to a reduction in the length and quality of programmes. This is in line with the recommendations of the "Delors Commission" Report (UNESCO 1996), which proposed the right to an educational time bank on which all adults could draw throughout their lives. Some countries, including Germany, have adopted legislation guaranteeing the right to paid educational leave (see Chapter 3). American vocational training programmes (P 1) give participants financial support, but tend to offer only extremely short sessions to provide, for example, "job interview skills".
Lastly, educational continuity is more than an individual matter. The 1982 Quebec Enquiry Commission on Adult Education (CEFA 1982: 387) proposed

that educational agencies play a role to help meet demand for collective services and support from social and community organisations not generally well served by institutions. The purpose is to provide them with learning activities incorporated into their collective activity and with resource personnel and expertise. This policy was implemented in some Quebec universities, including the University of Quebec in Montreal. Similar strategies help meet demand for education from local authorities in the Philippines (P 1), for the renewal of local democracy and trade unionism and community life in Eastern Europe, for health and safety committees in Brazil, etc. This could also help universities and colleges sink roots in their local and regional communities, and would be another way to extrapolate and extend into the social and cultural field the closer co-operation developing between universities and business (Otala 1993).

8.3. Broadening the framework for policy intervention

8.3.1. Policies on learning environments

The scope for adult learning policy intervention is growing. There is firstly the adoption of what we have called social demand for learning policies, but also the emergence of policies to examine and improve learning environments. It is not enough to develop an educational strategy and content, since the underlying culture of institutions, the family, business and society also engages in informal teaching. The environments in which learners live, study and work are as influential as the educational activities carried on in them. Motivations differ, as does the stimulation provided, with some environments more knowledge intensive or more favourable to significant learning. Each institutional context has a hidden agenda. Every learning activity takes place in a surreptitiously decisive environment that encourages or suppresses questioning, curiosity, a taste for learning, and the will to review ways of thinking and doing, and creates or destroys the space needed for the emergence of idiosyncrasy. One can speak today of an ecology of cognitive development. The environments where adults live and work influence their learning aspirations and the degree and nature of their participation in learning, facilitating or blocking the acquisition of knowledge, as already observed by UNESCO in 1972 (UNESCO 1972: 33).

Learning policies can no longer be purely educational. Learning environments and the learning incentives they encourage or discourage must be taken into account. Work environments do not all foster creativity and are not all "learning organisations" (Watkins and Marsick 1993; Draves 1995; Cohen and Sproull 1995), much less in-house "industrial democracies". It is no longer possible to ignore the far-reaching cultural influence of different urban and rural environments, the media, and other industrial cultures that can spread or curtail a plurality of expression, and permit or prevent the voices of "others" being heard. A number of local authorities are beginning to develop operational links between the various cultural infrastructures they support (United Kingdom, P 5-8; Belgium, CS: 5): museums, libraries, cultural centres and environmental parks (Frischkopf 1994; Chadwick and Stannett 1998). To this end, the regional government of Tuscany has even created an environmental teaching laboratory in Florence to develop methods to help adults learn in reflexive interaction with their different environments. The OECD initiative to promote the concept of learning cities based on a general mobilisation of public opinion to encourage the population to continue to learn in various ways is inspired by a similar broad vision of learning strategies (OECD-CERI 1992). The cultural environment and the attention given to written material in the context of everyday life are particularly crucial in countries with low literacy levels (see Chapter 10, sect. 2.2), where policies to promote printed material, the local popular book industry, wall newspapers, and the simple, clear quality of messages addressed to the population by government departments are now being studied with the support of different co-operation agencies like UNESCO, Unicef, the German Foundation for International Development (DSE) and an exchange network (OECD 1995). An international study has already shown that the number of books found in young people's immediate environments is one of the best predictive indicators of the mastery of written communication (Elley 1992: 6). It is worth noting that while public libraries in the developed countries have an average of 500 books per 1,000 inhabitants, the average is 60 for all other countries and only 20 for sub-Saharan Africa (UNESCO 1995).

New information technologies are also starting to be a subject of learning policies (ICEA 1994: 115-125). Information and communication technologies have real potential to help formal and informal learning, but many issues must be addressed if this is to be done in a creative and effective way: the unequal distribution of technological equipment, respect for the diversity of cultures, access to the skills and knowledge needed to use these technologies, the participation of the community in producing learning material, the restriction of the use of these new learning methods by the marketing of copyrights, etc.

Numerous creative and innovative examples of providing access to information and communication technologies in different national and regional contexts point to some existing alternatives.

8.3.2. Policy frameworks specific to adult learning

An analysis of adult learning policy shows constant tension between the integration of adult learning into the formal education systems and the organisation of specific approaches to the learning aspirations and conditions of adult populations. The crisis in structural adjustment and public budgets in the 1980s and the still weak institutionalisation of adult learning led many governments in this period to reduce their budgets or incorporate these new services within the regular structures and, wherever a general demographic decline prevailed, place adult groups in formal initial education programmes. In other cases, such as in Spain, general legislation on adult learning was based essentially on basic teaching for young people, to which a section on adult learning was added (Organic Law of 1990, Title 3, see P 1). Legislation on adult learning in this kind of framework often had a highly compensatory orientation, characterised by school curricula and regular diplomas and examinations. Second-chance education was then in danger of remaining compensatory. The situation is disturbing when all it offers is a second chance to backtrack and "repeat", instead of moving forward with all the experiential learning acquired since school. The regional governments of Spain successively endeavoured to rescue adult learning from the standardising logic of initial schooling and the concept of deficiency inherent in denying learners their previous learning biography, in short, to break with what we will later describe as "linear extension"-type continuity.

Education later in life differs from initial schooling. The latter is based on standard curricula backed by a social consensus, a predictable linear sequence of paths, a homogeneously organised student population based on "universal" initial schooling, compulsory enrolment (at least until a certain age), the long-term deferment of the concrete application of learning, and comparable accredited educational institutions. It is not necessary to insist on how adult learning contrasts on each of these points. The characteristics and conditions of on-the-job learning and community education are sufficiently illustrative. It was precisely in order to avoid losing the specificity and effectiveness of educational action and to reach the targeted public with new approaches that the Indian government decided to take the initial step of organising the National Literacy Mission outside the Ministry of Education, that Namibia decided to create a special adult education department that included its cultural services, that the Ministry of Social Welfare in Catalonia was placed in charge of co-ordinating adult learning, and that the general adult education services in Northern Europe are all situated outside the formal educational institution networks. American legislation (P 9) on literacy also removed this programme from the educational establishment, albeit without succeeding in preventing pressure for certificates to close the spaces needed to take into account living contexts and the diversity of learning projects.

New vocational and community programmes have emerged in the United Kingdom (CS: 156-161) that attempt to deal with social groups poorly served by academic approaches. These have also developed separately from educational institutions, including traditional adult education. A variety of measures have been introduced, including information and awareness campaigns, the expansion of learning sites and agents, greater diversity of programmes to meet specific interests, the separation of education and accreditation functions, the creation of open college networks, the strengthening of the open university, the creation of the university of industry, the development of diversified public and private financing (partly to help offset budget cuts), and the use of European structural funds for regions in need.

Finally, many new adult learning policies have developed separately from the educational authorities: in economic affairs ministries (labour, agriculture, trade, fishing, etc.), social affairs ministries (health, population, environment, social services and justice) and cultural affairs ministries (art, museums and libraries, and ethnic minorities). The education ministries do have an important role to play, but a different role with different relations with other partners. Indeed, at times this specificity is organised inside the ministries of education, where special directorates have been created for this end.

8.4. Conclusion: The ambiguity of lifelong learning discourse

The most common policies today tend to ensure the spatial continuity of adult learning services and programmes by creating bridges and promoting links among the different learning programmes and curricula. What is new is the growing tendency to ensure the continuity of learning biographies themselves and expand the framework for policy intervention to include diverse learning and cultural environments and reduce obstacles to participation. Of greatest significance is the adoption of different policies to support learners as they navigate their personal paths through the thousands of learning possibilities with their countless possible sequences.

No study of adult learning policies can stop at their contribution to freeing up learning pathways temporally and spatially. Learning continuity has another, more ideological meaning. In addition to the pursuit of lifelong learning, there is the possible and more problematic continuity involving the perpetuation of cultural orientations and the impact of the social reproduction of initial schooling. It is not possible to wind up this chapter with innovations in the temporal continuation of lifelong learning without questioning the tendency to latch onto and rely on a monolithic discourse on lifelong learning that conceals the contradictions of the projects it supports. It is one thing to ensure the independence of learning biographies and promote the plurality of learning projects, but quite another to maintain relations of academic dependence and initial schooling inequalities.

Two basic trends can be seen. The first can be termed a linear extension, where under the innovative cloak of lifelong learning, educational activity, now carried on throughout life, continues to function as the simple transmission and updating of knowledge and adaptive preparation for socially determined roles and positions. It ensures the ongoing adjustment of subjects to changing situations and expectations. This maintains the dominant authority of schooling and ends up perpetuating unequal social effects and the stratification of initial education. Nonetheless, this tendency to prolong academic inequalities and ceaselessly push individuals to conform, so typical of continuing education conceived as a "linear extension", is running up against the new requirements of far-reaching changes in production modes, the de-socialisation of social values and roles (Touraine 1997: 56 f.), uncertainty in organisational models and, as a consequence of all this, diversity in social learning demand. This tendency also conflicts with actors' aspirations for greater independence at work, in everyday life and in learning. This harks back to the themes taken up in Chapters 4 and 5 of "individualisation" and the "uncertainty" of reflexive societies.

This ambiguity in the discourse on lifelong learning and continuing vocational training can currently be seen above all in the field of waged employment, but social demand to develop productive and creative capacities is not confined to the formal economy. This trend to constantly "adjust" individuals to increasingly fluid socio-occupational positions and to constantly seek to socialise and re-socialise, i.e. to repeatedly internalise throughout life the dominant cultural orientations, which are presented as inevitable, brings us back to the debate on the "cultural" role of education. Here we are referring to critics of the information society who envisage a general growth in demand for qualifications and the gradual reorganisation of personnel based on managerial rationality (Bell 1976; Aronowitz and Di Fazzio 1994), to discussion of E. D. Hirsch's thesis (1987) on the need for "cultural literacy" and the continuing reproduction of historical values, and to debate on the return to the basic values that, according to Samuel Huntington (1996), citizens need to integrate.

We will call the second tendency "reflexive continuity". Like the first, it also entails temporal continuity, implying the continuous pursuit of organised learning throughout life. However, there is a break in continuity in the sense that the different actors concerned constantly need to re-examine and re-organise the relationship between action and education. In this discontinuous continuity, continuing learning begins to correct the initial educational trajectories set in motion by school. Learning aspirations and demand can then be defined in terms of strengthening the independence and creativity of the subjects, including their capacity to learn to question and to learn to learn.

The educational activity of community and non-governmental organisation networks and the autonomous "educational responses" (Philippines, CS: 30-39) found in almost all sectors in the Philippines ensured some temporal continuity in adults' educational life. They are significant because they provide extensive learning services and promote innovations that break with "school reproduction" models and challenge government programmes themselves in such areas as basic education, language training for minorities, programmes targeted at women, agricultural education and community development.

Concrete adult learning policies can thus be placed along a continuum, at the extremes of which can be found the two approaches, linear extension and reflexive continuity, i.e. the constant return to an obsolete order and the difficult return of the actor.

This new typology has great significance, for the temporal and spatial freeing up of learning pathways creates an ambiguous dynamic. The pursuit of lifelong learning does not necessarily lead to the emancipation of subjects' learning biographies. Indeed, the development of continuing education often changes little, and even conceals, in order to better maintain, the prevailing cultural orientations of academic education and their impact on social selection. Furthermore, it is also crucial to emphasise that, while temporal continuity does not necessarily lead to reflexive continuity, the latter cannot be attained without continuing organised forms of learning throughout life, and without continually strengthening capacities for action.

Chapter 9
The Transformation of the State's Role

Introduction: Variations and constants in defining the state's role

The origins of direct, open state intervention in the process of adult learning date back to the dawn of industrial society in the developed countries and the days of national liberation struggles and independence in the developing countries. Examples of learning, which has never been completely confined to the initial education of young people, can of course be found in the oral, artistic and scriptural traditions of different regions of the world. Nonetheless, sustained state activity in adult learning is a relatively recent phenomenon.

Among the rare historical examples of legislation on adult learning are the decrees approved in 1739 by Denmark making literacy a requirement for everyone (Titmus 1985: III). There is also Condorcet's 1792 report, which proposed that the legislative assembly of Republican France introduce adult education as part of educational policy. In 1777, the United States took measures to promote the basic education of soldiers in the Continental Army (National Advisory Council 1981: 10). During the 19th and early 20th centuries, many countries of the North enacted specific measures. These included Denmark in 1814, Spain in 1839, Belgium in 1842, the United Kingdom in 1889 and 1902, and the United States in 1917. At the initiative of Bishop Grundtvig, Denmark opened 60 folk high schools in 1864. Workers Institutes appeared in England during the same period, followed shortly thereafter by university extension services (Field 1992; Pöggeler 1996, Korsgaard 1998). Well before that, in the years 1650 to 1670, the European philosopher Comenius produced his Pampedia, which proposed lifelong education, divided into eight well-defined cycles (Groothoff 1973: 194). Some colonial governments attempted very early on to introduce programmes such as the "Castillanisation" of the indigenous peoples of Mexico in the 18th and 19th centuries, and evening schools in reading and writing the colonial power's language in 19th century India (San Roman Vasquez and Ibarrola 1994; Steele and Taylor 1995; Walters 1995). It was only when spurred on by the national liberation movements, starting in the 1860s in Mexico, in the 1920s in India and in the 1950s in Africa, that adult learning in the former colonies really became part of educational policy. Indeed, in the 1960s, the adoption of national adult literacy and education programmes even became a symbol and a weapon in the fight for independence.

These few bits of information point to the potential value of a transnational historical study of this field for a better understanding of the formative factors in the state's role in adult learning and for filling in the blank spots in our historical memory. One goal of such a study would be to understand when the historical process of declaring "social rights" first started in the field of adult learning, and how this process interacted with the rise of liberties and the redfinition of the state's role. Puellez Benitez's hypothesis assumes that individual liberties began to be expressed in law during the second decade of the 20th century, at the time of the Russian Revolution and the approval of the Mexican Constitution of Queretaro in 1920. He defines subsequent development in terms of a new "policy of mankind" not as an abstract generic entity, but as humans seen from the point of view of their particularity as minors, adults, the elderly, women, etc. This approach was adopted by the Weimar Constitution in Germany in 1919 and then the Constitution of the Republic of Italy in 1946, which assigned the state the task of eliminating economic and social obstacles to the full development of human beings (De Puellez Benitez 1993: 52 f.).

It was only in the 1950s that these isolated harbingers of the19[th] and early 20th centuries were legitimised in constitutional law. There was then steady growth world-wide in state legislative action in adult learning, including in regards to literacy, with the encouragement of the UNESCO Experimental Programme.

This phenomenon was not confined to countries involved in the process of national liberation, but was broader in nature. It was no coincidence that in the 1950s and 1960s existing theories were given a new lease of life under new names such as lifelong education and the learning society. Without minimising the role of progenitors like Comenius, the 19th-century Utopians and the Chautauqua Movement in the United States in the early 20th century, the concept of the state's central educational role in nation-building really took hold in the post-Second World War decades.

During this period, state intervention intensified and became more open. The Gramscian idea "that the state must be conceived as an 'educator' precisely because it is beginning to create a new type and a new level of civilisation" (Gramsci 1986) spread roots more broadly. States and institutions in general then increasingly began to play a more direct role in determining the dynamics regulating the population's learning process. In some cases, the way welfare policy evolved created fertile terrain for developments that pushed the state towards becoming an "educating state". In this climate of rapid growth, national liberation and overall optimism, UNESCO and then the OECD published their important reports on "lifelong education" (UNESCO 1972) and "recurrent education" (OECD 1973). The petrol crisis a few years later buried these projects in a series of counter-reforms. UNESCO as well as the OECD would wait another twenty years before proclaiming the idea of lifelong learning once more, this time in a very different context.

9.1. Crisis of the welfare state and the transformation of the state's role

Paradoxically, the years of financial crisis, welfare state crisis and World Bank structural adjustment programmes corresponded to silent growth in the state's role (at least in some states, including in the developing countries) in two areas: the scope of policy intervention, and in meeting economic needs.

9.1.1. Broader scope for intervention

In the typical welfare state context, adult learning policies comprised the dissemination of knowledge, the adaptation and updating of competencies and other auxiliary functions discharged by the systems and institutions specifically responsible for providing educational services. The crisis in this model reinforced the expansion and new structure of sites involved in the production of knowledge, which, in addition to traditional locations, now took place in a wide variety of spaces and times in personal and social life. Similar developments could also be seen in relation to new active labour policies and new integrated regional development policies that linked the cultural, educational and economic dimensions involved in an area's growth.

State policy could not deal with this new context simply by increasing spending and public intervention, but had to take control and provide some guidance by taking on key tasks beyond the direct provision of educational services. To strengthen its position vis-à-vis different actors, for example, the state gave itself the power to legitimate the new learning sites, agents and processes. To handle this problem, which was particularly acute in Central and Eastern Europe in the early 1990s, the state established special services that authorised the practice of educational activity. In its most developed form, this meant approving laws requiring that organisations adhere to quality standards set by public agencies. These involved, for example, the nature of the infrastructure and the activities offered. In regard to individual learning processes, as we have seen, the traditional instruments typical of the former model were now supplemented by a new mechanism. In particular, systems appeared for certifying knowledge and legitimating know-how and competencies acquired informally, even outside recognised institutions (Péarker, Leplatre and Ward 1994).

Perhaps even more importantly, many non-education ministries introduced educational programmes in their respective fields of responsibility, not only for their own personnel and non-governmental organisations active on the margins of their fields, but also for specific outside groups (farmers, fishermen, prisoners, etc.) and the general public (in health care, the environment, etc.). As already mentioned, budgets have been severely cut in the traditional official field of adult education, community education, popular education in the industrialised countries and adult literacy programmes in Africa. Yet these more visible and negative cuts should not, paradoxically, obscure the diversification and expansion of the state role in the vast field of organised learning activities provided for adults.

9.1.2. The state role is growing to meet new economic needs

The second factor driving the extension and change in the state's role concerns the new demands placed on adult learning policy by economic actors. The crisis in the welfare state is closely linked to the changing economy. Paradoxically, the growing trend towards a free-market economy is heightening demand for state intervention to raise workforce qualifications. It is above all at this historic moment that business is increasingly demanding that the state pay for part of the costs of the theoretical and practical training of the working population and that it creates counselling and support services for companies and individuals. Demand is likewise constantly rising for state co-operation in building new "knowledge superhighways", the expensive new information and communications infrastructures widely demanded in particualr by population groups involved in "symbolic-analytic activity".

More privileged individuals have now reached very high levels of capacity for individual initiative, and the participation in adult learning has reached new heights (see Chapter 1). In the United States, for example, the American Society of Training Directors has continued to develop a parallel adult learningsystem in industry. Companies spent US$ 45 billion on this in 1992, almost as much as was spent on the formal education system. In 1997, *Industry Report* estimated the year's business spending on education at US$ 58.6 billion, an increase of 33% over the previous three years alone, with 56.6 million participants in 1997 (summarised in: *American Training*, October 1997, p. 33-75) . According to a Canadian estimate, nation-wide business spending in 1991 came to Can$ 3.6 billion, enabling 36% of private sector employees to take part in education (Canadian Centre on the Labour Market and Productivity 1993).

This tendency, however, is neither new nor exclusive to the industrialised countries. In Brazil, observers noted the supplementary role played by business as long ago as 1942 (CS: 36). Government policy everywhere has encouraged this trend. There has been growing demand for greater state involvement, with mechanisms and forms adapted to the new dynamics. Since the 1960s, the Canadian government "has been working to encourage business to take part in the field of education", to develop a learning culture in the business world, to focus on-the-job training on those at work, and to focus investment in learning designed to promote productivity increases (CS: 14 f.). In the United Kingdom at the beginning of the 1990s, the White Paper *Employment in the 1990s* (P 3) prompted the creation of the Training and Enterprise Councils. These "independent" organisations were established at the instigation of the Ministry of Employment's Training Agency. They were responsible for analysing the need for "training credits" and distributing them among adults. Measures were taken in Australia to encourage businesses that promoted learning (CS: 20 f.), as they were in Japan too starting in 1969. Moreover, in Japan measures were implemented to encourage companies to handle the management of learning policy at the company level. To achieve this objective, the state asked industry to draw up a step-by-step, systematic programme to promote human resources development (HRD) and to appoint a human resources development promoter in each company (Japan, CS: 36).

Yet surprisingly enough, the combined pressure from economic actors and governments on an increasing number of companies, pushing them to invest in training their personnel, has not reduced government involvement and spending. The fact that business has become a new active subject in adult learning is leading and has led to four immediate results. First, the trend towards rising productivity has prompted both developments in company training and cuts in the number of employees, under the neutral heading of rationalisation, as well as demands for the state to organise "employability" programmes and train the job-seeking population, which on average corresponds to the percentage of unemployed persons among the "active" population. Second, while business has increased its investments in adult learning, it has also stepped up pressure on public institutions to pay for initial education, "second chance" education and the reintegration of workers, innovation, accreditation and monitoring, and to grant tax relief for company training costs. Third, greater occupational mobility has resulted in public education systems (vocational training centres and post-secondary institutions) being shouldered with re-training programmes that were previously organised by companies providing guaranteed "lifetime" jobs. Fourth, the expansion of production-related learning demand has given birth to an "education service industry", which has taken shape in the private sector as well as in public services and "partnerships". There has been an explosion in new types of demand from public institutions and services. This no longer simply amounts to financing or managing learning activities. It entails creating the special infrastructures and assistance needed for the new educational actors to fulfil their roles. The state becomes an important player in this expansion of the basic cultural and educational services, i.e. the learning hardware: information centres, specialised IT networks, satellites for distance education, libraries specialising in helping self-directed learning, research and documentation centres, etc. In other words, everything that goes into "collective intelligence", to pick up on Pierre Lévy's use of Gramsci's expression (Lévy 1997).

An examination of adult learning as a whole shows that, despite appearances, the state's commitments and responsibilities have grown, at least in the most dynamic institutions and those with real decision-making autonomy. This growth has been prompted by radical changes in the volume and quality of social demand for adult learning, combined with the complexity of the resulting responses and the constant increase in their costs. The state has consequently become more committed to supporting and developing diverse learning strategies and to monitoring and adjusting the targeting and distribution of learning resources.

This growth in the state's responsibilities is thus accompanied by new contradictions and antagonisms intrinsic to the production-learning relationship. Given the new economic model, with economic growth that fails to generate jobs, state educational policies must redefine their role. The automatic adaptations and linearity of the past are now a dead letter. Furthermore, increasing educational investment in a model that does not seek to generate full employment requires parallel growth in investment in social policy, in order, paradoxically, to offset the impact of job cuts caused by investment in productivity and education. A new state role has thus been created, correcting the paradoxes produced by the unregulated free market. This does not, however, signify a return to welfare models that promote public services. It entails instead the redefinition of adult learning policies and strategies to create new prospects for what the Swedes call "the participatory welfare state", or what could also be called the "learnfare state".

9.1.3. "Steer rather than row"

"Steer rather than row": Borrowing the expression from David Osborne and Ted Gaebler, Robb Mason (author of our country study on Australia) thus characterises the new adult learning approach taken by the Australian government in recent years (CS: 21). Australian adult learning, he writes, has become "a market that is guided rather than determined or directed by service providers or the government" (CS: 20). The government defines or co-defines priorities, the types of competencies to be favoured and the educational results to be expected, and tends to leave it up to market dynamics and civil society to see whether the different types of intervention will succeed or fail. An OECD typology limited to the formal economy posits that the main new state functions include policies and micro-economic measures to encourage participation in learning, direct and indirect support for companies that invest in adult learning, the promotion of partnerships, and other actions to regulate, orient and guide the educational processes (OECD-CERI 221). To this list should be added the allocation of public support to non-governmental organisations interventions in different fields (health care, the environment, democratic participation in community life, etc.) and new policies to open public formal education networks to adults (see the *Agenda for the Future*, para. 16-23, in: UNESCO 1997).

This undeniable change must however be interpreted more in terms of redefining the steering and managing functions rather than the domination of one over the other. Given the rapid growth in adult learning, and its expansion in all areas of life, it is clear that what was directly linked to the centralised model of the national school systems is being systematically replaced by a "networking pattern" in which the concept of a "centre" is gradually being eroded. In this new context, there are no predefined limits or boundaries to national adult learning policy, unlike the case of initial education policy. The inherent polymorphism in this new phenomenon must be respected if it is to be oriented, supported, regulated and administered. Policy renounces a reductio ad unum, and accepts and administers a plurality of various subjects, environments and approaches. The main focus or common denominator of these various policies and strategies is support for and development of capacities for the independent initiative of civil society and the creation of equal opportunities for empowerment throughout life as well as at life's starting points (Roemer 1996) — in other words, the liberation of the creative and productive forces.

Adopting a policy to promote the development of capacities for initiative in civil society does not, however, mean that public institutions should renege on their resonsibilities or their role of "managing". It simply means that this needs to be done differently. Thus we talk of "making do with", of "getting others to act" and of "only doing what is necessary" (i.e. subsidiarity), and above all ensuring that whatever is done responds to objectives, demands and aspirations. Another fundamental change should be considered at this point. School policy has always focused essentially on the management of institutional systems and the determination of curricula, even defining didactic methods and content in detail, and this has often been true of adult education as well. This may still be the case for some formal adult educational institutions, but these goals are no longer central in adult learning policy. Policy now directly intersects with physical and economic policy, labour and social policy, regional development policy, etc.

A more in-depth study of the meaning of the terms "steer" and "manage" requires an examination of the content of these functions. In the last decade few or no policies have been implemented to reduce the role of the state in the field of education. Whether or not George Bush actually deserved the title to which he aspired of "President of Education", it seems that neither he nor his predecessor ever gave up the idea of seeing the state play a role in defining national adult learning policy. Even the British Education Reform Act of 1988, which Margaret Thatcher deemed a radical, definitive turning point, while attempting to introduce market principles and free choice into education, never called into question the central role of the national government and local authorities. Under Prime Minister Major and then Blair, education once again became a priority. A new consensus was indeed forged that led to reviving the role of public authorities in initial education and to new roles for adult learning. The place of the welfare state in education was obviously shaken, and even seriously damaged, but, unlike other sectors, it survived (Lawten 1992). Public services were much more seriously affected in countries subject to structural adjustment programmes (Mulenga 1994).

The report by the "Delors Commission" explicitly states,

> "Education is a collective asset that cannot be left only to market forces (...). The state must assume certain responsibilities to its citizens, including creating a national consensus on education (...) and proposing a long-term view for the future" (UNESCO 1996: 182).

It especially emphasises specific functions that are the state's responsibility, such as managing social dialogue and medium and long-term programming.

Looking at deregulation policies from this point of view, it becomes clear that they did not negate the state's key duties. Some of their choices were certainly debatable, since they favoured the access to learning of certain social groups over others and they promoted the expression of some types of learning demand over others. This is relevant, for example, to interpreting President Reagan's initiative to reform the previous Comprehensive Education and Training Act, abolished in 1982, and replace it with the new Job Training Partnership Act (P 1). The reasons for the change, as expressed in the demands of the business world and politicians, included:
(1)   to eliminate certain welfare provisions and replace them with measures to promote the training of displaced workers;
(2)   to introduce performance criteria into the financing of activities;
(3)   to give State private industry councils a role in planning and evaluation;
(4)   and, finally, to modify and increase the responsibilities of the states.

Institutional adult learning policies should be viewed and analysed above all from a macro-educational point of view. The expansion of the managerial responsibilities of economic and social agencies and the rapid increase in the number of service providers is reinforcing and broadening the state's steering and managerial tasks, which are being pushed to deal with higher levels. The recent example of Senegal is significant. The ministry of basic education, which was solely responsible for a small literacy programme (with a budget of US$ 300,000) in 1990, had a budget ten times larger five years later. However, by this time, much of it was handled by partnerships or outsourcing. The government's tasks are now centred on orientation and monitoring, the co-ordination of agencies, and research and development! Looked at simply from the angle of the public literacy programme, this was a retreat. Yet viewed from the other end of the tunnel, it represented a larger new commitment to the state role, which now managed to provide basic education to ten times as many adults.

The goal of developing the capacity of different components of civil society for self-regulation needs to be pursued. The basic role of public institutions and the state centres on three key tasks:
1. The search for equal opportunities for all citizens, by adopting policies aimed at equal initial education (a task that goes beyond initial schooling) and at increasing equal access to organised adult learning;
2. The recognition of cultural rights respectful of different identities;
3. The expression of the broad demand from citizens for learning and support for the development of a variety of responses to the demands raised.
From this viewpoint, the state is still the agent that must assume responsibility for orienting and "networking" the different policies on which an overall lifelong-learning strategy is based.

9.2. Changes in the state's main role: The decentralisation and internationalisation of decision-making

The dialectic that is developing between the different decision-making levels (local, regional, national and transnational) has an educational dimension. It corresponds to a process of identification and democratic control by subjects who determine the educational pathways, from the global level to the local level and vice versa. The processes of strengthening the local dimension and developing the transnational dimension of adult learning both correspond to essential levels of policy management and development. The first brings decision-making power and the choices of concrete subjects closer together, and the second develops transparency and democracy in the management of relations between national actors and economic and military power at the global level. In light of this dual process of decentralisation and transnationalisation, it is essential to examine the new contradictions being spawned.

9.2.1. The new importance of local power

The local level has always been emphasised in theoretical, political and methodological discussions of adult learning. The assertion of the importance of the local or regional dimension in adult education decision-making has been part of an effort to make standardised academic approaches more democratic, participatory and flexible. Emphasis on the local or regional dimension corresponded to an alternate conception of decentralised public power that was closer to the citizens and their various grass-root organisations, to recognition and support for new cultural and ethnic identities (local minorities), and to the process of developing new organisational models of adult learning based on locally-integrated systems.

Intervention at the regional and local level was and still is a response to the contradictions generated by the forced unifications that accompanied the rise of the big nation-states and the corresponding models of educational systems structured on the lines of the big organisations and their need for a trained national labour force.

Over the last fifty years, since the first international UNESCO conference on adult education, consideration of the regional and local dimension has been an increasingly important constant in discussion and practice in the world of adult learning. Why? One reason is that reference to the local dimension has become part of the tradition of the great educational utopias. Still today, it nourishes the hope of carrying out, albeit only in small privileged arenas, programmes that are not immediately feasible on a large scale, with the hope that they will spread afterwards. In the spirit of Goethe, who said "God is in the details", Gandhi wrote, "Each village must become a republic or panchayat with full powers (...) This system of countless villages must be made up of ever expanding circles, and never take the form of ascending circles. Society must be an oceanic circle at the centre of which is the individual". In Senegal, Julius Nyerere developed a similar programme based on "Ujamaa" villages (Carnoy and Samoff 1990: 212 f.).

Beyond these utopias, it should not be forgotten that, with the coming of industrial society, the management of the educational process in a given territory stepped out of the pages of speculative visions of science fiction writers and became an integral part of the process of managing contemporary production relations. When, beginning in the 1950s, the big international organisations inaugurated the era of pilot projects and development projects in the depressed regions of Europe and the developing countries, they were merely updating the models of integrated territorial management (urbanistic, productive, cultural, educational, etc.) that had already been implemented in more rigid forms in the gloomy industrial cities of England described by Engels, in the new mining and agricultural cities chalked out in Italy by Mussolini, and in the new cities where the viceroy Toledo started systematically concentrating the Incas in the 1580s after the execution of Tupac Amaru. Further to the north, in 1555, the Mexican Church had already demanded at its first council that the native be "persuaded – or obliged if necessary, but with as little violence as possible – to gather in suitable towns and cities where they can live in a civilised and Christian way". (Benevolo 1993: 119 f.). It was in Mexico, too, that Vasco de Quiroga arrived to build two ideal cities inspired by Thomas Moore's Utopia in 1531 (ibid.: 122). Centralisation facilitates control, standardisation and unification.

All democratic states have now adopted the model of the decentralisation of authority in the management of the adult learning process. However, there are contradictory methods of implementing this common model, including such examples as:

a. The geographic decentralisation of central power by creating new functional linkages that grant decentralised bodies only the power to implement policies and programmes. This "prefect" model increases the central power's control over the periphery;

b. The decentralisation of decision-making power, but not of resources, in policy implementation. The Brazilian model corresponds to this type of decentralisation;

c. Marginal decentralisation, which involves adjusting and compensating for policies decided at central level, including through conflict. Developments in the United Kingdom during the 1980s provide one example of this. Here, given a central policy mainly aimed at work-related training, which resulted in collapsing participation in informal adult education activities, local opposition movements began to arise and create new informal learning opportunities (CS: 154 f.);

d. Real, not merely proclaimed decentralisation, including genuine power to intervene in educational matters, with genuine budgetary power, often including the power of taxation. This model can already be found in some autonomous regions of Europe, such as Tuscany and Catalonia. The local scene is thus not only open to utopian exercises, but also to political confrontation. Regional and local institutions are playing an increasingly important role in many parts of the world and taking over responsibilities from the big nation-states.

The post-modernist critique, which has exposed the arbitrary cultural standards behind the global references of dominant Western discourse and the unitary visions with their universalist pretensions, has greatly strengthened political and cultural proposals that advocate a return to the local level. This "reaction", which had its brief moment of glory in the 1980s, was bound to fragment. First, the most dynamic local initiatives soon required broader interventions precisely to protect or develop autonomous zones and build solidarity among them. For example, "local powers" quickly gave rise to transnational institutions in Europe, such as the Committee of Regions of Europe. This organisation has consultative powers with regard to the European Union and helps manage the programmes it finances, without any direct control by the "intermediary power" of the member state. These regions and the major European cities inaugurated the Assembly of European Regions, in which local institutional organisations from Eastern Europe also participate. Furthermore, global power, particularly economic, had become too great to be left to itself without the concurrent organisation of civil society locally and internationally.

9.2.2. The new supranational organisations

While all this has been taking place, the binding powers of new transnational organisations have been growing stronger world-wide. Everywhere supranational organisations with real powers (normative and financial) are being established or strengthened in the field of adult learning: the European Union, NAFTA, Mercosur, World Bank, Asian Development Bank, International Monetary Fund, Organisation of African Unity, etc. None of these supranational organisations functions in the same way as parliamentary democracies. The same holds true at European level: although the European parliament is elected by direct popular vote, up to now it has fewer powers than the Council of Ministers and the members of the European Commission, which is a true governmental authority but does not really derive its powers directly from Parliament.

It is well known that the new production organisation model is structured globally and is based on and integrates locally- and sub-regionally-related production systems. The economy is thus actually steered at both the transnational level, which is dominated by multinationals with budgets equal to or greater than those of many medium-sized states and by new supranational political and financial organisations, and at the regional and sub-regional levels by small and medium-sized enterprises and regional and local governments. Projects for European, North American and South American unification, and similar efforts in Africa and Asia, are not simply the results of prophetic visionaries and modern regionalists, but rather an institutional response to demand, mainly economic, to redefine and reorganise the role of the nation-state. These actual economic decision-making centres are adopting "unwritten rules" for managing human resources and imposing determinant orientations that are exempt from any right of supervision or adjustment by nationally constituted democratic authorities.

This globalisation is not only economic. Environmental hazards, the dangers of epidemics and demographic dynamics are also breaking down frontiers. Although the epicentre of the Chernobyl disaster was in Ukraine, the resulting dangers threatened an entire continent. Health-care prevention measures, or the lack of them, also ultimately have global impacts.

A new dynamic is developing in response to this transnationalisation and the resulting imbalance between new global decision-making sites and the national mechanisms for democratic control. There is growing interest in a new international order, in reforming the United Nations and in the still fragmentary emergence of a supranational civil society including global environmental non-governmental organisations, internationally linked popular movements and independent transnational media (Castels 1996).

9.2.3. The dialectics of global and local power

Just as key decision-making centres are being globalised, many democratic governments are implementing processes to decentralise authority in every sector of public life. Local and regional governments are taking on increasing powers in the field of public service management, including of educational policy. Their power to guide policy is growing steadily. These two trends – decentralisation and globalisation – increasingly interact, displacing contradictions. The new model of economic growth (predominance of multinationals, the internationalisation of money markets, marketing and labour, transition to post-Fordist production modes and "jobless growth") bases its operational strategy on local and sub-regional restructuring. In the 1980s, the slogan "act locally and think globally" held great appeal for many people. Yet the implicit division between "act" and "think" should have made its authors more circumspect. Real policy is now being developed at every level, including the globalisation of economic decision-making, along with efforts to organise and develop resistance at the global level too, the emergence of regional political power and the establishment of continental networks of voluntary groups, administrative decentralisation, privatisation and the revitalisation of local communities.

The issue here is not globalisation or decentralisation, but the dominant approach at every level and the capacity to counterbalance the new dominant powers at every level too. A key factor for adult learning is that the emergence of supranational powers, particularly economic ones, is leading to an increasingly perverse shift in "the equilibrium point between the efficiency and equity of systems", i.e. between the ability of the system to produce a profit at the lowest cost and the methods and criteria for distributing its benefits. Gaps in purchasing power and consumption capacities for all kinds of products, including educational services, are growing. For example, in the United States in 1960, the managing director of a large corporation earned about twelve times more than a worker in the same company. In 1988, however, a managing director's after-tax income was about seventy times greater than that of a worker (Reich 1991: 254 f. and 260 f.).

Methods of raising productivity, which are often closely linked to work-related adult learning policies, are lifting the standard of living of certain limited strata in the labour force and a few regional zones around the world, to the detriment of other subjects in other regions. Supranationalisation and decentralisation are thus taking on new meaning, in that they are related to the impoverishment of vast areas of the world and to the outbreak of new conflicts. These are expressed in the spread of anti-solidarity ideologies, the explosion of local wars and the weakening of democratic structures.

Accepting a development concept that is based on one region or country in the world, cut off from the search for solutions for the other regions and bereft of any notion of solidarity, ultimately comes down to accepting a model that increases unemployment and poverty. In this model, to use the Chicago school's reasoning, unemployment and poverty play an "educational" role as a constant reminder and threat for all economically vulnerable employees. No management of the new general economics of adult learning can simply dismiss this new "economic horror" (Forrester 1999) or the dynamics underlying the unequal developments of human resources.

9.3. Managing the new general organisation of adult learning

9.3.1. The macro-economic dimension

The crucial problems posed in managing adult learning can be analysed in relation to two types of problems: first, the changes in vision and strategy being effected by the shifting relationship between economic policy and adult learning policy, due to the globalisation of the economy, and second, the increasing inclusion of adult learning costs in fixing the prices of goods and services.

A new model of the general organisation of adult learning
With regard to the first problem, with the transition from an economy based on big national companies to one dominated by extensive global networks, we are witnessing the demise of a model of full-employment labour policies and of the strategic educational arsenal that was linked to it. This educational model was centred on initial schooling and continuing on-the-job training and was associated with the theory of human capital and "the filter". Education was seen as an investment that could increase productivity and lead to big advances, including for the workers themselves. Investments in this field took on even greater significance because there was an extensive amount of time in which the learning acquired by the subject could be turned to profitable use. Initial schooling was then continually rounded out or tailored by training acquired more or less informally on-the-job and preferably with immediate effect, to reimburse any invest-

ments made by the individual, the company or the government relatively quickly. In short, life-time jobs made possible and were based on lifelong education.

This statist model has hit a crisis with the globalisation of production and the increasing importance of the "symbolic-analytic" professions. According to Reich's thesis,

> "the economic well-being of any group of individuals with a given political identity no longer depends on the companies they own but on the value that they add to the global economy through their capacities and their imagination. Their living standards are increasingly determined by the activities they carry out, and not by the success of abstract entities like big companies, industries or national economies" (Reich 1991: 233).

At a time when national prosperity and the stable redistribution of wealth can no longer be guaranteed by continuing growth and full employment, the corresponding educational institutions and strategies are also falling into crisis.

This immediately undermines the synchronism of diploma > work > income. It is no longer certain that investment in human resources will be economically productive. Even prior to this, new contradictions appeared in the role and objectives of educational policies in a climate marked by "jobless economic growth". In this new context, adult training designed to increase the competency of people at work is reflected by an increase in their productivity. This means that adult learning enables fewer employees to produce the same quantity of products, and thus leads to a fall in employment. The ambiguities in adult education designed for those pushed out of the labour market has already been noted.

If a nation's prosperity increasingly depends on the "wealth and imagination" of its citizens, adult learning policy must also take into account this new strategic orientation. Educational investments made to promote growth and development can no longer be planned based on current employment or company projections. Investment must concentrate on building "dynamic learning communities" and heightening individual and collective intellectual capacities. One of the most significant examples of the rise of this new approach is the Document on the programming of structural interventions for objective 4, approved by the European Commission in 1994. In this document, adult learning ceases to be focused on the job definition and "strengthening the job position", i.e. based on the company as such, and instead emphasises "reinforcing the professionalism of each worker". The document explicitly prohibits "making any a priori references to any specific industries or sectors" in order to promote channelling funds towards actions that "take into consideration the general requirements of the workers" (European Commission 1994b).

The linear model is thus being replaced by a new model of the general organisation of adult learning, which we could define as holistic-transformative. It is no longer centred on particular educational or economic institutions. It treats the subject as the centre of developmental strategy and helps subjects to realise their full intellectual potential and remove any obstacles to achieving that. One measure of the effectiveness of this new approach is thus its capacity to define and modify the learning factors that hinder individual and collective development. These factors, which are linked to the conditions of daily life, consumption and work, inflict learning damage on individuals and the community. The resulting harm can be measured in terms of loss in aptitudes, competencies and knowledge, and in general difficulty in being creative or engaging in adult learning. The costs are inevitably borne by the individual and the community, and affect the prosperity of the nation as a whole and its prospects for growth. The general organisation of adult learning thus includes not only the organisation of educational services, but also the active and passive handling of the environments that promote or inhibit continuing lifelong learning. The risks of learning damage are as much a part of adult learning policy as ecological dangers are a part of environmental policy.

Setting the prices of goods and services is also related to the macro-economics of adult learning. Pricing goods and services has increasingly incorporated, in addition to the cost of materials (raw materials, machines and financial costs), the cost of health-care protection and social security and, more recently, the cost of environmental damage caused by production. In the same way, the new general economics of adult learning must now also incorporate the cost of learning on-the-job and move beyond a model that passes on the cost of learning and learning damage to the individual and the community. Some national and transnational policies have clearly already begun to move, however timidly, in this direction. The 1974 Geneva Convention on paid educational leave, approved by an ILO plenary session, was one of the first examples of reintegrating part of training costs into production budgets. Tax deductions for training purposes should also be seen in this light. A third example is the aforementioned decision by a growing number of countries to allocate 1%-2% of total payroll to training. This initiative is contradictory, however, due to the segmentation of the labour market and the consequent unequal development of learning opportunities.

Adult learning without money

More than a bright future, for most adult educators this heading evokes a familiar past and present. The concern that we would like to address at the end of this section is that if we abandon "the exchange" of learning products to the marketplace, that is, with money as the regulator of exchange, we will automatically eliminate the possibility for most of the world's population to become the active masters of their own development. As Tandon emphasises, "with the growth of specialization and increasing centralization of the knowledge industry, only a particular mode of knowledge production recommended and pursued by the dominant systems of knowledge production was accepted as the only legitimate mode of knowledge production" (Tandon 1988 : 8).

By imposing and accepting these models of knowledge production, a system of production, distribution, exchange and consumption is ultimately created where the purchasing power of individuals, social groups and countries determines their position and participation in the general organisation of lifelong learning. It is vital that the legitimacy of models of educational exchange based on market laws alone be challenged. The risks entailed are as much cultural, social and political as economic.

This problem has been studied by numerous governments on every continent. Adult learning freed from an absolute domination of money should ultimately be rooted in the dynamics of mutual solidarity and civil society. However, the solution to the problem we face does not consist in opening side markets and giving a complementary educational role to voluntary action, alongside and in support of an official, legitimate system for the production of knowledge. What can serve as the financial motor and driving force behind the intellectual development of everyone in every part of the world is the introduction of dynamics and methodologies specific to educational work in each sector of activity. Each action by individuals and communities at different moments of everyday life, including in the family, in institutions and at work generates a learning demand and calls for financial support closely related to the sectors and levels of activities involved. The only model for the general economics of adult learning that will prove lasting and meet everyone's needs will inevitably cut across sectors, and, like health care, be increasingly integrated with the general economy and at the same time try to take into account both costs and benefits.

9.3.2. The new policy on managing adult learning

The de-territorialisation of educational policy
As already emphasised, policy is no longer confined to the provision of educational institutions or the "product". Policy increasingly covers all learning responses. It targets individual and collective learning processes of every kind, including formal, non-formal, informal and accidental. The limited concepts of "space" and "time" so typical of initial formal education are taking on broader connotations ("lifewide" and "lifelong"). The space marked out for former educational institutions has undergone a process of "de-territorialisation", and these institutions have lost the exclusive roles previously reserved for them:

"The space for knowledge emerges from the collective destiny (...).
Collective knowledge reverses the relationships created by a given territory
between time and space (...). Territory creates its own time by the act of
being established (...). To control and shape the future, it uses spatial mechanisms: walls, canals, shop-counters, drawbridges, bureaucratic labyrinths, the
endless spirals of exclusion and belonging (...). A territory wants to make its
orders, hierarchies and structures eternal. The space for knowledge, in contrast, is in a state of continual re-birth. It emerges inexorably from the individual actions and histories that drive forward collective knowledge. It never
has an a priori structure, but on the contrary expresses, maps out and reveals
the tangled webs of subjective and inevitably unforeseeable durations"
(Lévy 1997: 182).

The transformation of the "space for knowledge" is being expressed in policies
that influence both individual learning pathways and the learning structure that
influences the vast number of learning spaces. This can be seen in legislation
adopted in France, Germany and the United Kingdom which certifies, i.e. ap-
proves for the purposes of an academic or professional career, knowledge acquired
in the most diverse times and places. In this case, response management policy
is aimed at supporting individual and collective pathways for the generation of
knowledge. Based on these kinds of considerations, several countries, including
France, have implemented measures to recognise the knowledge acquired by
adults.

"It is in the arrangements of knowledge trees, (...) it is the curricula of individual learning that structure the knowledge trees of a community. Yet these
curricula are not based upon calendar time – the dates when all the diplomas
are acquired are not listed. All that matters is the subjective growth of knowledge, and its imminent structure (...) In addition, the cognitive coats of arms
of individuals (...) no longer record what has been personally acquired, but
link each individual's competencies into an emerging collective order, the
community tree (...) Subjective temporalities compose a common space"
(Lévy 1997: 171).

The new concept of space in adult learning necessitates a re-examination of the
conditions facilitating the rise of "intelligent communities". Policy no longer
functions solely to add new products to the existing supply (cyberspace to academic institutions!). It tends instead to influence the learning structures active in
a society and in its different organisations, i.e. on learning processes that have
developed, intentionally or unintentionally. The conception of a learning society
and a "learning organisation", which is intended to help influence the different
components of any organisation where learning is likely to take place, will help
arm policy with an ecological management of the learning process that goes well
beyond the specific organised learning activity itself.

Policies to promote a metasystem of adult learning

The old concept of an adult education system must be redefined in the light of these new functions. Titmus' definition states that its basic elements include:

"(...) a plurality of educational enterprises or initiatives, which operate as individual systems. They may range from one-off enterprises of limited duration to continuing or repetitive ones of indefinite length. They may stand in isolation, as unique event, unrelated organisationally to other similar enterprises, to any formal agency or association, as when a number of people form a group in order to learn what may do to oppose proposals for a new power station in their vicinity which threatens to affect adversely their environment. At the other extreme, they may operate within a permanent organisation, part of whose continuing programs they form" (Titmus 1990: 197 f.).

This definition continues to be shaped by logic that treats adult learning as specific organised activity. It could also still lead to being "isolated" from the actual learning dynamics at work in society. Indeed, current policies already go beyond these limits. The new model is taking shape as a building block for the development and management of individual and collective processes, and not as an agglomeration of spaces, subjects and actions whose educational role has been legitimated a priori. The new model is based on variable geometry in that it reflects the learning dynamics of subjects, whether co-operating or in conflict, it pursues the numerous directions in which different and opposing educational interests push it, and it is opening up to the new spaces and moments of individual and collective life and knowledge. It does not exclude the traditional structures of formal, informal and accidental adult learning, but purposefully takes into account the "endogenous" dimension of the learning process. To pick up on an old slogan of pedagogical activists, we can say that this is a "system whose skeleton has no flesh" and that, by managing the "learning structure" operating everywhere (on the job, in the community and in everyday life), it is supporting the learning dimension at every point in people's lives.

Unlike the school system, this is a meta-network, linked to all economic, cultural, institutional and other subsystems, but not reducible to the learning activities taking place within each of them. However, this metasystem, "inescapably characterized by continuing tension and instability" (Titmus 1990: 203), often still leads to various centralising policies, and thus to uniformity, a reductio ad unum, like the models of any systemic logic. This new meta-network-type of orientation is in line with the proposal of the European Centre for Work-Related Training for continuum policies (Cedefop 1994). These policies focus on provision, and more precisely on two factors: co-ordination among the different organisations responsible for defining strategy and policy, and the creation of direct links among the various types of adult learning agencies and activities. These two goals are relevant to improving the organisation of policy implementation and can, if achieved, lead to economic benefits and above all to the elimination of the obstacles that block or hinder adult mobility within learning networks.

The perspective of the subject, however, is different. For the learning public, continuity is assured less by the existence of "intersystemic gateways" than by the subject's own learning trajectory, which can be more or less satisfactory, and is often channelled towards vast arid cultural deserts. The problem therefore is to introduce opportunities for ruptures or discontinuities in lives that have often experienced more "learning damage" and abandonment than benefit. From the subject's viewpoint, continuum policies are advantageous provided they aim at enabling each individual and the community to control and manage the subject's education in times, places and directions that have been freely chosen and where the subject's knowledge can grow effectively – so long, that is, as, based on the concept of "biographicity", "the potentiality of unlived life" is targeted (Alheit 1994).

A new organisational model
This trend towards a meta-network does not imply the absence of organisational models capable of ensuring the individual and collective control and management of learning processes. The relevant component of the new model is not so much the fields it covers as the subjects it aims to support, as they attempt to handle their own learning processes on or off the job, in groups or individually, on site or at a distance. Its key educational functions are not reducible to distributing predetermined knowledge. It is defined instead by the transversal educational functions – common to every field – that it can fulfil at different junctions in the cycle: the activation of the learning process and the distribution of learning opportunities, the opening of institutions and the recognition of informal learning, and creating free conditions for participation in organised learning throughout life.

With respect to this basic role, this organisational model can no longer be subject to compartmentalisation in subsystems (university, vocational training, literacy, informal education, culture, etc.). The latter continue to operate in a somewhat co-ordinated way, but it is not by first directing their immediate functioning that the new policies will in the main manage the learning process. To ensure the possibility of managing the entire cycle and the subsystems, the new organisational model is gradually developing based on three fundamental functions transversal to all the different subsystems and policy measures, including:

the organisation of the individual and collective learning processes, a phrase that designates all the actions designed to enable individuals to influence the learning conditions in their personal and collective lives and at the workplace, and to learn how to transform these. For example, the JOBS programme in the United States is an attempt to co-ordinate various laws and funds for women to create incentives that promote their participation in different learning activities (P 5);

the co-ordination, orientation and development of educational provision, including the improvement of their quality and their relevance, a description that covers all organised learning activities, including the different fields and sub-systems at every level;

the overall guidance, management and development of basic services and infra-structures, i.e. permanent transversal measures – not merely situated within particular sectors – designed to help subjects obtain basic elements (information, etc.) so as to promote their access to learning and their active control of the ongoing process.

We have already explored the first two functions in the preceding chapters and paragraphs. It is important now to delve into the function of the guidance, management and development of basic services and infrastructures, because it is relatively new and is assuming strategic importance in some countries.

In this regard, the new element to be emphasised is the transition from basic services providing internal support for various sub-systems to a policy of supporting learners. Information, orientation and guidance services are nothing new in work-related learning. What has changed is that, unlike in the past, they are now "personal services" that cut across and link the various sub-systems. Such is the case, for example, in Australia, where institutions have given birth to central and regional offices that "oversee the service agencies and play a role of co-ordination and planning" (P2 : 4). Similar structures can be found at the regional level for work-related learning in the United Kingdom and for all further education in Germany.

The rise of a policy promoting a basic infrastructure and services for adult learning has a double-edged, contradictory basis. On one side, these policies go hand-in-hand with policies to promote demand and with the gradual opening up and increasing flexibility of adult learning generally. Insofar as learning opportunities are being pushed to adapt to the trajectories of individual lives, it is increasingly important to offer services capable of informing, guiding, assessing and motivating adults in their learning pathways.

But on the other side, these policies can of course be defined and used in the framework of neo-liberal strategies and policies to reduce direct state intervention and relegate it to a function of co-ordination and quality control, and replace the "policy of provision" model by reduced services designed simply to ensure supply-and-demand equilibrium for learning available on the market. This approach would encourage a withdrawal of public services.

However, as already noted, the new policies tend to include public measures for the active expression of demand, individual financial support programmes, directives to open public institutions to adults, support for non-governmental organisations, the establishment of inter-corporate funds and the modernisation of programmes for unemployment benefit, health care and the environment, public education services to offset inequalities, etc. In short, whatever the contradictions they may run into, these new policies, as already emphasised, tend overall not to reduce the state's role but to transform it. Although the political economy of adult learning is quite different from that of initial education, the state is no less present – it may no longer be the main provider, but it is at the heart of the synergistic dynamics.

New basic services and infrastructures
To understand the potential importance and role of this type of organisational model, consider the case of policies on basic infrastructure and services in Tuscany (Italy). A policy adopted by the Regional Council of Tuscany in July 1996 introduced two types of basic services (Regional Council of Tuscany Del. 251 of 25 July 1996) into continuing work-related learning: services for citizens and business, and services to manage educational services and ensure the quality of education offered.

There is a wide range of services for learners, business and other organisations. The information services are responsible for distributing information on all education on offer in the Tuscany region. These multimedia services operate at the regional, sub-regional and local levels. The information services are a key tool for the inter-organisational integration of services provided by the different educational agencies at work throughout the region. They are able to collect and widely distribute information on all available learning opportunities so that individuals and organisations can plot their learning pathways.

The development of services for the recognition of experiential learning and competencies is also foreseen in the form of specialised "counters" as well as orientation, guidance and follow-up services (including job-seeking). Services to finance individual learning demand will be responsible for handling the relationship with each citizen entitled to "study coupons", to inform interested parties of their rights, to apply the relevant measures and make the checks required for recognition of the activity provided by the educational organisation. Services to analyse business learning needs, to be managed in collaboration with the relevant sector associations and trade unions, are designed especially to help any small and medium-sized enterprises that find it impossible to develop their own learning strategies.

Monitoring the different learning activities and verifying the quality of learning are part of the mandate of special services (Hasan and Tuijnman 1997). These services include the evaluation and guaranteed recognition of the quality of the services (applying the ISO 9000 system to the regional vocational training system), research on the regional system's functioning, and experimentation with and promotion of pilot projects. The service for training instructors is still at the experimental stage and is based on both traditional educational methods (courses, in-service training, applied research, etc.) and individualised tutorial methods, providing each participant with "training coupons" so they can directly consult a predetermined network of specialists based on their individual needs.

Policy on inter-ministerial and inter-sectoral co-ordination
These new functions will help change the role of public services. Adult learning policies are breaking with the typical linear planning strategies of state initial education ministries, and aim at "making do with" and "getting it done"; they help facilitate communication and promote greater co-ordination among the diverse adult learning activities. Government ministries, hitherto the main providers of adult education, are increasingly cutting back on their direct educational activities, except to correct inequities and maintain innovative centres, to develop support policies for adults and various educational agencies, and to play a transversal role among the various educational agents. Efforts are underway to link all the activities and actors on the increasingly diversified and dispersed scene of adult learning. On the other hand, inter-ministerial horizontal co-ordination and umbrella committees and local and regional further education councils that are part of the government itself, like in Japan (P1), Botswana and the Catalonian region of Spain (Inter-ministerial Council on Adult Education, Law of 18 March 1991), cover the entire field. Nonetheless, apart from these unusual cases, all new policies have limited their information, communication and co-ordination activities to the economic sector, and above all attempt to develop links among educational agents in the world of work. This initial breakthrough should promote a closer rapport between in-company training, vocational training centres and training institutions. Yet there are many other actors in the new, broader panorama of adult learning!

9.4. Conclusion: Lifelong learning – going back, or restructuring

Although the last decade has seen a revival of 1970s-style discourse on lifelong learning, the perspective today is quite different. The goal of broadening opportunities for learning throughout life can no longer be based on the belief that the economy will steadily grow, that there will be full employment and that the welfare state will go on expanding as it did during the three golden post-war decades. The goal of education for all can no longer ground itself in a monistic vision of development and ignore cultural differences. What we have today is a quite different model, or rather models, of lifelong learning. We return to this theme in the conclusion. But first, we shall retrace and analyse changes in the practice and policies of adult learning in the specific sector of adult literacy.

Chapter 10
Promoting Adult Literacy: A Revealing Field

The adoption of adult literacy and basic education policies is not a recent development in education history. Back in 1964 UNESCO, its member states and many multilateral agencies adopted an "Experimental World Literacy Program" (EWLP)[1], and two years later they inaugurated International Literacy Day and at the same time established the international prizes granted every year on 8th September.

Up to 1990, the main sources of explicit demand for "fighting illiteracy", as the problem was called then, were multilateral agencies and governments racing to gain their national independence.[2] From 1961 to 1982, African ministers of education held five regional conferences to discuss basic education.[3] Thereafter, aside from the independence movements that for a while associated the promotion of widespread literacy with the struggle for national liberation, it was mainly economic development agencies that emphasised the need to raise the basic skills of the adult populations, first in the developing countries and later in the post-industrial countries. The exceptional nature of the brief but remarkable popular mobilisations in countries like Cuba, Namibia, Nicaragua and Ecuador confirmed this general trend. The history of the growing importance of literacy in the developing countries is well known (Verhaagen 1999), as is that of the rise of written communications in the industrial countries. Notably, these were due to the interplay of different religious, social and economic factors, and not merely school factors (Cipolla 1969; Havelock 1976; Furet and Ozouf 1977; Graff 1979).

However, by the early 1980s, economic recession and the limited results of basic education, which had not taken sufficient account of cultural diversity and the need to be functionally integrated into the community, had relegated literacy programmes to a secondary priority. By the end of the 1980s, the total elimination of illiteracy was being announced routinely. This was followed by proclamations that the "scourge would be stamped out" by the end of the next decade.

It was not until the early 1990s that there was a complete change in priorities in

---

[1] This programme was proposed during the second International Conference on Adult Education, held in Tokyo in 1960, and was launched four years later. It was subject to a systematic evaluation in 1975/1976 (UNESCO 1976b).

[2] For example, in 1950, China launched a vast literacy programme and, in 1965, the Arab countries created the Arab League Literacy Organisation. Tanzania declared 1970 the year of adult education to help step up the programme it had started several years earlier.

[3] Addis Ababa (1961), Abidjan (1964), Nairobi (1968), Lagos (1976) and Harare (1982).

both the developing and highly industrialised countries, and it was longer still before changes came about in the way literacy programmes were perceived and organised.

As a result of these changes in priorities and perspectives concerning literacy, today the trends, tensions and debates taking place in this area are characteristic of the entire field of adult learning.

10.1. The on-going redefinition of social demand

The United Nations proclamation of 1990 as International Literacy Year gave this area a new impetus. In Jomtien in March, three months later, UNESCO, the UNDP, Unicef and the World Bank called an "International Conference on Education for All". The call was taken up by 155 member states, with more than 150 non-governmental organisations taking part. The delegates adopted a global statement and an action framework that set priorities for the next ten years (Unicef 1990). The revisions made in educational policy priorities reflected agreement on some key points. It had become clear to international co-operation agencies as well as to UNESCO member states that development would continue to falter as long as people's basic education needs were not met. It is impossible to meet the goals of improving healthcare, promoting women's rights and achieving sustainable economic growth and democracy without the active participation of men and women and without opportunities for them to increase their capacities to act.

This conference had a significant impact on many countries and the co-operation agencies. The Jomtien Declaration was a landmark because it moved towards making initial basic education an "absolute" priority and affirmed that this was impossible without expanding the different formal and informal approaches to basic youth education and implementing effective policies for adult basic education. This complementarity between basic education for children, young schoolleavers and adults is echoed throughout the Declaration and the Action Plan (Unicef 1990).

10.1.1. Recognition of demand is belated and uneven

However, the balance proposed at Jomtien between initial basic education action and adult literacy action was not reflected in concrete policies and programmes. Such was the assessment made six years later by the Amman forum in the mid-1990s. One of the most important recommendations of this meeting (UNESCO 1996) was specifically concerned with the redevelopment of programmes for adults and young school-leavers over the age for compulsory school attendance. The following year, the fifth International Conference on Adult Education underlined the necessity of guaranteeing adults the right to basic education, thus giving them "a gateway to fuller participation in social, cultural, political and economic life" (cf. *Agenda for the Future* para. 24, in: UNESCO 1997). Today, as the year 2000 starts, adult basic education has become, at least formally, a priority recognised by all, even, as we shall see in the third part of this chapter, the World Bank.

This changing approach to learning policy should also be associated with an increasingly broad re-definition of demand for adult literacy and the growing numbers of those involved in defining it, besides education ministries and pioneering associations. A decisive factor in government recognition of demand for adult basic education in the 1990s was the acceptance that growth could only be sustainable if it were based on what officialese called major investment in human resources, especially in basic education for young people and adults (Holland 1998). Since then, the UNDP has used progress in basic education as an indicator of a country's development. A similar process took place during this period in the industrialised countries.

Nonetheless, although economic agents and governments, now including the ministries of health, labour and economics, women's affairs and agriculture, increasingly proclaimed the need to raise the level of basic skills, rising social demand for basic education also reflected the influence of other social forces, thus pointing to other explanations. The increased importance of adult literacy was rooted above all in changes in civil society. New trends in research on democracy and citizenship brought to light the relationship between the use of written communications and the functioning of contemporary society, where demand for literacy is increasingly felt (Roche 1992).

The environment of written communications needed for political life in contemporary society is too often taken for granted. The very notion of citizenship is based on the fact that each citizen, although unable to personally contact all their fellow citizens, remains in contact with them by means of the media. Everywhere, there is a transition towards large-scale society, from *Gemeinschaft* (community) to *Gesellschaft* (society), towards living environments where the capacity for long-distance written communications is becoming essential. Indeed, the massive use of written forms of communication and the democratisation of basic education are implicit conditions for the development of modern states, especially as they develop today towards post-industrial societies.

The question is not whether literacy inherently leads to democracy. Posing this question in the abstract, without distinction between different types of literacy, has no meaning. The real question is whether democracy is possible in mass societies without the technologies for social communication that have developed continuously since Gutenberg in 1457, and without universal access to them.

Demand for literacy has been fuelled by the rise in democratic aspirations. Rapid urbanisation has created communities where oral communications among people no longer suffice to create a feeling of belonging and generate the structures needed to express and handle conflicts. Habermas has analysed how written communications enable and facilitate a process of dialogue and negotiation among social groups (Habermas 1987). Yet the spread of written communications –in terms of both the passive capacity to receive messages and the more active capacity to interpret them and respond locally and throughout society – reinforces the application of the social contract between state and civil society only insofar as everyone can exercise their right to acquire basic competencies and be able to participate fully.

More and more, it is representatives of different social groups who express popular aspirations for greater qualifications: women's groups, local communities, trade unions, immigrant associations, linguistic minorities, senior citizen groups, etc. These social groups tend to focus their learning demands on their own social projects or at least on demands to improve their living conditions. These demands, linked to social projects and marked by similar claims by different social groups, are growing and giving rise to negotiations. Some political parties and movements are now beginning to pick up on these demands and relate them to socio-economic needs.

10.1.2. The developing countries

Consider a few examples of this recent rediscovery of the importance of basic education, first in the developing countries. In some countries this rediscovery preceded the Jomtien Declaration by several years. In India, the limited results of the National Programme for Adult Education — a 40% drop-out rate, with 20% returning to functional illiteracy (Ahmed 1991: 225-229) – required a drastic change in approach. So, at the end of 1988, the New Delhi government set up its well-known National Literacy Mission (India, CS: 87 f.). Yet what is remarkable about the new Indian policy is the way this massively funded Mission (see Chapter 1) turned towards a more all-encompassing policy on human resources development aimed at making India, in the words of the prime minister's speech launching the Mission, a genuine industrial state. The demands of economic agents, which included raising agricultural productivity, were reinforced by the recognition that it would be impossible to meet population targets without widespread basic education for the current generation of parents. The well-known success story of literacy policy and its economic impact in neighbouring rival China loomed over this entire debate (Ahmed 1991: 225-229).

Another factor influencing the adoption of this new policy was the fact that this Mission enabled the federal government in New Delhi to directly reach a significant proportion of the adult population in order to strengthen a sense of Indian identity in an enormous country torn by many centrifugal forces. Even more importantly, however, these socio-economic demands found an echo in the population's own significant explicit or latent aspirations. This was certainly reflected in the extensive participation of civil society in this campaign. From 1992 on, the various Mission programmes counted some 40 million participants annually.

There have been similar developments in the Philippines (CS: 124). A 1989 survey had already sounded the alarm by revealing that the official 90% literacy rate had to be reconsidered, given that a quarter of the population (27%) were unable to use written communications in their daily lives (CS: 125). Three years later, the Philippines government adopted a medium-term development plan, with an "Education 2000" component that made adult basic education and literacy top priorities. In government circles, the literacy programme was discussed and ultimately adopted out of concern for the needs of the market, agriculture and healthcare. It set up a Council for Co-ordinating Literacy.

The public supported the programme, but while its learning aspirations were also related to economic needs, they were more comprehensive, incorporating the need for basic skills in terms of individual empowerment, increasing capacities for individual initiative and improving general living conditions. Recognition of demand for adult basic education was also influenced by the cumulative results of literacy programmes conducted by non-governmental organisations. These results clearly showed that, first, adult literacy demands could effectively be met and, second, this kind of educational action could significantly help community development. It was not until the end of the 1990s, however, that this official recognition found expression in significant public investment.

Morocco (CS: 99-102) had already been the scene of general literacy programmes, including a significant campaign in 1956 and 1957, a functional literacy programme in the 1960s and a new literacy programme linked to the Ministry of Social Affairs in 1970. In 1990, however, the situation had barely improved: the overall illiteracy rate for the population aged 10 and over was 55% – 40% for men and 68% for women. Very few women in the countryside (3%) had ever had access to a basic education programme.

The International Literacy Year marked a turning point, with a Royal Appeal that set new targets and led to the adoption of new policies. In 1991/1992, the programme had already reached 100,000 people, but the target was 200,000. This was itself limited in view of the 10 million people needing help. After 1997, two ministries undertook complementary efforts, the Ministry of Social Affairs, already involved in the field for ten years, and the Ministry of Education, which set up a literacy department in 1998.

In the Ivory Coast, the situation was very different. Despite numerous demands by the non-governmental sector, this country had not adopted any national literacy policy before 1997. This was all the more surprising since, in addition to the non-governmental organisations, the business world had already (CS: 50 f.) expressed significant demand for it, since it felt that a lack of literacy hindered raising the technical skills of the workforce. It is only recently, in 1998, that a national programme (PNDEF) has been inaugurated, a national literacy committee (CNAL) established and a national funding mechanism (FNAA) created.

In Latin America, the recent history of recognition of social demand for literacy has developed differently. For example, after the well-known 1989 literacy campaign in Ecuador by the bishop Mgr. Proano, the country needed to ensure follow-up to the intensive work in 1989/1990. This led to the 1992 adoption of a basic education and literacy programme. Unfortunately, a lack of funds prevented this programme from really meeting existing needs (P 1).

In Brazil, 1985 saw the end of the Mobral Programme. The programme had suffered constant criticism related to the military regime's support for it. The constitution adopted in 1988 set up a new system guaranteeing basic education by means of "evening courses". In that same year, the federal government adopted a national education plan with the declared goals of "the elimination of illiteracy" and universal initial schooling for young people. To help promote adult literacy, the Educar Foundation was set up, but unfortunately, like the corresponding National Literacy Programme, its work virtually ceased due to cutbacks in federal funding. Since then, no overall programme has been set up at this level to meet the literacy and post-literacy needs of millions of Brazilians. In this country where, as in South Africa, the right to basic education for young people and adults has been written into the constitution, the laws and budgets needed to exercise this right are much too weak. Federal policy also provided for co-operation with local authorities to enable the latter to play a more effective role and make use of their proximity to the target populations. This policy, also adopted as part of the International Literacy Year, remained loosely implemented. Despite this, a certain number of initiatives were undertaken by local government and also by civil society, the voluntary sector and business, even though the latter's national representatives had helped block government intervention, as noted previously.

Despite continuing contradictions, there has been genuine renewed emphasis in the developing countries on basic education and especially adult literacy since 1990. Moreover, as we shall see later, this change is taking place everywhere alongside marked changes in the definition of social demand and the dynamics driving it.

10.1.3. The industrialised countries

This renewed emphasis on adult basic education in the 1990s was not exclusive to the developing countries.

In the industrialised countries, once the goal of universal primary schooling had been achieved, adult literacy was no longer considered an important issue. It was felt that the problem was solved, and efforts were concentrated on extending schooling beyond primary education. Umbrage was taken at questions concerning the basic competencies of adults. Literacy rates even disappeared early on from official statistics, as in Germany in 1912. Except for a few isolated initiatives in the English-speaking countries in the 1970s, adult literacy was only taken up again at an International Council of Adult Education seminar in Eastbourne, England, in September 1981 and at the forum on European Youth in November of that same year in Langen, Germany.

Until 1990, however, adult literacy remained the concern of pioneers seeking to raise awareness and to conduct micro-experiments (Hautecoeur 1997). A growing number of awareness-raising seminars were also held during the 1980s. In September 1985, the Belgian association Lire et Ecrire held a national conference, where the call was raised for a campaign to "raise awareness of the need for literacy". At UNESCO, the first official document mentioning the problem of literacy in the industrial countries was the report of the fourth International Conference on Adult Education, held in Paris in 1985 (UNESCO 1985). On the basis of a recommendation adopted by this conference, the UNESCO Institute for Education held a technical meeting in Hamburg on the prevention of "functional illiteracy" in the industrialised countries. This topic was taken up again at a May 1989 follow-up seminar to which the UNESCO Austrian Commission invited experts from 17 countries. Particular note should be taken of the international seminar of the International Council on Adult Education in October 1987 (Gayfer 1987). There, 300 delegates from the industrialised countries of North America, Asia and Europe underscored the urgent need for government action to support adult citizens' initiatives and proposed a broader vision of social demand, linking it to the fight against poverty.

Other than the public awareness campaign launched in the United Kingdom by the Adult Literacy and Basic Skills Unit (ALBSU, later the Basic Skills Agency) in 1981 and the 1979 American report "Adult Illiteracy in the United States" (see Hunter and Harman 1985, preface to the new edition), it was not until 1990 that the governments of the industrialised countries began to take this problem seriously (see Quigley 1997, Chapter 3).

As declarations about the need for the continuing education of the workforce were rising sharply (see Chapter 1), the OECD released an important report in 1995 pointing out how the poor basic skills levels of a large part of the working population were impeding economic growth (Benton and Noyelle 1991). Together with the OECD, UNESCO (UIE 1992) carried out a series of national studies to evaluate the extent of this problem.[4] These studies, particularly those of the OECD and Statistics Canada[5], used a variety of approaches and showed that an important part of the population, between 7% and 35%, had difficulty achieving a sufficient command of written communications and basic mathematics to take part in contemporary society, whether at work or in community activities. This raised awareness significantly in all of these countries and led to the adoption of new policies.

Hence on 8 September 1988, following the creation of the ALBSU national agency in the United Kingdom ten years earlier and the Group for Combating Illiteracy (GPLI) in France in 1984 (GPLI 1999), the Prime Minister of Canada announced the creation of the National Literacy Secretariat (Canada 1995). In 1990, the Belgian and Dutch authorities also adopted national literacy programmes (Hammink 1990). There were similar developments in Australia and Spain. The Nordic countries and Central Europe only went into action in 1997, while the governments of other countries like Germany and Switzerland supported local initiatives but did not adopt national policies.

---

[4] The shocking declaration of the Spanish Ministry of Education in 1986, that 38.7% of the adult population was functionally illiterate, certainly had a significant influence on preparations for the 1990 organic law with its third article on adult education (P1). Fortunately, these kinds of negative, alarmist declarations were followed by more multidimensional quantitative and qualitative studies that placed the development of written communications skills within the broader panorama of individual learning biographies and investigated the numerous causes of cultural inequalities (Barton and Hamilton 1990).

[5] The most systematic studies, which took account of the complexity and everyday use of written communications skills, were those of the OECD and Statistics Canada, which covered seven countries in 1994, five in 1996 and more than six others thereafter (OECD and Statistics Canada 1995; OECD and HRDC 1997).

10.1.4. An international issue with differing definitions

As the 1990s draw to a close, adult basic education has become a major issue in all regions of the world. Although official statistics (despite their unsystematic nature) and household surveys raised awareness of the extent and persistence of the problem, the precise nature of the problem was more clearly identified by national debates and qualitative studies by voluntary groups and local centres. The main voices evoking the need for basic education were cultural, educational and rural development centres, crafts organisations and agricultural extension services, local health clinics, *maisons rurales* and women's groups in the South, and national and regional literacy associations in the North.

More silent, but even more important, was the response of the public to educational provision, which confirmed the extent of social demand. In all countries, the rising number of participants wanting to take advantage of the opportunities for basic education ultimately came up against the capacity of budgets to meet demand. It is telling that as opportunities for education expanded, so did explicit demand. Government agencies have intervened to slow down or even block this trend, as in Brazil (CS), India (P 2), Morocco (P 4), Spain and Quebec (ICEA 1994).

Yet while adult literacy has become an official priority, national responses everywhere are failing to meet needs. Soaring population growth is obviously one factor here. In India, for example, the rate of female literacy rose from 8% to 40% from 1951 to 1991. Yet population growth of 125% resulted in an absolute increase of 32 million in the number of illiterate women. As all national and international reports point out, budgets are not keeping pace with statements of intent.

Much literature has criticised the general lack of attention to obstacles to participation in these programmes and the reasons for dropping out (Giere, Ouane and Ranaweera 1990; Wikelund, Reder and Hart-Landsberg 1992; Quigley 1997: Chapter 3). Women, who make up two-thirds of adults world-wide who have not had the opportunity to master written communications, have particularly suffered at the hands of policies limiting access. The issue of adult literacy is being discussed ever more broadly, with social exclusion viewed with increasing cynicism as the flip side of globalisation. The importance of basic education as part of an overall adult learning policy is related precisely to the continuing persistence of inequality.

Imposing the same programme tends to ignore the differences among potential participants with regards to literacy and limit accessibility. Even if an initial group of adults takes part, there will be those who, although motivated, do not participate due to various obstacles. Some adults who desire to improve their abilities may be reticent because of previous off-putting experiences of formal schooling. There will also be some who have managed up to now on their own, picking things up as they go along, but are facing increasingly demanding situations (Beder 1991). Finally, there is the particular situation of linguistic minorities (Wagner and Grenier 1990).

The extent of social demand for basic education is not the only issue. Dwelling on this could even result in overlooking its complexity and diversity. The renewed importance of literacy is expressed differently in each society due to different education systems, the dominant forms of labour organisation, forms of political participation, off-the-job lifestyles, and the influence of different values and objectives on educational programmes.

Thus debate abounds on the definition or, more precisely, the definitions of literacy (Venezky, Wagner and Ciliberti 1990; Street 1996a). This concerns firstly the expansion of the notion of basic education — comprising reading, writing and basic arithmetic — but now also encompasses all the competencies and knowledge needed to improve living and working conditions and the situation and collective needs of the local community. Different social actors have different literacy programmes, and any definition of basic competency is inherently ideological (Street 1995 and 1996b). There are differences in learning methods, of greater or lesser significance, diverse approaches to learning, such as whether to focus on deficits or assets, differing approaches to individual learning pathways and variations in strategies to manage written environments, limiting or reinforcing the use of written communications and the taste for learning, and expanding or reducing the diversity of the environment itself (Hautecœur 1997). Written communications are used in a variety of ways to meet the different linguistic, cultural, ethnic and geographic environments and situations specific to a given social milieu or to the men and women of a given milieu. Programmes that fail to take into account these differences will result in selection and exclusion (Fingeret 1992).

In short, we are dealing not so much with literacy as literacies. National and international policies inevitably make choices. These include choices between a strong trend towards an economist definition of social demand linked to policies for integration into the labour market or immediate productivity gains in agriculture or fishing or in the local management of a rapidly growing informal economy, and more community-oriented trends based on a broader vision of needs and aspirations. Choices are also made that take account of or ignore sexual and linguistic identities. The big debate on the use of native languages, especially on the African continent, is significant (Ouane 1995). The Segou Conference represented a real turn towards recognising "the cultural identity of the learner" and re-examining complementarities between formal and informal education (Mali 1995).

Moreover, definitions and hence policies vary over time. Literacy policy in Brazil, for example, has gone through three phases. The initial phase took place under the influence of the peasant movement where Paulo Freire's conscious-ness-raising method was developed and applied. A second phase came about in the 1970s when the military regime created Mobral, a large-scale technocratic "top-down" programme. The third phase followed the return of democracy in 1985, when literacy programmes gained support from local authorities, the voluntary sector and above all from businessmen and their sector and regional associations, which promoted the participation of the working population in general education programmes (UIE 1999: fasc. a).

International conferences and regional and national literacy seminars have pro-vided favourable opportunities for expressing a diversity of perspectives and approaches. Differences have been spelt out and attempts made to reach diffe-rent kinds of consensus. However, the current situation is still marked by ambi-guities.

On the one hand, there is a convergence of economic and community views which, in the terms of the United Nations, is developing around the need for basic education to promote people's active participation in socio-economic development and help improve living conditions.[6] Social demand is thus being expressed in terms of economic productivity, the potential contribution of the adult generation to children's education and the empowerment of individuals to adopt new practices in healthcare, the environment, family planning, etc. In short, the combined demands for more developed communications and more active participation at work and in the local community and everyday life make it possible to forge the consensus needed for adopting new policies.

On the other hand, once the basic policies have been adopted, their implementa-

---

[6] In this regard, the *Hamburg Declaration* (see para. 1, 2, 11 and 12) of 1997 and the *Agenda for the Future* (see para. 5) give a good summary of declarations at the various past United Nation summits on health, the situation of women, population problems, social development and the habitat: "Literacy, broadly conceived as the basic knowledge and skills needed by all in a rapidly changing world, is a fundamental human right. In every society, literacy is anecessary skill in itself and one of the foundations of other life skills. There are millions, mostly women, who lack opportunities to learn or who have insufficient skills to be able to assert this right. The challenge is to enable them to do so. This often implies the creation of preconditions for learning through awareness-raising and empowerment. Literacy is also a catalyst for participation in social, cultural, political and economic activities, and for learning throughout life." (*Hamburg Declaration* para. 12, in: UNESCO 1997)

tion, including the budget allocation, can easily end up undercutting the initial convergence and multidimensionality.

As we have repeated throughout this book, the adoption of policy constitutes a social process that, while reflecting the dominant relationships, can in certain situations also enable the actors to modify them. Yet the transformation of the debate and the increasing acceptance of an expanded, pluralistic definition of literacy grows out of a more profound change in dynamics which, through the interplay of the aforementioned contradictions, will doubtless promote both more comprehensive goals in basic education and the groups that support them.

10.2. Changing problematics

In both the North and South, we are witnessing sharp criticism of and even ideological ruptures with the visions that have heretofore underpinned literacy policies. This process and the ongoing transformation of dynamics mainly involves three issues: a renewed focus on the actor, a conflict between a linear and ecological vision of the processes at work and continuing difficulties in integrating literacy into a lifelong learning perspective. More is involved here than the already mentioned acceptance of a range of literacies. Prognoses are changing, analysis is breaking with the modernist paradigm of progress and the educational focus is becoming increasingly broad and long term.

10.2.1. Renewed focus on the actors and their projects

The discourse that long dominated the literacy scene took stock first of the economic and social changes required for modernisation and growth, and the new "technical" skills these required, and then assessed their absence in a certain percentage of the population to consequently set up programmes to raise basic levels of competency. The policy was thus to correct "deficits", eliminate cultural obstacles to a development programme that was viewed as an indisputable given, make adjustments for any inadequacies, and help the population conform to task requirements. Target populations were thus defined by an absence of the skills demanded, lack of adaptability, ignorance of the required knowledge, and the lack of a cultural capital defined by a higher political or economic power.

The efforts of the last twenty years to break from this view are increasingly bearing fruit. In Hamburg in 1997, for example, there was no longer talk of "eradicating illiteracy" as if it were a disease. The *Declaration* adopted by UNESCO emphasised instead that, "basic education for all means that people, whatever their age, have an opportunity, individually and collectively, to realise their potential." Posters representing the populace as people heading blindfold towards a precipice are increasingly rare (Giere et al. 1992). There is instead a renewed focus on the subjects, on the act of learning and on removing obstacles to the pursuit of learning biographies, where mastering written communications is integrated into a particular environment and is thus necessarily exercised in a wide variety of patterns and sequences.

Evaluation and analysis converge in this respect. Adults are increasingly insisting on due consideration of their experiences, competencies, previous learning and, more fundamentally, their objectives and identities. Individuals and local communities have a learning history that no more begins with literacy than the Americas began with the arrival of Columbus!

An acknowledgement of the failure of remedial schooling strategies is fuelling this change in perspective, as literacy policies to adapt populations to the dominant standards of behaviour are no longer working. Some external definers of learning demand are beginning to recognise not only the functional need for a new focus, but also its socio-economic relevance. The active, autonomous participation of local communities, and hence a free-flowing increase in competencies, have become essential for developing different sector policies (Fingeret and Jurmo 1989).

This critique obviously seeks to take into account the broader issue that actors are involved in a specific community where they make efforts to improve their living conditions or simply survive (Pieck 1999). Although work-related literacy programmes tend to be relatively instrumentalised, the issue is not bringing about a rapprochement between basic education and vocational training, but the orientation of educational practice, regardless of whether it is in a work environment or a local community voluntary group. The point is not choosing between vocational training and general education, which in any case increasingly overlap, but refocusing both of these on empowering the actors (see the bibliographic review by Holland of literacy and the new economic order: Holland 1998). As already underscored in Chapter 5, raising economic and social productivity first requires strengthening the producers' capacity to act, and thus empowering participants.

Adaptation-oriented literacy is not designed to enable subjects to achieve "metaliteracy" (Gnamus 1990), where actors know how to exercise their new competencies, and where they know that they know and so can play around and choose among the arbitrary elements of acquired knowledge, integrate this with past experiences and master it in the course of their own activities.

This movement to refocus basic education policies and programmes on the actor

is highly diversified. In some places it is limited to women's groups, more organised local communities (Medel-Añonuevo 1996), non-governmental organisations alone or a few companies. In other places it is more nation-wide.

The American case is especially significant for discussions on the basic
approach of national adult literacy programmes. Since the 1980s, the United
States has hotly debated basic education policy. On one side, a fundamentalist
position proposes basic education that teaches the fundamental values underpinning American civilisation (Bloom 1987; Hirsch 1987). On the other side is the
position of educators who seek to focus basic education on the acquisition of
concrete competencies capable of empowering the learner subject, while taking
into account different cultural contexts and identities and respecting each individual's learning pathways. In short, the debate puts a continuity based on the
arbitrary canons of a society's broad cultural orientation up against a more
reflective normative continuity based on the capacity of actors to play a creative
role and master the dialogue skills required in pluralist societies, i.e. a choice
between going back to basic values and strengthening the autonomy and solidarity of culturally-rooted subjects. Proponents of the first position believe that
social problems in the United States are due to a lack of socialisation in basic
values and propose re-socialisation to correct these deviancies and ensure maximum behavioural conformity. Proponents of the second position believe that
adults with written communications difficulties are nonetheless already productive at work, in the community and at home. They are thus individuals undergoing a process of development who need to be given the opportunity to acquire
new competencies and adapt them to their own environment. This crucial debate
is taking place in all societies (Aronowitz and Giroux 1988). It should be followed closely.

Any basic education programme thus inevitably involves an implicit or organised process of negotiation between a population's aspirations and expectations
and the way government and economic agents define their needs. Social demand
for basic education is the ever-changing, inherently unstable result of this often-
diffuse process of negotiating between the trend to "set" policies that continually
"correct" lags and the resistance to externally imposed knowledge. Canieso-
Doronila has analysed these conflicts over orientation in the Philippines
(Canieso-Doronila 1997). King has also shown, for example, how official literacy programmes vary with the political climate in Mexico as regards their recognition of the native population's identity, aspirations, and written and oral culture (King 1994). Similarly, in French-speaking Canada outside Quebec,
Wagner (Wagner and Grenier 1991) analysed the numerous effects on minorities
of negating their mother tongue and the importance in such a context of resitua-
ting literacy policies in the broader perspective of the collective action of these
minority groups.

Hence the insistence by adult education movements on a policy of expression of demand that goes beyond functional initiatives to promote information and stimulate motivation and more fundamentally improves the still unequal balance of power in negotiating the definition of social demand.

10.2.2. Linear or ecological vision

The linear progression model of literacy is also coming under increasing criticism, and is being opposed by a more ecological vision (Hautecœur 1997). Adult literacy policies were colonised by the universal schooling model and governed for a long time by a postulate that situated literacy and most importantly school as the starting point for the rise of learning societies and particularly literate societies. However, an analysis of the emergence of such societies (Havelock 1976; Furet and Ozouf 1977; Graff 1979) demonstrates that this is historically inaccurate. Research in adult basic education (Giere, Ouane and Ranaweera 1990; Giere and Hautecœur 1990) also shows that this is misleading from the point of view of individual biographies. Literate societies started with religious campaigns to universalise access to the "good book", co-operative initiatives linked to the industrial revolution, and cultural campaigns. A learning biography starts with the subject and their personal environment and life path, meaning that many factors other than school come into play in the rise of literate societies (UIE 1999: fasc. b). For adults there are thus many trajectories and starting points, and not simply a "second chance" to re-do a standard route.

This search to develop an ecological vision is also being stimulated by the micro and macro interpenetration of the different dimensions of social demand for adult basic education. For the individual, the learning experience can only be significant, in Rogers' sense of the term (Rogers 1972), if he or she is able to adapt the knowledge acquired to the different circumstances of work, health, the family and community life on a daily basis. Outside the educational framework and alongside national and general literacy programmes, educational activities are also being developed as elements of policies on population control and healthcare, work and agriculture, women's equality and the fight against poverty.

Even more important is the radical shift in the conception of literacy from an activity essentially concerned with training individuals to a project for developing an active literate society. The objective is now to build and reinforce a literate environment where there is an interchange of oral and written communications and the practice of writing is integrated into living and work environments. Yet this can only take place when basic educational efforts are aimed at every generation, when it becomes an intergenerational enterprise, when the written output of information needed in daily life is accessible and meets perceived needs, when oral traditions are celebrated in written materials, especially the mass print media, when local newspapers and newsletters reflect community life and open a window onto the outside world, and when a taste for learning is encouraged.

Unequal access to written communications, needlessly complicated written communications methods, and written communications as a means of "distinction", like other symbolic practices, can only lead expanding learning opportunities into a dead-end and reinforce prejudices about the effectiveness of adult basic educational activity. If the intelligence of learners is not solicited or even worse ignored, if there is no space to develop projects and take a step into the future, if there is no room for questioning, if curiosity is not aroused, if learning does not lead to activities where it can be expressed so learners can improve their living conditions, then education, however andragogic and active, will change little. This implies pedagogies suited to local environments, learning environment policies, publications policies, and policies on access to written materials, including newspapers, books, magazines, databases, etc. We will come back to these points later.

The literacy environment and the learning environment more broadly are now key elements in learning policy. Literacy policies must therefore give priority to the widespread use of acquired competencies, a stronger presence of written materials in everyday life, and broader opportunities for using the different forms of written communications in daily activity.

10.2.3. Literacy and lifelong learning

Lifelong learning refers to all learning activities in a society; it can be broken down into three specific constituents: initial schooling, adult learning and the aforementioned learning environments themselves (Bélanger 1994). In practice learning is obviously more complex, as these components interact, educational agents migrate, transitions take place and increasing opportunities for informal self-directed learning merrily cloud the issue further. Here we wish simply to outline several basic trends in the redefinition of initial schooling and adult learning and in their specific features and complementarities.

Initial education
As soon as learning starts to take place throughout life, the role and importance of initial education is transformed. Schooling is no longer final. Now the initial phase of learning biographies, it extensively influences subsequent learning. The higher the adult population's level of initial education, the higher its participa-

tion rate in adult learning and socio-cultural activities. Adult learning policies risk ignoring a key factor influencing participation in further education if they overlook the issues of the accessibility, quality and relevance of the initial education of young people.

A major issue for lifelong learning is indeed this cumulative character of learning biographies. This is evident in both industrialised and developing countries. Inequalities in schooling tend to generate two-tiered learning societies in the North and the South. In short, this initial phase of schooling already partially shapes the future development of adult learning.

Fortunately, as an increasing number of facts demonstrate, educational inequalities are neither automatically nor systematically reproduced throughout life. School policies incorporating positive discrimination have made it possible to reverse the dominant trends in many disadvantaged communities. Likewise, despite financing problems, adult literacy and the informal education of youth outside school now form part of the educational arsenal in many developing and developed countries (Hoppers 1999). Yet while these trends may be reversible, existing corrective measures are still far too limited to effectively counteract them. This is a key issue and important indicator in the transition towards lifelong learning models.

The overall level of schooling worldwide is clearly rising. It already stood at 65% in 1991. Brazil and the Philippines, for instance, now offer initial schooling for ten years. However, marked inequalities in the development of education also need to be pointed out. The average duration of initial schooling is only two years in sub-Saharan Africa, whereas it is more than fourteen years in the OECD countries.

From the viewpoint of lifelong learning, initial education, which guarantees a basic education for all, as well as the adoption of positive measures to ensure accessibility, are part of an overall policy. They are genuine measures of prevention. The same is true of policies affecting the critical period of early childhood and inequalities in cultural backgrounds.

Refocusing initial education on independent learning and creativity to prepare for active learning biographies is another issue in the reorganisation of initial education based on a continuing education perspective. The outcome of the debate in every society over the definition of the quality of initial education and whether to factor in developing the creative potential and autonomy of young learners will have major cultural repercussions on individuals' learning pathways, as well as on the likelihood that the given societies will become learning societies.

Initial schooling is diverse. Discourse on education for all can lead to confusion: does this mean the same education for all, or providing the same opportunity for everyone to learn, but in close relationship to each person's environment and culture? The quality of education is not a neutral concept. Discourse and practice oscillate between two poles: a tendency to return to (or at least evoke) "basic values" and an arbitrary but supposedly universal definition of these values; and practical, critical and reflexive learning projects with more respect for cultural identities.

It is in this context that the temporarily neglected concept of creativity takes on new importance in debate on initial education. The concept of creativity discussed here is not an attribute of exceptional talent, but rather a potential within the reach of everyone: the possibility to learn by oneself, a desire for new experiences, for new relationships, for testing out differences, empathy with "others", curiosity, the desire to question, the taste for exploring different ideas, the ability to formulate problems and explore solutions individually or in groups, and the capacity to do all this in a reflexive way and to enjoy it. Adult learning policy cannot ignore this debate on the orientation and accessibility of initial education. Unfortunately, such concern is lacking throughout the adult learning policies analysed in this transnational study.

A third aspect of the change in relations between initial education and continuing education is the impact of institutionalised forms of certification obtained upon completing initial education and their social significance for pursuing continuing education. The more a diploma obtained upon completion of initial formal education is decisive for the entire professional career of an individual, the less he or she is inclined to take part in subsequent educational activity. This relationship is particularly clear in Japan (Okamoto 1994: 12 f.). The impact of the initial education diploma is so significant on the Japanese labour market that it tends to undercut any motivation to pursue education, since upon completion of initial education "the dice are already cast". Yet the need for education is no less important. The recognition of this dysfunction is one of the main reasons why Japanese decision-makers adopted legislation in 1990 encouraging participation in adult learning. The measures taken concerned increasing flexibility in the accreditation of initial education, recognising continuing education credits, particularly in the fields of learning a second language and information technology, and opening universities to adults. Moreover, the National Council on Continuing Education proposed reintroducing into initial education certain elements of "social education"[7], in particular individual expression, so as to stimulate greater curiosity and a taste for learning among young people at this stage.

---

[7] The name given in Japan to adult general education, which corresponds to the Scandinavian "enlightenment".

In short, the point was to prevent the exchange value of initial education, its selective function, from usurping its use value, i.e. learning to learn.

The specific nature of adult basic education
The specific nature of adult education is not mainly pedagogic or andragogic. It is related above all to the social learning demand of adult populations, their different needs, their many previous routes to learning and the particular conditions of different groups of men and women. Its unique character is thus bound up with a multiplicity of learning projects, subjects and sequences, as well as times and places to learn. It embraces a learning plurality whose consistency is found not in a common core curriculum, as in initial education, but in the idiosyncratic unity of individual learning biographies and, organisationally, in the new general adult learning organisations, which will be discussed in the third part of this chapter.

Hence, in contrast with the national standard targets of initial schooling, the programming of adult basic education inevitably must be "tailor-made" in order to take account of subjects' previous learning and experiences, their immediate expectations and the community environment in which this learning will be used. From this point of view, for example, adult literacy programmes in Belgium integrate elements of reading, writing and basic arithmetic into the broader content developed in co-ordination with local community voluntary groups, as well as other technical training elements demanded by participants. While the experience of non-governmental centres in Belgium, both French (Belgium 1999) and Flemish (CS: 13), is not unique, it still only represents an emerging trend seen mainly in the voluntary sector.

The patterns of initial schooling still weigh heavily on the design of adult basic education. In Morocco, for example, literacy policy is dictated by broad national objectives and is centred at the ministry of social welfare on issues of population education and family planning and at the ministry of education on remedial schooling for young school-leavers. The process of developing concrete literacy programmes is not very open to issues like revitalising local and regional cultures and meeting the needs of educating local neighbourhoods in keeping with their different situations. An analysis of the curricula of basic literacy programmes in adult public education services from Vietnam through Canada to Spain raises the same questions.

This debate is also taking place in the Philippines, where a national literacy policy primarily targeted at remedying deficits is opposed by groups intending instead to reinforce current efforts to empower communities and individuals. The latter orientation seeks to enable groups to situate their programmes in such a way as to make learning more relevant and maintain an ongoing relationship between learning content and their own life experiences (Philippines, P 7: 21-24; Bernardo 1998). Similar criticisms of the authoritarian imposition of content and a desire for social control (CS: 32 f.) were among the reasons why Brazil terminated its Mobral programme.

Policy on adult education programmes is also distinguished from school policy by the much broader scope generally given to the mother tongue (Ouane 1995). For example, one of the chief characteristics of the national literacy plan in Namibia was the radical change it instituted in the use of indigenous languages. The decision was taken at the beginning to organise the literacy programme in each of the native languages of the different linguistic communities of the recently liberated country. This required an effort to standardise certain languages as well as reworking learning materials and pedagogical tools. A positive assessment (Lind 1996) of the use of these languages provided additional support for views asserting the importance of using native languages right from the initial stages of learning written communications. The Namibian example is also interesting because of the gradual transition throughout the three stages of the native language literacy programme towards a certain bilingual development, thus taking into account the official national language of English. In urban areas, however, given popular demand, programmes were provided directly in English.

In many countries, adult education programmes are giant experimental laboratories in the use of native languages in basic education. This subsequently has repercussions on the curricula of primary education itself.

Another way the new literacy policies differ from initial education policy is the tendency not only to recognise specific linguistic features, but also to pay special attention to the situation of women and their participation in the programmes and to revise these programmes to deal with their specific concerns. Admittedly, too many national literacy programmes still tend to ignore the particular experiences and fields of interest of learners, but resistance and demands from women are growing in this area (Medel-Añonuevo 1995; Jung and King 1999). Literacy rates in Africa and the Arab-speaking countries are still more than twice as high for men as for women (UIE 1999: fasc. c). Women's groups are increasingly active in developing programmes for the national literacy mission in India, literacy programmes related to reproductive health in Morocco, the Tostan Programme in Senegal (ibid.) and community literacy projects in Belgium, Canada and Spain. Methodologies are now being proposed to monitor basic education with regard to the impact of gender (Medel-Añonuevo 1999).

From the point of view of continuing education over time and in different sectors and fields of interest, the rise of literate societies in South Africa, Latin America and Asia (China, Thailand and the Philippines) has been accompanied by a shift in priorities towards the widespread access of adults to post-primary education and diplomas. Several national literacy programmes provide for a series of two or three stages in basic education. Post-literacy policies and programmes expanded throughout the 1980s (Dave, Ouane and Perea 1989). Forms of post-literacy studies have been diversifying to include learners who want to continue formal education. Two paths for post-literacy studies have been developed in Vietnam: the provision of informal post-literacy programmes and the establishment of formal basic education centres leading to a certificate that opens the doors to the regular networks of formal secondary and professional education (P1).

In this respect, a tendency is developing in a number of countries to separate education from certification and create services for the recognition and accreditation of learning. The separation of education from certification makes education programmes more flexible. The pressure from economic factors and adults themselves to obtain accreditation in order to gain access to higher educational levels and potential employment has a retrospective impact on the standardisation of content. From this point of view, there is always tension in literacy programmes between the use value of learning, requiring that it be situated and rooted in participants' experience, and its exchange value, requiring a standard way to measure the value of learning for the purposes of selection and promotion.

The emergence of a literate society where written communications become widespread and interactive derives from the simultaneous efforts of several generations. Raising the general level of basic competencies can no longer be accomplished solely through the formal education of young people. Even making schooling widespread requires a dual approach targeting young people and people outside school, including the generation of parents. This is why complementary policies on adult literacy and initial education for children are becoming increasingly common, especially in societies with low literacy levels. The light shed by a numerous studies on the impact of the parental environment on children's learning behaviour and the significant correlation between parents' level of schooling and children's actual learning – in short, the intergenerational dimension of education – is also helping to expand the field of basic education policy.

10.3. The changing role of the state

These changing dynamics are altering the environment in which adult basic education policies are decided. The increasing diversity of policy fields, the growing number of actors, the emergence of new measures both up and downstream of conventional educational activity and the adoption of new approaches to the very organisation of adult learning are transforming the state's role and models of functioning.

10.3.1. The nation-state: between global actors and civil society

Furthermore, the state is exerting less and less control over the flow of both capital and information and knowledge. This phenomenon is affecting all state interventions in education and culture. For example, the growing number of efforts to extend the global free market to culture and thus to publishing (De Brie 1999), along with general policies on the selective financing of education, are undercutting the nation-state's capacity for action and leading it to meet these new challenges by intervening beyond its frontiers and stepping up co-ordination.

Indeed, supra-national and sub-national actors have such an extensive influence on parliamentary and governmental decision-making in adult basic education that it is no longer possible to analyse the field simply by examining the national situation.

The local impact of global policy
Even though basic education activity and the national policy framework are experienced at the local level, they depend increasingly on the way literacy is treated at the supra-national level.

Consider the basic trends in overall budgetary policy. In all the countries analysed, except India and Namibia (see Chapter 1), which respectively spend 1.03% of the total central and state administration budget (i.e. 5.05% of the central budget allocated to education, see National Literacy Mission 1999) and 2% of the total education budget on adult literacy, budgets have not kept pace with statements of intent on adult literacy policy. In this regard, all the authors of our country studies mention the influence of external decisions, particularly structural adjustment programmes. Global standards imposed by the World Bank since the 1980s and targeted at holding down public health and education budgets (Carnoy and Samoff 1990; Reimers and Tiburcio 1993) have had a significant impact. They have slowed and sometimes even blocked the development of national adult literacy programmes (Mulenga 1994) and literally frozen the allocation of international funds for adult basic education. Schooling and adult literacy are set against one another, with the upshot being the assertion that, given the lack of funds, the former takes precedence.

Mammoth national debt repayment requirements have also had an impact on the capacity of countries to maintain their adult basic education budgets. When a country like the Philippines decides by decree in 1977 that 40% of the national budget must automatically be allocated to debt repayment, the room for manoeuvre for considering new social demands is tightly constricted.

Complex situations and ever present tensions enable social dynamics to make themselves felt. The political wills of national governments to implement their declared policies vary immensely, without even considering the pressure and resistance of the people and possibilities for catalysing forces internationally. Consider the example of the World Bank and its long-standing refusal to make adult basic education a priority. It is true that in practice the Bank's sector-based policies supported certain basic education programmes that were combined with active policies to restructure Ivory Coast fishing and support for the informal economy in Ecuador (P1), but these were not recognised or identified as components of adult learning policy. It is also true that some Asian countries like India, Indonesia, the Philippines (via the Asian Development Bank) and Vietnam have managed to negotiate adult basic education loans from the Bank during this period.

Nonetheless, everywhere else the refusal to inject funds remained the rule for a long time. In Africa, as far as we know, the only countries to obtain direct aid from the Bank for adult literacy programmes were Ghana in the 1980s and, more recently, Senegal. If Namibia was able to stand up to the Bank's refusal and regardless launch its adult literacy national programme, it was thanks to support from Sweden and above all its own national political determination. At the time the programme was adopted, the Namibian parliament also unanimously adopted a resolution recognising the universal right to an education and thus the state's obligation to meet the adult population's learning demands, to which, as mentioned above, it allocated 2% of its national education budget. Despite difficult situations, some other governments have also managed to maintain minimum national programmes, including Burkina Faso, which was aided by Switzerland.

The African countries have never given up their demand that basic education be exempt from the budgetary rationalisation requirements imposed by the Breton Woods organisations. They succeeded in having UNESCO's 1993 general conference adopt a resolution along these lines. This demand had already been formulated at Jomtien and was repeated in the important "Segou Perspectives" adopted by the ministers of education of eleven African countries, from West Africa to Central Africa, gathered in Segou, Mali, in March 1995 (Mali 1995). This demand and a reminder of the priority of adult basic education were strongly echoed in Hamburg in 1997, in the speeches of the government and non-governmental delegates and in the final *Declaration* (see para. 2, 9 and 11). The International Commission on Education for the Twenty-First Century, chaired by Jacques Delors (UNESCO 1996: 204), even demanded a debt swap for the less developed countries precisely for the purpose of basic education.

It is no coincidence then that the World Bank, which, with the few exceptions noted, while not exactly ignoring adult literacy, at least resisted investing in it from 1980 to 1997, has since revised its previous prognosis on which these restrictions were based and finally recognised the positive impact of such investment and begun to modify its policies. In 1999, adult basic education, under the name "Adult Outreach Education Program", became one of the eight focus groups of the Bank's new human resources development programme (World Bank 1999).

In the industrialised countries, following the awareness-raising activities discussed previously, the OECD also changed its policy on adult basic education during this period. In 1992, it published a report on adult illiteracy and its economic impact (Benton and Noyelle 1992). It noted that the low levels of basic skills in the knowledge-intensive economies of the industrialised societies undermined the economy and social cohesion, and it demanded the adoption of policies on adult basic education. The OECD took up this cause once again in 1995, and again in 1997, emphasising that adult literacy was now a core policy concern of the developed countries and that economic globalisation obliged them to raise the basic level of the working population to ensure their comparative advantages and meet the requirements of the new production modes and societies increasingly based on written media (OECD and Statistics Canada 1995; OECD and HRDC 1997). The European Union has undertaken similar initiatives since 1989.

State policies thus arise not only within an environment structured by decisions taken by multilateral agencies and the actors influencing them, but also within the more fluid context of the global economy, where decisions are made concerning employment, the collection of tax revenue, human resources development, the concentration of information resources, technology transfers, copyrights and educational material, literate environments, and where national authorities are often unable to intervene (Beck 1997). In this regard, the post-modernist proposition that only local resistance or escape is possible amounts to a policy of hiding one's head in the sand. Global action is essential for developing responses and creating transnational movements capable of restraining the arbitrary roles of actors who know no boundaries (Castels 1996). The influence of international actors in national decision-making also includes the transnational organisation of resistance, solidarity actions and support for alternative projects, participation in conferences to influence decisions, and co-ordination to secure the development of new programmes.

The public, the voluntary sector and the market

With regards to literacy and basic education, national governments are being compelled to share their power with increasingly important supra-national actors and deal with an increasing number of non-governmental and private education agents. To reduce national spending, they are also being tempted to decentralise and shift educational responsibility onto local authorities. This trend to restructure the roles of the state, civil society and the market with regard to literacy is common to the developed countries and the developing and rapidly developing countries.

The distribution and organisation of roles in the structure of education services varies, and includes: national campaigns and programmes supervised by the state with the support of national liberation-type movements (Namibia and Nicaragua), national programmes based on a public network of education institutions (Quebec), programmes directed at the national level but decentralised to the provinces (Brazil, non-Quebec Canada, India and Spain), national programmes based totally or in large part on non-governmental organisations (Belgium, Quebec and Senegal), state-supported non-governmental organisations (Germany), non-governmental programmes with national scope (Bangladesh and Switzerland) and projects headed by local communities or business (Brazil and the Philippines).

The various strategies on the provision of educational services mean that almost everywhere the state must play either a minimum role of support, co-ordination, monitoring and setting a framework, or a more important role in defining programmes and in service provision. These functions can either be carried out by a single ministry, which could be education, culture, social welfare or labour, or by several or even many ministries.

The arrival of these new actors changes the balance of forces. Differences can be seen throughout India, depending on the vigour of civil society and the voluntary sector in the different states. In some, non-governmental organisations and student and intellectual movements have become involved in the literacy campaign and have developed alternative programmes with deeper roots in local community concerns. Business and trade unions have also become more involved. The situation is very different in other states where there is no active participation from civil society and the programmes conform more closely with national guidelines and recommendations. The situation can also change over time: in Ecuador, following a literacy campaign covering 520,000 people from 1989 to 1992, the national programme lost support and carried on with more limited means and less involvement from civil society and the local community.

The fact that the state is turning increasingly to non-governmental organisations, business and/or local authorities to achieve its national objectives gives the latter a lever to negotiate content and adapt the development of competencies to local priorities and the desires of the educational agents involved. This dynamic is increasingly important: with national literacy programmes having to increasingly draw on the voluntary sector, educational content is becoming more decentralised, localised and pluralistic.

10.3.2. The changing role of the state: New roles

In this new context, the role of the state is both expanding and shrinking. The centrifugal tendency to disperse educational activities, for example, in the new general organisation of adult basic education, is producing paradoxical results. We are seeing a redefinition of more limited functions in educational service provision and, even more importantly, a centripetal tendency for the state to adopt new policies on the expression of social demand and exercise new roles designed to pursue its basic objectives by promoting synergy among various activities and continuously monitoring educational activity and its impact.

Policies on the expression of social demand
First, an ambiguity needs to be pointed out concerning the adoption of policies on the expression of social demand for education. Such policies must not be confused with the only too frequent practice of alerting public opinion by reducing the importance of raising basic competencies in written communications to a calamity afflicting some dramatic percentage of the population. These alarms make headlines, but obscure the more complex reality behind the rise of literate societies.

The new policies on the expression of demand are based on a very different analysis. A great deal of research carried out over the last twenty years (Barton and Hamilton 1990; Giere, Ouane and Ranaweera 1990; Holland 1998) has led to a reconsideration of the basis of adult literacy policies (Barbe 1998). This does not entail challenging the need to make basic skills widespread, but it does mean acknowledging the arbitrary nature of interpretations of what this involves and, consequently, creating spaces to negotiate the definitions to be used. The unequal distribution of basic skills and the high percentage of the population who are cut off from active literate society are not due to a lack of interest from men and women in continuing to learn and improve their condition, as if they had ceased to hope and dream of better lives. If too many adults hesitate or are not inclined to pursue their education, or if they feel themselves incapable or lack information about the different possibilities of doing this, it is above all the social environment that is blocking their participation and stifling their hopes. Their living conditions and the accumulated burden of a life of inequalities are smothering their dreams. Hope is nonetheless present, albeit tacit, and social demand is still implicit. Too many institutional obstacles, financial burdens and cultural dictates undermine the expression of these aspirations. Contrary to the simplistic interpretations of the would-be budget slashers, an analysis of adult education drop-outs in India, Morocco and Namibia confirms this analysis of the weight of these cultural and structural factors (Wagner 1987; Ahluwalia and Sharma 1995; Lind 1996: 24 f.).

Expressing and unleashing learning demand in populations who have not yet had the opportunity to acquire certain basic skills, linguistic or otherwise, is a multidimensional process. Measures to achieve this obviously include a component of information and public awareness-raising (information campaigns, local reception and reference services) and a series of immediate financial support and time-release measures. Intervention is also needed in the very process of defining and correcting policies, by creating opportunities and spaces where problems, needs and responses can be redefined and contextualised, and where broad debate on the priority of adult basic education and policy goals can be launched and pursued. This is why, for example, Unicef financed a national literacy policy and legislation conference in the Ivory Coast in 1994 in an effort to kick off programmes specifically designed for women and girls who had never had access to school. It is also why the National Literacy Department in Benin organised a week of debate and publicity on adult learning in every region of the country in September 1998, and why non-governmental organisations in different countries have demanded and obtained nation-wide debates. The repeated holding of national and international conferences and seminars, noted at the beginning of this chapter, should be viewed in this light as well.

Policies on the expression of demand also affect factors on very different levels that influence the active participation of populations in literate societies in the longer term. There is the question of adopting policies and measures that foster the emergence of what we have called, with Bernstein (see Chapter 5), the general structures promoting participation: measures to encourage reading and establish public libraries in local communities (Petit 1998), including the creation of local reading centres, support for the production of local newspapers and popular literature in the native language (UIE 1999: fasc. b), the organisation of adult learner weeks (UIE and NIACE 1999), support for the more interactive development of information, communication and education programmes in the different ministries, policies on learning environments, etc. These measures call for the presence in the local community of cultural infrastructures that nourish learning aspirations and the satisfactory exercise of recently acquired abilities. They concern the quality and relevance of written communications and messages that adults encounter in their daily lives, whether government information, information on various consumer products or publicity. As in Australia and Canada, they emphasise the use by public and private organisations of simple accessible written language and begin to monitor the quality of the language used in the fields of health care, local government, etc.

Such policies can be applied to vast areas. In order to incorporate elements of basic education, diverse contents need to be integrated and various organisational structures combined (Pieck 1999). These policies require inter-sector and inter-ministry co-operation between labour, culture, social welfare, healthcare, the environment, agriculture, justice, etc. They also necessitate co-operation with non-governmental organisations in the voluntary sector, with the press and electronic media, and with business and local authorities. In India, for example, fostering a proper environment was a key element in the activities of the national literacy mission. For this purpose, non-governmental organisations, organisations of women, students, teachers, artists and writers, the major media, local theatre troupes and folklore and traditional art groups all contributed to creating a stimulating environment; they organised cultural caravans, created folk operas, published wall newspapers, inserted advertising into the media, held races, etc.

The organisation of educational responses
The role of the state has also changed in terms of the organisation of educational responses. As the number of educational agents grew, the state's role concentrated firstly upstream on support for research, innovation, discussion, exchanges among organisations, trial experiments and training educators. Then it shifted downstream, with a focus on the recognition of experiential learning and accreditation as well as on evaluation and monitoring. It concentrated thirdly on the co-ordination of actors and financial support for individuals and training organisations, and finally on the organisation of public adult education services. Thus, the state plays a leading role and helps correct inequalities. In the developing countries, the complementarity between initial formal and informal educational activity and adult literacy has become a key element in the new orientation of basic education policies (UIE 1999: fasc. d; Hoppers 1999).

In the context of overall policy and in order to involve the various actors, some governments precede policy formulation with a consultation process and thereafter publicly monitor implementation.

The emergence of this model has begun to prove itself in the industrial countries. For example, Canada has created the National Secretariat on Literacy, France the Group for Fighting Illiteracy and the United Kingdom the Agency for Literacy and Basic Skills. This can also be seen in developing countries such as Brazil (CS), India (P 2), Namibia (P 1) and Mexico (Pieck 1999). It has also been confirmed at the supra-national level, in Africa with the "Segou Perspectives" (Mali 1995), in the French-speaking industrialised countries with the adoption in Namur, Belgium, in June 1999 of the declaration "Perspectives for the 21st century" (Belgium 1999), and in the new approach contained in the *Agenda for the Future* adopted in Hamburg in 1997.

In Brazil, for example, the federal government is playing more of a role in developing general guidelines and optimising resources, while relying on the local authorities. In India, the national literacy service was first institutionalised as an extra-ministerial "mission" to facilitate co-ordination with the various public organisations and ministries (especially the ministries of youth, sports, social welfare, women's affairs and national education) and enable it to communicate and directly interact with sub-provincial authorities, in particular the districts. This also gave it the flexibility needed to co-ordinate organisations around the public institution network. Once the organisation was set and the programmes established, the mission was then integrated into the super-ministry of the development of human resources.

10.4. Conclusion

Basic trends in different global regions are appearing in adult basic education policy. There is growing recognition that more is needed than the formal initial education of young people to achieve the objective of education for all adopted at the Jomtien Conference. A dual approach is required, aimed at both young people and the out-of-school population. The general structure of adult basic education and the policies shaping its direction and supporting it respond to specific models that are different from those applied by educational policies in the ministries of education in previous eras when education and schooling were one and the same.

Destructured and separated from the past models that had colonised them, the object and field of application of adult basic education policies are now being totally reorganised around the focal points of the creative participation of subjects and the development of active literate societies. Literacy policy thus in-cludes but extends beyond literacy education.

In the new economics of adult basic education, change is taking place in the roles of all the actors on the learning scene, including the nation-state, local authorities, social groups and associations, the socio-economic partners and global actors. Local literacy programmes cannot be isolated from the national and global arenas, which have such an extensive influence on the decisions being made today. The general restructuring of adult literacy is not, however, taking place along free-market lines. The role of the state is not disappearing, but changing. The sweeping reorganisation of the state's role is being driven by many factors, including the dysfunctions resulting from market models, the economic and social costs of inequalities engendered by the market, the need for public regulation of quality and accreditation, and the increasing interpenetration of basic education and other development policies. New adult literacy policies are being organised around two main points: the expression of social demand for basic learning and the synergistic organisation of educational responses, including the co-ordination of numerous governmental and non-governmental actors.

We are witnessing a dual rupture, first with the pathological discourse on individual deficits that has held back development, and second with the linear theory on the continuing adaptation of "human resources" to modernisation.

The convergence and contradictions of economic, social, political and cultural demands for basic competencies raised by various populations and the changing dynamics of adult literacy make it a revealing field for current lifelong learning policies in general. And, as with all adult learning, while social demand is growing, concrete responses are lagging behind. Inequalities are being reproduced throughout learning biographies. Policies can make a difference and, as we have seen, some do. The dynamics and development of policy are characterised by the varying influence and integration of three ever-present basic objectives: accessibility, the recognition of differences and instrumentality. In addition to the problem of cultural rights, the following dilemma is also posed everywhere – basic education for all, of course, but serving and relying on the continual adaptation of competencies to external requirements, or serving and relying on the empowerment of the actors and the strengthening of their capacity for initiative?

Adult basic education policies are very much prototypical of the entire field of adult learning.

Conclusion

1. Adult learning policy goes beyond adult education

First reconstruct the adult learning situation

To understand the changes underway in the different areas of adult learning, first it is necessary to reconstruct the fragmented reality of adult learning as it has developed around the world today. This means first and foremost taking a new look at past definitions from a perspective that transcends ministerial bounds and semantic exclusions which only render visible learning demands that have found responses. It entails looking beyond the existing institutional framework that obfuscates the reality most crucial to the analyst, namely, the actors' projects and their contradictory relations with the policies and strategies being implemented.

We have endeavoured to carry out this reconstruction by taking into account all the growing variety of organised learning activities as well as the rapidly increasing number of interventions upstream and downstream of learning that influence adult participation. Doing this required going beyond conventional boundaries to identify the various actors and policies involved in expressing and meeting adult social learning demand and in organising and monitoring the many varied responses.

Once traditional definitions are broken with and all facets of adult learning grasped, it is clear that, to the surprise of many observers, it takes on increasing importance in national educational environments.

Demand for adult learning has grown steadily, virtually booming over the last twenty years: adult literacy training, the enrolment of adults in day and evening college and university courses, professional refresher courses, training in business and in the informal economy, agricultural extension services, the integration of education and information components into sector-based policies, training offered by local healthcare and environmental protection centres, a dizzying increase in the number of public and private organisations offering courses in second languages and computer technology, growth in adult education centres and open universities, a rising number of men and women using their free time for self-help projects, the expansion of voluntary-sector educational activity, growth in open learning and distance learning organisations, increased access to museums, national parks and libraries, and so on. The growing need and demand for an increase in competencies cannot await the next generation of adults. This would take thirty years. Changes are increasingly taking place now, with the current generation of adults.

Amidst this centrifugal growth in learning opportunities and the increasingly fragmented learning environment, each individual is compelled not only to link the different formal and informal learning experiences acquired throughout their lives, sometimes obtaining official recognition, but even more importantly to seek to construct subjective coherence to enable these experiences to be converted into a cumulative, and ultimately empowering process. This process of individuation, the independent monitoring of one's own life narratives (Beck and Beck-Gernsheim 1990; Giddens 1992) and learning life, is paradoxically closely related to the reconstruction of the fragmented general organisation of adult learning. It calls for corrective centripetal motion and, to this end, a new role for the state. The intimate and idiosyncratic process of constructing one's learning biography both prepares the grounds for and demands new policies for liberating and democratising the act of learning.

In the developing countries, the examples cited throughout this book from Brazil, India, Morocco, Namibia, the Philippines, Thailand and Vietnam indicate strong demand for adult learning. In most of the post-industrial countries, the number of adults taking part in organised forms of learning, even without counting informal education and self-directed learning, exceeds the combined student population at primary and secondary level (see Chapter 1).

In every country, attention is increasingly focused on adult basic education, the recognition of adults' right to learn, demands for an increase in basic skills levels for the adult population and the active participation of civil society, as well as the widespread demand for a rise in jobs skills throughout the occupational hierarchy. Adult education is becoming a burning social issue. Moreover, since the factors driving adult education are on the rise, albeit with differing intensities, the field will continue to expand.

The more adult learning grows and becomes a strategic social issue, the more it will become the subject of debates and policies for interpreting social demand and "managing" the development of responses. These new dynamics are thus involving government ministries, various economic agents, collective actors from many different fields, and countless local community and voluntary groups.

It is impossible to understand adult learning policies without placing them in the context of the relations typical of each social formation. This book has been informed by a constant concern to understand the constraints and determinations affecting policy, without ever allowing these to shackle thought, and to seek in the process of policy development the language of "the possible" brought forth by the actors themselves – in short, to always seek out and bring to light the space for change.

The current expansion in direct and indirect adult learning policies has come about precisely in response to adults' rising aspirations for increased empowerment and capacity for initiative as well as to the external need for their more active participation due to the restructuring of work and the changing relationship between state and civil society in the implementation of sector-based policies. Reconstructing the learning scene also means focusing on an analysis of the concept of adult social demand for learning. We have constantly referred to social demand. This is firstly because the forces driving the rise of adult learning are complex and sometimes contradictory. On the one hand, they reflect and articulate aspirations and needs felt by individuals as well as groups of adults. On the other hand, they set or impose demands and requirements defined by established economic and political powers. Second, this is because there is a constant process of often-diffuse negotiations between social actors and the political authorities. Reconstructing thus means going beyond the specific purposes of each policy to determine the basic issues involved.

We have also sought to understand how the different adult learning policies in contemporary society constitute social measures intended to increase, in various fields, the capacity for action of certain social groups. While basic trends can be found, due precisely to a certain convergence in learning aspirations and requirements for increased competencies, policies today are increasingly diverse due to differing environments and the uneven outcome of "negotiations" among the groups concerned. The projects of collective actors, like the responses or lack of responses, thus go beyond the framework of formal adult learning policy. Adult learning policy can only be analysed in relation to the different groups involved in it. This obviously includes social actors capable of expressing collective interests, and proposing responses or resisting those proposed. To understand the policies adopted, consideration must be given to the processes that paved the way for them, because it is here that the various interests are expressed and the conflicting aspects of social demand become visible. Each of the 122 policies here has been examined beforehand from this perspective in order to determine some of the core issues in new adult learning policies.

2. The basic issue of adult learning policy and its components

We have reached a historic moment where the risks facing humanity cannot be addressed without the active participation of the adult population. From 1992 to 1996, a series of conferences raised world awareness of crucial global problems: the environment in Rio de Janeiro in 1992, human rights in Vienna in 1993, the population issue in Cairo in 1994, social development in Copenhagen in 1995, women's issues in Beijing in 1995, the habitat in Istanbul in 1996 and food in Rome that same year. Yet on each of these occasions, the delegates devoted more than half their recommendations to measures to promote the activity of civil society as a key component of their strategies. The 1997 International Conference on Adult Education clearly echoed this new trend.[1]

We have reached a historic moment when the actors' capacity for initiative and the full development of the creative and productive forces have acquired strategic importance. Emancipating the subjects has become not only a goal but also a condition of the survival of contemporary society. Society can no longer meet the looming economic, social and cultural risks without relying on the active, reflective participation of civil society. Just as the mid-19th century industrialists had to take the risk of rapidly developing the productive forces and thus the workforce, society today is being challenged to move to a new stage in unlocking the productive and creative forces and to once again take the risk of an accelerated, wide-ranging development of human resources, i.e. the resources of the actors themselves.

Ensuring people's participation and liberating the productive forces, the actors' capacity to act and "produce", is all very well – but from whose perspective? This is one of the fundamental issues affecting all adult learning policies. Each policy could be situated on an ideological continuum running from a model of "knowledge societies" organised in a continual process of teaching and adjusting to new technologies and prescribed knowledge to, at the other end, a model of learning societies that are closely integrated with an active civil society centred on the actors and their individual and collective creativity. The central question is whether to control or strengthen the actors' capacities for initiative and whether to regulate and maintain or transform adults' learning conditions.[2] Obviously, between these two abstract models lies a continuum of possibilities and realities. Indeed, the reality is more complex. The options are no less clear.

Social changes in the world of work, community life and private life have slow-

---

[1] "The challenges of the twenty-first century require the creativity and competence of citizens of all ages in alleviating poverty, consolidating democratic processes, strengthening and protecting human rights, promoting a culture of peace, encouraging active citizenship, strengthening the role of civil society, ensuring gender equality and equity, enhancing the empowerment of women, recognising cultural diversity (including the use of language, and promoting justice and equality for minorities and indigenous peoples) and a new partnership between state and civil society. Indeed, to reinforce democracy, it is essential to strengthen learning environments, to reinforce the participation of citizens, and to create contexts where the productivity of people will be enhanced and where a culture of equity and peace can take root." (*Agenda for the Future* para.11, in: UNESCO 1997).

[2] An environment more or less favourable to continuing learning, the presence or absence of learning infrastructures conducive to self-directed learning, opportunites for learning in different work sectors, support for participation, etc.

ly combined to eventually challenge and even transform models of participation and citizenship. Strong underlying trends working over decades and imperceptible, almost fleeting, micro-changes have had the cumulative effect of gradually building up learning aspirations. This has led to an increase and transformation in adults' social demand for learning today.

The slow, but steady and sustained advance of initial schooling for young people in all societies has also transformed the cultural aspirations of today's adults. New inequalities are taking root on the outskirts of the constantly shrinking primary labour market. Gradual, but sustained reductions in the paid working week and longer life expectancies are creating new spaces and times where independent non-market activities are becoming sites for liberating the productive forces (Piotte 1990: 118 f.). Life models are fragmenting and becoming desynchronised, the bases for identity are changing and spatial mobility is increasing. All of this is giving rise to "life choices" that are not determined beforehand. Women are using different cultural models to create alternative lifestyles, breaking with traditional life cycles and sequences. The emergence of a new, more youthful older generation gives room for the pursuit of productivity which can then be extended beyond the context of "paid production". An end to an absolute belief in "quick-fix" scientific and technological solutions is fuelling scientific doubt and pushing each individual towards greater intellectual independence. Linear models of growth and "progress brought about by modernisation" are being increasingly challenged, and the ecological and ethical limits of a limitless rise in living standards are taking us into an uncertain world. All that is solid melts into air (Berman 1982). We are at a turning point.

This transition towards a "risk society" (Beck 1992), or "reflexive modernisation" (Beck, Giddens and Lash 1994) in terms of an autonomisation of actors, is strengthening a trend towards a broader definition of social demand for learning. We are reaching a historic moment where the established political and economic powers must take the risk of fundamentally relying on the actors and their creative participation. This recognition of the need to unleash the productive and creative capacities of the adult population is behind the boom in social demand and the current push for an expanded reinterpretation of how to deal with it. The economic need for a work force that is capable of handling information, solving problems and being consulted about production techniques and methods is leading to a type of learning and individualisation that is very different from the linear adaptation to changes in job positions so typical of the "simple modernisation" phase (Lash, in: Beck, Giddens and Lash 1994: 113). We are coming to a point, where the act of learning, questioning, redefining problems and taking an independent position, all of which have become daily necessities, could disrupt basic trends. The situation resembles the 19th century, when entrepreneurs in search of new workers recruited extensively from traditional rural society and thus had to take the risk of liberating the productive forces. It is clear that this liberation did not stop at the creation of urban centres, childhood schooling and the use of new tools. The "need", i.e. the demand and the associated risks, is the same now as then: to strengthen the capacity to produce and reinforce the independent action of the subjects.

This leads to a certain ambiguity, for this is not an inherent process or one that is becoming universalised. As we explained in Chapters 4 and 5, reflexive modernisation is itself very uneven. In the face of the challenges, societies might take refuge in the blind pursuit of continued growth, reducing the risks and contradictions to problems of functioning and attempting to "adjust" or adapt their populations. Other societies might seek refuge in fundamentalist values. What is important is that the rise in people's cultural aspirations is very real, as real as the broader redefinition of economic and non-economic demands for the liberation of the productive forces, and as real as turn-of-the-century society's growing trend and capacity for self-reflection, so that it increasingly becomes the object of reflection itself.

The real question is not whether adult learning policies empower the subject. This is a false question anyway, as outcomes depend on orientations and policies that are never neutral. The real issue is to understand that the new environment, with all its contradictions, is unleashing a new dynamic. The challenge is the capacity to integrate these advances into collective and individual projects, raising and broadening the learning demand of the adult population. The debate is no longer about the pros and cons of lifelong learning. The real debate now is about its different orientations.

After all, what is behind this world-wide emergence of adult education policies, programmes and activities, with all their contradictions, if not the return of the actor (Touraine 1988), increased room for the actors to manoeuvre vis-à-vis the structures (which is the very definition of "reflexive modernisation"), and the rediscovery of the intelligence and the creative and productive capacity of people? The new economic demands are opening new perspectives.

No production without the actors
Our perspective challenges the still widespread tendency for Manichean analysis that sets professional training against general education. The issue is not whether work-related training is currently the most important source of growth in the adult population's learning demand (Hasan and Tuijnman 1997). Nor is the problem the "hyper-professionalisation" of adult learning, as if adult learning were developing within a closed budget managed according to the principle of com-

municating vessels between technical training and liberal education.[3]

In our opinion, the recognition of the need to draw on subjects' capacity for initiative and their empowerment in the formal economy's most advanced sectors, which is currently taking place faster there, marks a crucial point in the broader process of liberating the creative and productive forces. This process is being furthered by the trend towards broader redefinitions of productivity, the renewed importance of the actors and their "empowerment" at the core of the production process and new productivity measures, the sharp rise in investment in adult education, and the growth in policies to promote these investments. It is nonetheless necessary to grasp the contradictions in this initial phase to understand the full significance of these dynamics, which could be as easily blocked as unleashed. The uneven development and orientation of learning responses is raising many questions.

The increase in social demand for work-related adult learning has been marked by the employment crisis, the segmentation of the labour market and the transformation of labour relations. There is, of course, a tendency to deal with global competition and the crisis in productivity by concentrating on a single variable, the cost of labour, and thus to find where labour is cheapest world-wide and shift production accordingly. This policy on the external flexibilisation of labour markets is developing concurrently with a trend towards greater internal flexibility, relying on training and higher skills, which is assuming increasing importance.

The development of adult learning is thus marked by the international division of labour, as noted in Chapter 4. Adult training is much more developed in the modern enclaves of the so-called peripheral economies, in the formal economies, and even more so in the "symbolic work" sectors and the higher levels of the occupational hierarchy. And it is no coincidence that the majority of women are found in the secondary labour markets and McDonalds-type jobs! The trend towards "reflexive production" (Lash, in Beck, Giddens and Lash 1994: 121-127), though real and strong, is also very uneven. There are reflexive winners and reflexive losers, i.e. "the underclass" (Wilson 1987), those excluded from reflexive modernity and the information society.

Furthermore, whereas education is becoming lifelong, jobs are moving in the opposite direction. This means that, while employers overall have an interest in investing in the active participation of the workforce in the information-intensive economy, each employer as an individual, conscious of the new intercorpo-

---

[3] On the contrary, the current trend involves the diversification and expansion of investment in adult learning. To see this, however, it is necessary to look beyond the budgets already identified in this sector with the ministries of education and human resources!

rate mobility of their personnel, is less and less inclined to spend company funds on it. Hence the renewed interest among corporate executives for public action in this field.

The ambivalence of current policy on training the unemployed in the post-industrial countries reveals the reciprocity of the statement "no production without the producer" and the impossibility of understanding the significance of training policies without also looking at policies that are not immediately educational. The past decade has seen a gradual spread of active labour market policies to enable the unemployed to take part in training.[4] Yet these policies pose the same dilemma everywhere. It makes sense to actively use this "waiting time" gain qualifications. The question is how this relates to jobs. The problem is that if the waiting and training lead nowhere, "train while waiting" programmes lose their credibility. Cut off from its stated purposes, this learning process becomes alienated and leads to undesired results, ultimately becoming "anti-learning". Faced with a deteriorating situation that is very much "the product" of the motivation to learn, the tendency is to decide against the learner and require him or her to carry on the training even when it has lost all meaning. Training for the unemployed thus becomes, as in Canada (CS: 10-13), compulsory or at least a requirement for receiving unemployment benefit. The circle of the non-work economy (see Chapter 4, sect. 1.2) is thus complete! Rather than freeing up creative energy, training tends to play the role of "parking", of anaesthetising aspirations and shifting the responsibility for unemployment onto the shoulders of the individual – a striking example of policies which nullify the subjects' capacity for initiative (see Chapter 6, sect. 2.4).

In this situation, the change in the paradigm at work in reflexive production, which has fuelled advances in adult learning, is blocked. The problem is not the workers' demands for qualification and their learning aspirations. Current active labour market policies for the unemployed have been built on premises that are no longer valid. They are based on economic models that are no longer capable of ensuring everyone steady, decently paid work. They now reproduce and reinforce labour market segmentation through the use of continuing education itself. There is clearly no solution without providing learning opportunities, but the training solution alone is meaningless, a fact that the unemployed have obviously been quick to understand. Legislators are increasingly recognising the need to develop the productive forces. The problem is that they are all-too-often still trying to do this without considering changes in the national economies and reas-

---

[4] In Canada, these policies are called employability policies, and in 1994/1995 they received US$ 2.5 billion (two-thirds from the unemployment insurance budget). In the United States, they come under headings like "Return to Work" and "Labour Force 2000", and in Switzerland under the banner "Continuing Training Offensive" and are based on discourse drawing on "dormant qualifications potential".

sessing past dogmas on unlimited growth and jobs for all, and without an in-depth look at economic strategies and job-sharing. Training producers without production negates the producers, their productivity and their contribution to society; it undermines their dignity and sense of worth. It is profoundly unpro-ductive.

Questions also arise as to the orientation of educational responses. The jobs cri-sis is also a cultural crisis. In other words, the ability of individuals to express themselves through their work is in crisis. Social demand for learning still focu-ses too much on job positions and not enough on the individual producer. Educational responses are often one-dimensional with weak roots in local envi-ronments and individuals' learning projects. They thus come up against the sub-jects' multidimensional motivations and the growing recognition of the cumula-tive, transferable character of learning acquisition and individual capacities to act.

The problem of work-related adult learning – whether in the formal or informal economies, industry, services or even agriculture – is not its rapid growth in some sectors at the expense of others. This trend is actually an advance and even helps transform the dynamics. The problem is its uneven development and the tendency towards a reductionist, adaptive approach to responses, thus limiting the pursuit of learning and above all any increase in the actors' capacities for initiative. The problem is the often-noted contradiction between statements that recognise new learning demand and concrete policies that confine this break-through to a narrow framework and a "work-qualification" system that leads to undesirable results.

This is the challenge facing all new adult learning policies in any form of econo-mic production: to promote increased investment in this field, to create the spa-ces needed for expanded definitions of social demand to be expressed, to over-come inequalities, to recognise advances in innovations with respect to the goals adopted, and to encourage a synergistic development of capacities for action both for organisations and individuals.

There is also the challenge of making use of openings in work-related training to extend these dynamics to all fields of activity.

Extending social demand for active participation to all sectors of society
The pertinent question is not whether to support an increase in productivity, but how to support it in all its aspects, including creativity, for everyone, for all sec-tors, ages and cultures in an orderly fashion and amidst chaos.

In this context, social demand for adult learning is not merely increasing, it is changing in meaning.

There can be no increase in productivity without a prior increase in the economic, social, political and cultural productivity of the actors. This gives adult learning policies a new meaning: there is no production without recognition of the actors. With this revised, expanded concept of productivity, we are rediscovering the producer-subject whose capacity to act is at the heart of the process. For now, this is most visible in economics, but the same dynamic is increasingly evident in other fields – and it is spreading. Indeed, the active general social participation of the population is becoming an urgent demand and explicit aspiration everywhere. Faced with the deadlocks existing in the world of work and in new fields such as environmental protection, healthcare and the liberation of groups facing discrimination, government proposals and other collective actions are now marked by the widespread demand for the liberation of the creative and productive forces.

When we started this study, we asked our 24 national teams to include among the national policies they selected for study what were then called indirect policies, that is concerning adult education, but developed and implemented outside the field of education and professional training. 40 of the 122 polices studied were of this type (see Appendix II, table 2). These included polices on women's rights, population education, the promotion of healthcare, the introduction of occupational health and safety measures, environmental education, support for agricultural and forestry innovations, cultural development, and the promotion of native languages. We have seen that the demand for productivity and creativity does not stop at the doorways of high-tech industries, that the need for the development of people's competencies is not restricted to certain activities, and that this demand is becoming widespread.

Limiting opportunities for lifelong learning will undermine the functioning of today's reflexive societies. Contemporary society will not be able to address the risks of epidemics, environmental damage or conflicts between groups without the participation and development of its citizens' abilities.

Although these trends are becoming clear, it is still difficult to change policy and, even prior to that, analysis. The development of the productive and creative forces is still often limited to certain fields. Change is closely linked to the capacity of the social actors in each society to expand the notions of productivity and the creative potential of the subjects; to free them from an exclusively economic framework and make them cross-functional; to apply them to all fields of social activity, including the economy, where they will then in turn have a synergistic effect; and to integrate the "increasingly interactive capacities" component into their social projects and invest in them.

Moreover, as is clear in these new contexts, excluding a social group from the new general organisation of adult learning is tantamount to depriving them of their right to act as citizens. In this respect, changes in adult literacy policies are revealing. Freed from initial schooling models, adult basic education policies everywhere are being redefined based on the goal of developing active literate societies. In the past decade, the convergence of economic, social, political and cultural demands to increase the basic competencies of the adult populations, although relative and internationally uneven, has led to a renewed emphasis on adult literacy, from the national level up to the World Bank. The subject's independence and capacity for expression have become the agreed goals of new adult basic education policies.

The subject's independence and capacity for expression

Let us step back for a moment. What is the meaning of the new learning dynamics and the recognition of acquired job skills? What is the meaning of the new dynamics of people's active social participation? What are the implications of the new emphasis on basic education, broadly speaking, i.e. the possibility for women and men to express themselves differently? What are the implications of the return to the actor and the subject (Ollivier 1995), if not, most profoundly, a process of widespread subjectivation, where the individual's need and demand to take initiative becomes linked with their search for identity (Sainsaulieu 1995)?[5]

In other words, social demand for adult learning is the locus of the encounter and confrontation, i.e. the negotiation, between, on one side, the demand on employees and citizens to expand their competencies and capacities for initiative and, on the other side, the subjects' aspirations to make individual choices related to their personal development and the group's or community's will to make an endogenous choice concerning its own social projects. There will be no reflexive actors on the job and in the local community nor any actual capacity to invest in them without the search for and discovery of meaning for the subject.

"The individual investment of each person is no longer focused on economic goals alone, but simultaneously on developing space for relationships with others that at the same time inspires productive creativity and social creativity." (Sainsaulieu 1995: 459 f.)

The rejection of repetitive work is definitely a cultural issue and a question of

---

[5] Here, the new sociology of adult learning ties in with the sociology of the new popular movements, which places the question of the subject and the actor as well as the search for identity at the heart of the forces transforming contemporary society.

mental health (De Bandt, Dejours and Dubar 1995). It has also become an economic issue. Today, neither politics nor economics can ignore the individual's intelligence and experience. Yet whereas each citizen ought to develop their intelligence and competence, now they are more and more demanding this as their right!

Thus increasing productivity and creativity does not express the entire process at work in the development of social demand for adult learning. The object of this process is the very meaning of the empowerment sought by men and women, the search for a higher quality of individual and community life, self-expression, the diverse expression of identities and the celebration of their difference. This process also involves demands regarding the distribution of the profits of increased productivity and the democratisation of the quality of life.

The dynamics at work here should not be obscured purely by the fact that the emphasis in the current relationship between the development banks and actual development is still placed on debt repayment and that the bias in the relationship between business and producer-subjects is still in favour of external demand!

The celebrated "joy of learning" proclaimed in Hamburg in 1997 reflects neither some Pollyanna-type definition of learning nor a comfortable capitalisation on the mastery of expected responses. On the contrary, it refers to the intimacy of the act of learning, to ingenuity in handling a problem, the adventure of questioning, to curiosity and the risks of the unknown, the anxiety before a cross-road, and to the difficult reconstruction of an inherently fleeting personal synthesis (Lengrand 1994).

This process of increasingly widespread subjectivation is political. It is the source of the development of learning projects, and it demands the rejection of economistic, monolithic approaches. It is giving rise to new policies that invest in the subjects and create room for them and for the spaces needed for their expressions. It is political because it is closely linked with the dynamics of citizenship and the democratisation of liberal democracy. It is also political because of its inherent tendency to spread, and because of its demands for equality and for policies to overcome inequalities. The trend at work here towards individualisation is not some abstract norm, but an observable programme that derives from the subjects themselves in their different life environments. It is rooted in the process of widespread subjectivation taking place amidst very uneven conditions, including in businesses that do not all allow room for individual expression and ingenuity.

Accessibility and equal opportunity

Although accessibility and equal opportunity are proclaimed in all legislative preambles and speeches, it is less common to find them actually pursued. This "less common" is a result of observation and does not indicate a determinist view of social reproduction. It cannot be repeated too often that there is a basic trend in adult learning towards learning continuity that, in all its contradictoriness, bears both the promise of lifelong learning for anyone with a good start and the accumulation of disadvantages for anyone else.

There is a dichotomy in learning opportunities: "the rich get richer". Nonetheless, in addition to this basic trend, we have observed several situations where policies do make a difference. The determination of initial inequalities is never conclusive. There have been examples of this throughout the book, including the high levels of accessibility and success, however relative, of adult literacy programmes, the increase in participation resulting from outreach measures[6], the success of "learning weeks" with groups traditionally remote from the educational milieu, the educational impact of national liberation movements, and the new popular movements for women's rights and environmental protection.

As we described in detail in Chapters 7 and 8, the trend towards the perpetuation of initial educational inequalities throughout life calls for the adoption of a wide range of measures to help the adult population overcome the structural and institutional barriers to participation. In the longer term, this would also involve changing initial education. One indicator of future trends in adult learning is indeed the way in which different countries restructure initial schooling to ensure more equal opportunity and the development of creativity during this critical initial stage of lifelong learning. Adult learning policies as a whole cannot ignore policies on initial schooling.[7]

Oddly, outreach policies, however essential, are not the only or main policies that can widen accessibility. This is clear in practice. The goal of equal opportunities to learn throughout life will become feasible only to the extent that available learning opportunities are important to the subjects and relevant for the economic and social agents, that healthcare services introduce training with con-

---

[6] Information services and campaigns, financial support (i.e. paid educational leave, training credits, grants, loans, reductions and reimbursement of direct training costs, and tax exemptions) and time-release measures (i.e. childcare services, time-sharing measures and job-rotation schemes).

[7] Alternative adult literacy practices (multilingual approaches, attention to male-female differences, regional identity, etc) provide a unique opportunity to set the example to free academic education from the chains of standardisation that shackle it by providing a range of alternatives to initial schooling. In this sense, the new general organisation of adult learning is also a historic opportunity for initial schooling.

crete applicability, that vocational training corresponds to the reality of the work environment concerned, that agricultural extension services deal with farmers' concrete concerns, that available formal adult education is not merely a second chance to repeat the first experience, and that adults deal in environments that stimulate their curiosity and self-directed learning. The expansion of the types of intervention required and their integration into overall strategies is leading to a new model of the general organisation of adult learning.

New models of the general structure of adult learning

Despite appearances, what we are witnessing is not a withdrawal of the nation-state from adult education, but a restructuring of its role (see Chapter 9).

The role of the nation-state in adult education is being redefined in two ways: by supra-national economic and political demands and pressures and by sub-national demands and pressures for the decentralisation of decision-making so as to take into account local environments, and also by shifting government action to deal with the specific characteristics of this field.

At global level are the large multilateral organisations and the new supra-national regional authorities. Throughout this book we have seen that these organisations play significant roles. This new supra-national influence in the national decision-making process is expressed in a number of ways. There is the effect of the structural adjustment programmes on adult learning in the developing countries, which until recently was devastating, the decisive impact of the 1990 joint action of UNESCO, Unicef, the UNDP and the World Bank for renewed emphasis on basic education, and the stimulatory effect of financial support from the European Union through its structural funds[8] and the Leonardo and Socrates programmes.[9]

There is yet another, more diffuse global force affecting national decision-making. We are referring here to the new, less easily controlled global economic forces whose corporate executives make market-based decisions and adopt human resources management policies that weigh heavily on national policies, including shifting production and concentrating workforce skills. One aim of the member states' efforts to establish a decision-making Europe is to help the na-

---

[8] In the 1990s, the three European structural funds, the Social Fund, the Regional Development Fund and the Agricultural Development Fund, invested enormous sums in work-related educational programmes, in particular in the restructuring countries and regions (Bélanger and Bochynek 1999).
[9] These are, respectively, the European Commission's general education and vocational training programmes.

tion-states offset the impact of these arbitrary decisions via the investment of funds and the promotion of common policies. Standardisation and awareness-raising activities by United Nations organisations and other multilateral agencies in the form of conferences and the adoption of conventions and action plans (Bélanger and Mobarak 1996) are other mechanisms that can also help member states to correct the trends engendered by this new global "laissez-faire" system. There is, nonetheless, a great disparity in power.

The transition taking place today thus does not represent a drastic withdrawal or absolute minimising of the welfare state, although there have been attempts at this over the past two decades, but rather a move towards what the Swedes call a "participatory welfare state". We now understand that there can be no economic recovery, that healthcare policies that have been smothered by punishing inflation cannot be renewed, without redefining the state's role, implementing active labour and healthcare policies and ensuring the active participation of civil society.

The most remarkable expansion and change in the state's role in adult learning in recent years has clearly been the new emphasis on national policies for the expression of social demand for learning. This change in perspective, grounding adult learning policies firstly in the expression of learning needs and aspirations, finds even greater significance in the above-mentioned context, where nation-states and civil society together seek to counterbalance global economic decisions that are beyond their control and to correct the unequal social relationships involved in defining social demand for learning. Chapters 6 and 7 detail this turning point in adult learning policies. Here, we can only give a general sense of this transformation. Unlike initial schooling, which is based on a common programme and managed by a ministry of national education, adult learning is much more diversified in time and space. It is based on reasoning and assessments that are often external to education. It involves individual choices that are costly in people's time and resources. It is carried out in very diverse learning conditions. It faces specific obstacles and is integrated in a thousand ways with learning biographies that are as diverse as individuals themselves. Attempts to plan adult learning in a linear way based on future job projections have proved futile and are increasingly giving way to policies on broad qualifications and the personalisation of learning projects. Here, the boundary between general and vocational becomes meaningless and the dual expression of demand, external and endogenous, becomes necessary to ensure the sustainable, well-rooted development of learning.

A policy on demand expression entails first and foremost implementing measures to support individuals (information counselling services, financial support and time release) and the pursuit of their learning projects, measures to support the evaluation of learning needs by economic and social agents, the creation of space for the expression and negotiation of learning needs and requirements, and the improvement of learning environments. Learning policies should no longer be exclusively educational and ignore the media, other culture industries, libraries and museums or the cultural impact of urban physical environments. Policies to promote the expression of demand should go further, and take into account living and working conditions that foster or hold back intellectual development, the space available for the subjects' capacity for initiative in the community and at work, and encouragement for continuing learning projects. Information and awareness-raising campaigns, which in many countries have taken the form of adult learners' weeks, are part of this new trend.

To this end, the nation-state no longer acts alone, but increasingly relies on measures to establish networks with economic agents and non-governmental organisations. The ministries of education and employment also do not act alone, but rely on significant inter-ministerial co-operation. In this context, the state's role has changed greatly. It now focuses on defining national goals, on co-operation among government agencies, business and the voluntary sector, and on ensuring a range of services upstream of learning to guarantee the expression of demand by different groups.

The state is also involved in the organisation of the growing number and type of learning responses. Governments are of course continuing to play a significant role in the provision of educational services to adults everywhere, but this is beginning to be done differently. Business, the media and the voluntary sector have become important providers of education, and "non-educational" ministries have incorporated their information and education services into their sector-based policies. The state is still a service provider, but in a different way, and it is one among many. In practice, the ministries of education and human resources are maintaining specific services for adults to ensure a distribution of learning opportunities based on particular interests and regions, and they are asking their own "regular" educational institutions to open their doors to adults. The pivotal role of the state in the organisation of responses is expanding. It is also playing a role in developing networks and co-ordination, monitoring (including statistics) educational services and participation, guaranteeing the quality of education (by means of recognising institutions, training educators, and research and development) and the recognition of prior and experiential learning acquisition. The nation-state is also developing diverse mechanisms to finance education, support non-governmental organisations and provide assistance to individuals.

A look at the number of ministries and public institutions, local authorities and extra-governmental organisations involved in all these measures gives a sense of the importance of the new synergies, inter-sectorial communications and linked strategies that all this demands. In Botswana, China, Japan, and Catalonia in Spain, this process is already giving rise to new umbrella mechanisms that go under titles such as "the continuing education council" or "the adult education advisory board".

The decentralisation and restructuring of the state's role does not necessarily mean greater democracy, despite the claims of the statements accompanying these measures. Civil society has a real influence in these programmes, mainly via the organisation of learning activities, using the room it creates there to make necessary changes and develop alternatives. Except for rare exceptions when space is made in the decision-making process itself, participation in negotiations over social demand remains a diffuse process and takes place in the course of the activity itself. The decentralisation and diversification of state-supported educational agents in practice nevertheless creates new spaces for redefining and contextualising programmes, for recognising different linguistic, regional and gender identities, for facilitating the participation of local communities in deci-sion-making and for integrating literacy into the community development pro-cess itself.

The new general organisation of adult literacy clearly reflects this new model of the general structure of adult learning. All those involved in basic education are seeing their role transformed; non-governmental organisations are multiplying. The links between basic education and other development policies, and the inte-gration of educational measures into sector-based policies, are also part of this expanding reconstruction of the field of adult literacy policy. The new basic education policies include measures for enriching literate environments, streng-thening local communities, providing educational support for collective action by grass roots movements, supporting basic education in business and, as pre-viously mentioned, supporting "employability" programmes. Literacy policies extend beyond literacy education, just as adult learning policies extend beyond adult education.

3. An open-ended process
Policies reflect the state of social relations, but they also have an independent impact as the product of a never-ending process of negotiation. They build, legi-timate, modify and guide, or they can curb and disorient the movement. There is room for the actors. Policies develop differently in different contexts, showing that alternatives exist. The die is not cast.

The adult learning policies that we have observed in different countries develop and function amidst ever-present tension between the participation of social groups called on to meet external demand and the process of communities taking charge of their own development. It is here at the frontiers of social and political policy where the democratic life of contemporary society is being determined today. We say "tension" because policy approaches are always complex or even contradictory. Exogenous demands need the support of civil society to find the required resources and mobilisation to create environments conducive to the empowerment of the groups involved. This is apparent in the participation of the local groups and women's groups "called on" in India.

Indeed, the die is not cast. Who has access to adult learning? What is done with it? The questions are more open than ever.

Dialogue, co-operation and solidarity

The development, negotiation and implementation of adult learning policies are marked by globalisation and, if only because of their common trends and knock-on effects, have an international impact.

Globalisation itself ceases to be one-dimensional. The globalisation of risks is giving rise to global responses and resistance, and to alternative models that are leading to the hybridisation of hitherto monolithic discourse (Matelard 1994). In the field of adult learning and literacy, the consolidation of the UNESCO Institute for Education as the adult learning research and development centre of UNESCO is a good example. The International Council of Adult Education and its recent re-definition is another one. In the face of globalisation, local action is not enough. The global conditions increasingly influencing local activity cannot be ignored; global dialogue and action are needed to improve the situation.

With this book, we hope to help disseminate information about current trends and experience so as to support the process of renewing national adult learning policies. Above all, however, we hope to further transnational dialogue about the importance of rising demand for people's active participation in every field of life and the different responses this is engendering. We seek to reopen discussion on analysis and priorities, the universal demand for the right to learn and question, the recognition of identities and the context in which this takes place, and the alliances and expertise needed to draw investment into the creativity and independence of actors. In short, we seek to reopen discussion of the basic issue here: the challenge of unlocking the creative forces.

Invest, yes invest

This book has taken the question of investment very seriously. Invest, by all means, but above all in men and women. Invest to unleash the latent reserves of the cultural, social and, of course, economic productivity of today's adults.

Unlocking the creative forces has now become both a goal and a prerequisite of the 21st century – and thus an essential investment as well. At stake is not so much the rise of knowledge or information societies, but, potentially and most fundamentally, the development of active and creative citizens. This is the crux of the debate: the democratisation of the capacity to act, by which we mean the democratisation of opportunities, conditions and environments favouring, amidst diversity, the creativity of everyone, the diffuse capacity for initiative.

Eliminating the obstacles to the flourishing of intelligence, curiosity and ingenuity throughout the life of every individual is not a luxury. It is a deep-seated aspiration and an essential condition for the survival of our societies.

Appendix I
Adult Learning Policy Framework

A Repertoire of Adult Learning Policies

To translate the evolving reality of the field, a repertoire of adult learning policies needs to be based on an expanded definition of the policies and the field
covered in order to take into account a wide range of official documents and
public action plans as well as the current fragmented state of adult education
provision. Three types of documents have been distinguished: legislation, governmental decisions and policy papers (see the introduction to section 1 of the
bibliography for a definition of these three types). Given this, we have identified
eight categories of policies:

1. Policies for the expression of learning demand
2. Policies to ensure the continuity of learning throughout life
3. Provision-focused policies
4. Policies on the accessibility of adult education provision
5. Work-related adult learning policies
6. Adult learning policies related to social issues
7. Financial policies
8. Policies on the role of the state and non-governmental agencies

There are also general adult learning policies that integrate different measures
within a national policy framework, formulate overall objectives and propose
mechanisms for inter-sectoral coordination, but until now this kind of policy
development has been an exception.

1. Policies for the expression of learning demand

Policies for the expression of learning demand include, but extend much
beyond, specific demand-focused policies, dealing with broader social and cultural processes. Their objective is the transformation of conditions influencing
the expression of people's demand for learning at the work-place, in the community and at home. They aim to facilitate synergies between the different policies
that help develop and diversify the capacity of initiative within civil society.
They include:

a. General policies (and/or elements relating to adult learning that are integrated
into different sector-based policies) to create learning communities and promote
active and informed citizenship and greater participation in decision-making

processes from national to local level;

b. Policies to create the conditions under which demand for learning can be effectively expressed and addressed. These include:
- Information and counselling services which allow adults to make informed choices about learning,
- Recognition of prior learning (through systems for the recognition and accreditation of learning gained in the widest variety of contexts),
- Giving a voice to learners and mobilising educational agencies (organisation of an "Adult Learners' Week" within the framework of the "International Adult Learners' Week", including the celebration of the International Literacy Day; promotion of campaigns like the "One hour a day for learning" appeal),
- Recognition of the media's key role in promoting learning and increasing motivation, especially among excluded groups,
- Strengthening learning environments, i.e.:
  recognise and support cultural institutions as centres and resources for adult learning,
  develop and open museums, libraries and theatres to alternative forms of adult learning,
  preserve the cultural heritage and promote its educational use,
  enrich literate environments through the promotion of accessible and popular reading materials and the development of simple language and suitable (reader-friendly) language in public written communications.

2. Policies to ensure the continuity of learning throughout life

Policies in this category aim at:
  Recognition of adults' right to learn, including the universal right to basic education for anyone at any age,
  Ensuring that initial school education is accessible to all and truly part of a lifelong learning approach,
  Allocation of time for education through the reduction of working hours, time-sharing measures, paid educational leave, a dual approach to apprenticeship, job-rotation systems, active labour market measures for unemployed people, "One hour a day for leaning" campaigns, etc.

3. Policies to develop and monitor the provision of adult learning programmes and activities[1]

Policies to develop, organise, monitor and co-ordinate the provision of adult

learning programmes and activities cover many fields, including literacy and adult basic education, general adult education, vocational education and retraining, language education and civic education. The educational provision in these different areas of adult learning can be offered by and/or in public institutions, private organisations and non-governmental associations. They include policies:
- to ensure direct public provision,
- to support provision by non-governmental and private organisations,
- to ensure equal opportunities for access to adult learning through normative measures and individual support for participants,
- to open the formal post-secondary institutions to adults (through new admission clauses, extended time schedules, flexibility in access to existing provision, the creation of programmes specifically developed for adult learners, etc.),
- to reinforce the educational function of the media,
- to create and support open and distance learning systems,
- to ensure general access to new information and communication technologies and facilitate the use of new technologies to promote alternative ways of learning,
- to promote research on adult learning and support the initial and further or in-service education of personnel engaged in diverse adult learning programmes and activities in order to ensure their quality and sustainability.

4. Policies on the accessibility of adult education provision

Policies on accessibility aim at eliminating all forms of discrimination in organising learning throughout life, widening participation to those currently excluded, and facilitating access to learning at work, in the community and for those in rural and remote areas. These include policies:
- to ensure gender equality and equity (eliminate gender disparities in access to all levels and areas of education using legal, financial and economic measures where necessary; promote women's participation in decision-making and political structures),
- to ensure accessibility through financial means (ratify and apply the ILO "Convention on Paid Educational Leave" of 1974; implement measures like paid educational leave, scholarships for adults, learning credits, educational vouchers, time-sharing measures, fee-free provision, fiscal exemption, fee reimbursement, childcare services, etc.; offer long-term scholarships, i.e. more than ten months, for adults with limited initial education),
- to eliminate all forms of discrimination in adult education participation (ensure access for all, including older people, to all aspects of adult learning;

---

[1] Provision-focused policies can also be included in the accessibility policies mentioned under (4); see below.

provide appropriate learning opportunities for people from minority cultures and comprehensive education and training opportunities for refugees and other migrant populations; make all forms of learning and training accessible to people with disabilities and learning difficulties; provide prison inmates with information and counselling on educational programmes including those of non-governmental organisations and, where appropriate, facilitate access to these programmes,

- to make admissions standards more flexible and provide transferable academic recognition,
- to provide information and counselling services, and to facilitate the recognition of prior learning.

5. Work-related adult learning policies

These include policies:
- to ensure that work-related learning provides specific competencies and transferable skills as well as basic and comprehensive qualifications,
- to include, within the framework of an active labour market policy, adult education and re-training programmes for the unemployed as well as those at risk of losing their job,
- to promote co-operation between employers and representatives of employees for the development of adult learning at the workplace,
- to ensure that work-related learning opportunities are accessible to all, including women, older workers, the self-employed, ethnic minorities, migrant workers and persons working in the informal economy,
- to use work-related learning to break down barriers to women and minorities entering non-traditional occupations,
- to include, in work-related adult learning policies, the new active policies in agriculture, fishery and forestry.

6. Adult learning policies related to social issues

The environment, health, population, nutrition, the economy, security, local governance and culture are intricately linked to one another and to non-formal education in the framework of policies for sustainable development. These policies include adult learning components and bear indirectly on adult learning policies. Policies in these different areas set out:
- to recognise the potential of active participation and adult learning in facing new challenges;
- to promote and support organised learning activities and education programmes which enable people to make informed personal and collective

216

decisions on issues and to debate issues with decision-makers;
- to include Information-Education-Counselling (IEC) strategies in sectoral policies and make IEC strategies more inter-active;
- to link national adult literacy programmes to national economic, social and cultural policies.

7. Financial policies[2]

Financial policies for the promotion of adult learning are characterised by the following objectives:
- to invest a fixed percentage of a country's GNP in education and to allocate an equitable share of the governmental budget to adult learning,
- to encourage the social partners to support education programmes in enterprises and to fund them appropriately,
- to require employers to allocate a minimal percentage (1-2%) of the enterprise's payroll budget to adult learning,
- to propose that every development sector (e.g., health, the environment) includes an adult learning component in its programmes and provides it with a proper budget,
- to invest an equitable share of resources in women's education,
- to assess all technical cooperation projects (supported by external agencies) in terms of their contribution to adult learning and the strengthening of local expertise.

8. Policies on the role of the state and of non-governmental agencies

Policies on the role of the state and of non-governmental agencies in the field of adult education propose inter alia:
- to recognise the inter-ministerial and cross-sector dimension of adult learning and facilitate information exchange and co-operation between agencies,
- to secure the integration of different legislative measures into a national policy framework,
- to monitor the wide range of adult education participation and provision (including by developing new statistical approaches),
- to facilitate inter-ministerial coordination and co-operation between governmental, private and non-governmental agencies,
- to decentralise policy implementation.

---

[2] Financial policies can also be included in the accessibility policies mentioned under (4); see above.

Appendix II: Table 1
Policy Documents (by country and subject matter)

	Aus.	Bel.	Bra.	Cz. R.	Ecu.	Fin.	Ger.	Gre.	Hun.	In
Adult Edu. (General)	2, 4			1, 3		1	1, 2, 6		1	
Literacy/Basic Edu.	5		5, 7		1					2
Vocational Edu.	7		6	2, 8	2			1	6	
Non-Governm. Ad. Edu.	3	1	3	6, 7			3, 4, 5		2, 4	
Public Adult Edu.							4			
Language Edu.										
Civic Edu.										
Access to Edu.										
Population										1
Environment			2		3, 4					
Agriculture/Economy										
Health	1		1, 4	4, 5					5	
Culture	6									
Local Govern./Commun.									3	
Women										
Minorities/Indig. Pop.										
Total	7	1	7	8	4	1	6	1	6	2

Ita.	Iv. C.	Jap.	Lith.	Mor.	Nam.	Phil.	Slo.	Spa.	Swi.	UK	U.S.	Viet.
		1, 2	2				5	1, 2	1-5, 9, 12, 13			1
	3			4	1	7				1, 2, 3	9	
1, 12, 13	4					6			8, 11		1, 5	
8			3, 4	2						4, 5, 6, 7, 8		
			1			3						
						6					7	
2, 4, 7, 10									10		2	
				1, 3								2
3, 11	2		5, 6	5		2	1, 3, 4		7		3, 8	
5	1						2				6	
14									6		4	
6, 9						1						
						4						
						5						
14	4	2	6	5	1	7	6	2	13	8	9	2

Appendix II: Table 2
Politicy Documents (by subject matter and region) [1]

	Explicit Policies									Indirect Policies							
	Ad. Edu. (Gen.)	Litera./ Basic	Voca-tional	Non-gov. Ad. Edu.	Public Ad. Edu.	Lang. Edu.	Civic Edu.	Access to Edu.	Populat.	Environ.	Agricult./ Econom.	Health	Culture	Loc. Gov/ Commun.	Women	Minorit/ Indig. Pop.	Total
Africa & Arabia	-	3	1	1	-	-	-	-	2	-	2	1	-	-	-	-	10
America (South)	-	3	2	1	-	-	-	-	-	3	-	2	-	-	-	-	11
America (North)	-	1	2	-	-	-	1	1	-	-	2	1	1	-	-	-	9
Asia	5	3	1	1	-	1	1	-	2	-	1	1	1	1	1	1	20
Europe (Central & Eastern)	5	-	4	6	-	1	-	-	-	-	5	4	-	1	-	-	26
Europe (Western)	14	-	9	5	5	-	-	5	-	-	3	1	2	2	-	-	46
Total	24	10	19	14	5	2	2	6	4	3	13	10	4	4	1	1	122
per cent	20%	8.2%	15.5%	11.5%	4%	1.6%	1.6%	5%	3.2%	2.5%	10,7%	8.2%	3.2%	3.2%	0.8%	0.8%	100%

1 For an explanation of the categories used (country, subject matter, explicit or indirect character of policy) see the introduction to section 1 of the Bibliography (below)

Appendix II: Table 3
Policy Documents (by country and formal type) [1]

	Legislation	Governmental Decision	Policy Paper
Australia	1, 2, 4	-	3, 5, 6, 7
Belgium	-	1	-
Brazil	1	1	2, 3, 4, 5, 6, 7
Czech Republic	5	2, 3, 4, 8	1, 6, 7
Equador	-	1, 4	1, 2, 3
Finland	-	-	1
Germany	1, 2, 3, 4	-	6
Greece	1	-	-
Hungary	3, 6	4	1, 2, 5
India	-	-	1, 2
Italy	1, 2, 3, 4, 5, 6, 7, 8, 9, 10, 11, 14	12, 13	12
Ivory Coast	2, 4	2, 4	1, 3
Japan	1	-	2
Lithuania	-	1, 3, 4, 5, 6	2
Morocco	-	-	1, 2, 3, 4, 5
Namibia	-	-	1
Philippines	1, 2, 3, 4, 5, 6, 7	4, 5, 6	4, 7
Slovenia	3, 4, 5	1	2, 5, 6
Spain	1	-	2
Switzerland	2, 5, 6, 7, 8, 10, 11, 12	7, 10, 12, 13	1, 3, 4, 9
United Kingdom	-	4	1, 2, 3, 4, 5, 6, 7, 8
United States	1, 2, 3, 4, 5, 6, 7, 8, 9	-	-
Vietnam	-	2	1, 2
per cent	40,5%	20,5%	39%

[1] Documents may appear in more than one category

221

Appendix III
Researchers Participating in the Country Studies

Aïcha Belarbi (Morocco)
Lucien Bosselaers (Belgium)
Maria Luisa Canieso-Doronila (Philippines)
M'Badiala Cisse (Ivory Coast)
Phyllis M. Cunningham (United States of America)
Olga Drofenik (Slovenia)
Richard Edwards (United Kingdom)
Alfons Formàriz (Spain)
Sérgio Haddad (Brazil)
László Harangi (Hungary)
Stanislav Hubík (Czech Republic)
Fabio Masala (Italy)
Robb Mason (Australia)
Derek Mulenga (Zambia)
Julia Namene (Namibia)
Edmundas Normantas (Lithuania)
Pierre Paquet (Canada)
Ila Patel (India)
Peter Raggatt (United Kingdom)
Rudi Rohlmann (Germany)
Juan Samaniego (Ecuador)
Katsuko Sato (Japan)
André Schläfli (Switzerland)
Irene Sgier (Switzerland)
János Sz. Tóth (Hungary)
Magda Trantallidi (Greece)
Nguyen Truong (Vietnam)
Jorma Turunen (Finland)

Bibliography

1. Policy Documents

All 122 Documents are listed by country, covering 23 of the 24 countries in the study (for Canada, a wide-ranging comparative analysis of policies directly resulted in the country's policy study; see below, (2) Country Studies).

The following are given for each document:
a) general subject matter;
b) formal status;
c) complete bibliographical data.

Under (a), the following policy subject matters have been distinguished:

Policies bearing directly/explicitly on adult education in the fields of

Adult Education (General)
Literacy and Adult Basic Education
Vocational Education and Training
Adult Education in the Non-governmental Sector
Adult Education in the Public Sector
Language Education
Civic Education
Access to Education

Policies bearing indirectly/implicitly on adult education in the fields of

Population
Environment
Agriculture / Economy
Health
Culture
Local Governance / Community Life
Women
Indigenous Peoples and Minority Groups

Under (b), three types of documents have been formally distinguished:

Legislation   policies adopted, or in the process of adoption, by the legislative bodies of the country (including constitutional provisions);

| Governmental Decision | policy decrees, orders, etc. issued by the executive of the country; |
| Policy Paper | policy proposals, programmes, plans, reports, commissioned analyses, implementation guidelines, manuals, etc. issued by governmental or non-governmental agencies; |

Under (c), document titles are given in English where an official translation has been provided; otherwise, titles appear in the original, with a summary in English appearing in brackets.

Australia

1. Health
   Legislation (regional law):
   "Victorian Tobacco Act". Parliament of Victoria. Melbourne: 1987.
2. Adult Education (General)
   Legislation (regional law):
   "Adult Community and Further Education Act, No. 9/1991". Parliament of Victoria. Melbourne: 1991.
3. Adult Education in the Non-governmental Sector
   Policy Paper:
   "Adult Community Education: National Policy". Ministerial Council on Education, Employment, Training and Youth Affairs. Canberra: 1993.
4. Adult Education (General)
   Legislation (regional law):
   "Council of Education Act 1981 (amended 1991)". Parliament of Victoria. Melbourne: 1991.
5. Literacy and Adult Basic Education
   Policy Paper:
   "Australia's Language: The Australian Language and Literacy Policy" (including a companion volume to the policy paper). Commonwealth of Australia Department of Education. Canberra: 1991.
6. Culture
   Policy Paper
   "Creative Nation. Commonwealth Cultural Policy". Commonwealth of Australia. Canberra: October 1994.
7. Vocational Education and Training
   Policy Paper:
   "Working Nation: Policies and Programs". Commonwealth of Australia. Canberra: May 1994.

Belgium

1. Adult Education in the Non-governmental Sector
   Governmental Decisions, Regional Government of the Flemish Community:
   1.1. "Decree on the Subsidizing of Socio-Cultural Education Activities
        for Dutch-Speaking Adults within Voluntary Associations" of
        July 4, 1975. Ministry of National Education and Dutch Culture.
        1975.
   1.2. "Decree on the Subsidizing of Socio-Cultural Activities for
        Dutch-Speaking Adults in Various Institutions" of March 3, 1978.
        Ministry of National Education and Dutch Culture. 1978.
   1.3. Decree on institutes for political education. 1985.
   1.4. Decree on general educational activities and specific target groups
        and problems. 1985.

Brazil

1. Health
   Legislation and Governmental Decision:
   "Federal Congress Law 6514, 22nd December 1977" and "Labour Ministry
   Directive 3214, 8th June 1978" (on safety in the working place). Federal
   Congress and Labour Ministry. 1977, 1978.
2. Environment
   Policy Paper:
   "Qualification and Training of Trade Union Leaders Concerning the
   Environmental Issue". Central Unica dos Trabalhadores (Central Workers
   Union). 1991.
3. Adult Education in the Non-governmental Sector
   Policy Paper:
   "Education and Community Action for Work". Center for Education and
   Community Action for Work (SENAC). Sao Paulo: 1991.
4. Health
   Policy Paper:
   "Programa Nacional de Controle das DST e AIDS. Campanhas de Prevençao
   a AIDS" (educational campaigns for AIDS prevention). Ministério da Saúde,
   Secretaria de Assistência a Saúde (Ministry of Health). Brasilia:
   (1993/1994).
5. Literacy
   Policy Paper:
   "Programa Nacional de Alfabetizaçao e Cidadania: marcos de referência"
   (National Literacy and Citizenship Programme). Ministério da Educaçao et
   do Desporto, SENEB (Ministry of Education and Sports). Brasilia: 1991.

6. Vocational Education and Training
   Policy Paper:
   "Programa de Reciclagem Profissional" (Professional Retraining Programme
   of the Federal Government). Ministério do Trabalho, Secretaria de Formaçao
   et Desenvolvimento Profissional (Labour Ministry). Brasilia: 1993.
7. Literacy and Adult Basic Education
   Policy Paper:
   "Plano Decenal de Educaçao para Todos" (Ten-Year "Education for All"
   Plan of the Federal Government). Ministério da Educaçao et do Desporto
   (Ministry of Education and Sports). Brasilia: 1993.

Czech Republic

1. Adult Education (General)
   Policy Paper:
   "Principles of Further Education Bill". Czech Republic, Ministry of
   Education. August 25, 1993.
2. Vocational Education and Training
   Governmental Decision:
   "Ministry of Labour and Social Welfare Decree on Conditions of Assuring
   Job Applicants' and Employees' Re-qualification. January 7, 1991". In:
   Federal State Book Part 5, pp.108-110. Praha: 1991.
3. Adult Education (General)
   Governmental Decision:
   "Ministry of Education Decree on Education of Workers from Socialist
   Organisations. November 9, 1983". In: *Czechoslovakian Socialist Republic
   State Book* Part 27, pp. 763/764. Praha: 1983.
4. Health
   Governmental Decision:
   "Ministry of Health Decree on Medical Workers and Other Professional
   Workers in Health Services. July 21, 1981". In: *Czechoslovakian Socialist
   Republic State Book* Part 19, pp. 401-416. Praha: 1981.
5. Health
   Legislation:
   "Czech National Council Act on the Czech Medical Chamber, the Czech
   Stomatological Chamber and the Czech Apothecarys' Chamber. May 8,
   1991". In: *Czech Republic State Book* Part 44, pp. 1047-1051. Praha: 1991.
6. Adult Education in the Non-governmental Sector
   Policy Paper:
   Programme for the KOVO (Metalworkers Union) Educational System.
   Archives of the Federal Council of the Czech-Moravian Chamber of Trade
   Unions (CMCTU), Praha: 1994.

7. Adult Education in the Non-governmental Sector
   Policy Paper:
   System of Trade Unions Education after the Institution of the Trade Unions
   Academy and Transformation of CMIO (December 1993). Czech-Moravian
   Chamber of Trade Unions. Archives of CMCTU, Praha: 1993.
8. Vocational Education and Training
   Governmental Decision:
   "Ministry of Labour and Social Welfare Decree on Conditions of Assuring
   Job Applicants' and Employees' Re-qualification. May 27, 1992".
   Amendment to the Ministry of Labour and Social Welfare State Book Part
   66, pp. 1818-1819. Praha: 1992.

Ecuador

1. Literacy and Adult Basic Education
   Policy Papers and Governmental Decision:
   1.1. "Agenda para el Desarrollo del Consejo Nacional de Desarrollo
         (CONADE)" (extract from the chapter referring to education).
         Consejo Nacional de Desarrollo (National Council of Development).
         Quito: 1993.
   1.2. National Education Policy of Ecuador, 1992-1996. Ministry of
         Education and Culture. Quito: 1992.
   1.3. "Decreto Ejecutivo No. 634 de Reformas al Reglamento General de
         Educación del Ecuador" (Decree on the Reform of the General
         Regulation of Education). Government of the Republic of Ecuador.
         1993.
2. Vocational Education and Training
   Policy Papers:
   2.1. "Proyecto de Educación de Adultos y Formación Profesional (PRE
         DAFORP). Resumen Ejecutivo del Proyecto" (Adult Education and
         Professional Training Project). Servicio Ecuadoriano de Capacitación
         Profesional (Ecuadorian Service for Professional Training - SECAP).
         Quito: 1993.
   2.2. "Caracterización Global del Componente 2: Capacitación al Sector
         Informal" (Training in the informal sector). Servicio Ecuadoriano de
         Capacitación Profesional (SECAP). Quito: 1993.
   2.3. "Plan Operativo Anual para 1994 del Componente 2: Capacitación al
         Sector Informal" (same as 2.2). Servicio Ecuadoriano de Capacitación
         Profesional (SECAP). Quito: 1994.
3. Environment
   Policy Paper:
   "Términos de Referencia para el Plan Ambiental Ecuatoriano" (Terms of

Reference for the National Environment Plan). Comisión Asesora Ambiental adscrita a la Presidencia de la República del Ecuador (The Environmental Commission of the President of the Republic of Ecuador). Quito: 1993.

4. Environment
Governmental Decision:
"Politicas Básicas Ambientales del Ecuador" (Basic Environmental Policies) Decree no. 1802 (1st June 1994), off. reg. 456 (7th June 1994). Comisión Asesora Ambiental adscrita a la Presidencia de la República del Ecuador (The Environmental Commission of the President of the Republic of Ecuador). Quito: 1994.

Finland

1. Adult Education (General)
Policy Paper:
"Governmental Plan for the Development of Education and Research in Finland for the Years 1991-1996". Ministry of Education. Helsinki: November 1991, revised 1993.

Germany

1. Adult Education (General)
Legislation (regional law):
"Gesetz zur Förderung der Erwachsenenbildung vom 13. Januar 1970" (Law on the promotion of adult education). Parliament of the Regional State of Niedersachsen. In: *Niedersächsisches Gesetz- und Verordnungsblatt* 2/1970, pp. 7-10.

2. Adult Education (General)
Legislation (regional law):
"Gesetz zur Förderung von Einrichtungen der Erwachsenenbildung (Erwachsenenbildungsgesetz) vom 24. Juni 1974" (Law on the promotion of adult education services). Parliament of the Regional State of Hessen. In: *Gesetz- und Verordnungsblatt für das Land Hessen* Vol. I/No. 21/1974, pp. 295-300.

3. Adult Education in the Non-governmental Sector
Legislation (regional law):
"Erstes Gesetz zur Ordnung und Förderung der Weiterbildung im Lande Nordrhein-Westfalen (Weiterbildungsgesetz) vom 31. Juli 1974 in der Fassung vom 2. Mai 1982" (Law on the organisation and promotion of continuing education). Parliament of the Regional State of Nordrhein-Westfalen. In: *Gesetz- und Verordnungsblatt für das Land Nordrhein-Westfalen* 1974, p.

769, and 1982, p. 276. 1982.
4. Adult Education in the Non-governmental Sector/Adult Education in the Public Sector
   Legislation (regional law):
   "Gesetz zur Förderung der Weiterbildung und des Bibliothekswesens für Baden Württemberg. Vom 16. März 1975 in der Fassung vom 20. März 1980, zuletzt geändert in der Fassung vom 4. Juli 1983" (Law on the promotion of continuing education and the public library services). Parliament of the Regional State of Baden-Württemberg. In: *Ges.Bl.* 1975, p. 853; *Ges.Bl.* 1980, p. 249; *Ges.Bl.* 1983, p. 265. 1983.
5. Adult Education in the Non-governmental Sector
   Legislation (regional law):
   "Gesetz über Volkshochschulen. Vom 12. Mai 1970" (Law on folk high schools). Parliament of the Regional State of Hessen. In: *Gesetz- und Verordnungsblatt für das Land Hessen* Vol. I/No. 23/1974.
6. Adult Education (General)
   Policy Paper:
   "Dritte Empfehlung der Kultusministerkonferenz zur Weiterbildung. Beschluß der KMK vom 2.12.1994" (Further Education). Sekretariat der Ständigen Kommission der Konferenz der Kultusminister der Länder in der Bundesrepublik Deutschland (Committee of the Ministers of Education of the Regional States). 1994.

Greece

1. Vocational Education and Training
   Legislation:
   "The National System of Vocational Education and Training". In: *Government Gazette* Vol. 1/18 (February 14, 1992). Parliament of the Greek Republic. Athens: 1992.

Hungary

1. Adult Education (General)
   Policy Paper:
   Conceptual Draft for a Law on Adult Education and the Free Education of Citizens. Hungarian Adult Education Association. In: *TIM/Society, Information, Education* February 1994, pp. 9-10.
2. Adult Education in the Non-governmental Sector
   Policy Paper:
   Small Manual for Folk High Schools. Steering Committee, Népfőiskolai kis

kalauz (Hungarian Folk High School Society). Budapest: February 1992.
3. Local Governance / Community Life
   Legislation:
   Fundamental Acts on Local Self-Government in Hungary: Ministry of the Interior Act LXV. Budapest: 1990.
4. Adult Education in the Non-governmental Sector
   Governmental Decision
   Decree 30/1989 (November 19, 1989) on the Integrated Educational Institutes. Ministry of Culture and Education. 1989.
5. Health
   Policy Paper:
   "The Process of Restructuring Hungarian Health Care: The Hungarian Health Care Reform, Basic Principles and Process. 1990-1994".
   Parliamentary Secretariat of State, Ministry of Welfare. Budapest: 1994.
6. Vocational Education and Training
   Legislation:
   Act LXXVI of 1993 on Vocational Training (passed July 12, 1993). In: *National Vocational Training Institute. Collection of Acts.* Budapest: 1994.

India

1. Population
   Policy Paper:
   "National Population Policy" (Draft Proposal Compiled by the Expert Group on Population Policy, appointed by the Ministry of Health and Family Welfare). Ministry of Health and Family Welfare. New Delhi: May 1994.
2. Literacy and Adult Basic Education
   Policy Paper:
   "National Literacy Mission". Ministry of Human Resources Development. New Delhi: 1988.

Italy

1. Vocational Education and Training
   Legislation:
   Legge 845/21.12.1978: "Legge-quadro in materia di formazione professionale" (Framework Law on Professional Training). 1978.
2. Access to Education
   Legislation (regional law):
   Legge Regionale 73/06.09.1982: "Intervento di preformazione professionale e per l'inserimento al lavoro delle personne handicappate" (Professional trai-

ning and introduction into the workforce of the disabled). 1982.

3. Agriculture / Economy
   Legislation:
   Legge 160/20.05.1988 (formerly Decreto Legge 86/21.03.1988): "Norme in materia previdenziale, di occupazione giovanile e di mercato del lavoro, nonché il potenziamento del sistema informativo del Ministero del lavoro e della previdenza sociale" (Legal norms for social security, youth employment and the labour market). 1988.

4. Access to Education
   Legislation (regional law):
   Legge Regionale 22/23.03.1990: "Interventi a sostegno dei diritti degli immigrati extracomunitari in Toscana" (Rights of resident immigrants without citizenship status in Tuscany). 1990.

5. Health
   Legislation:
   Legge 135/05.06.1990: "Programma di interventi urgenti per la prevenzione e la lotta contro l'AIDS" (AIDS prevention). 1990.

6. Local Governance / Community Life
   Legislation:
   Legge 241/07.08.1990: "Nuove norme in materia di procedimento amministrativo e di diritto di accesso ai documenti amministrativi" (Norms ruling access to administrative documents). 1990.

7. Access to Education
   Legislation:
   Legge 125/10.04.1991: "Azioni positive per la realizzazione della parità uomo-donna nel lavoro" (Affirmative action for the equality of women and men at work). 1991.

8. Adult Education in the Non-governmental Sector
   Legislation:
   Legge 266/11.08.1991: "Legge-quadro sul volontariato" (Framework Law for the Voluntary Sector). 1991.

9. Local Governance / Community Life
   Legislation:
   Legge 381/08.11.1991: "Disciplina delle cooperative sociali". 1991.

10. Access to Education
    Legislation:
    Legge 104/05.02.1992: "Legge-quadro per l'assistenza, l'integrazione sociale e i diritti delle persone handicappate" (Framework Law on Financial Assistance, Social Integration and the Rights of the Disabled). 1992.

11. Agriculture / Economy
    Legislation:
    Legge 236/19.07.1993: "Interventi urgenti a sostegno dell'occupazione" (Employment measures). 1993.

12. Vocational Education and Training
    Policy Paper and Governmental Decision:
    "Accordo fra sindicati, confindustria, con la partecipazioni del Governo, del 23.07.1993, sull'occupazione" (Official agreement on employment). 1993.
13. Vocational Education and Training
    Governmental Decision:
    Decreto Legge 462/18.11.1993: "Lavori socialemente utili, piani per l'inserimento professionale die giovani privi di occupazione, norme in materia di contratti di formazione e lavoro" (Professional training for unemployed youth working as volunteers). 1993.
14. Culture
    Legislation:
    Legge 153/01.03.1994 (formerly Decreto Legge 26/14.01.1994): "Interventi urgenti a favore del cinema" (Emergency measure to support the cinema). 1994.

Ivory Coast

1. Health
   Policy Paper:
   "Rapport sur l'éducation sanitaire dans la politique de santé publique en Côte d'Ivoire" (Report on health education). Ministry of Public Health. 1988.
2. Agriculture / Economy
   Legislation and Governmental Decision, Republic of Ivory Coast:
   2.1.   "Loi n° 77-332 du 1er Juin 1977 sur l'organisation du monde rural en vue desa modernisation et de sa responsabilisation grâce aux structu res d'encadrement mises en place et aux textes en vigeur: Statut général de la coopération en Côte d'Ivoire" (Organisation of the rural sector with respect to its modernisation). 1977.
   2.2.   "Décret n° 93-777 sur la création de l'Agence nationale d'appui au développement rural (ANADER)" (Decree on the Creation of the National Agency for Rural Development). 1993.
3. Literacy and Adult Basic Education
   Policy Paper:
   "Actes du 1er Séminaire national sur l'alphabétisation et l'éducation des adultes, tenu à Abidjan le 18 février 1983" (Papers of the National Seminar on Literacy and Adult Education). Ministry of Youth and Sports in collaboration with the National Literacy Committee. 1983.
4. Vocational Education and Training
   Legislation and Governmental Decisions:
   4.1.   "Loi n° 91-997 sur la création du Fonds de développement de la formation professionnelle du 27 décembre 1991" (National Development

and Professional Training Funds).
4.2. "Décret n° 92-316 sur la création de l'Agence nationale de la formation professionnelle du 15 mai 1992" (National Professional Training Agency). Ministry of National Education. 1992.
4.3. "Décret n° 93-... sur la création de l'Agence d'études et de promotion de l'emploi du 3 février 1993" (Agency for the Study and Creation of Jobs). Ministry of National Education. 1993.

Japan

1. Adult Education (General)
   Legislation:
   "Law Concerning the Development of Mechanisms and Measures for Promoting Lifelong Learning". June 29, 1990.
2. Adult Education (General)
   Policy Paper:
   "Measures for Promoting Lifelong Learning Corresponding to Future Social Trends. Report on Lifelong Learning Council". Ministry of Education, Science and Culture. Tokyo: July 1992.

Lithuania

1. Language Education
   Governmental Decision:
   Decision No. 314 on "Qualification Categories for the Knowledge of the State Language". Government of the Republic of Lithuania. In: *Lietuvos Respublikos Auksciausiosios Tarybos ir Valstybès Zinios (The State News of the Republic of Lithuania)* No. 18/1992.
2. Adult Education (General)
   Policy Paper:
   "General Concept of Education in Lithuania: (b) Concept of Adult Education". Ministry of Culture and Education, Publishing Centre: 1992.
3. Adult Education in the Non-governmental Sector
   Governmental Decision:
   Decision No. 332 "On the Confirmation of the Rules Concerning the Establishment, Reorganisation and Liquidation of Educational Institutions", with supplements: "The Rules Concerning the Establishment, Reorganisation and Liquidation of Educational Institutions" and "Composition of the Licensing Commission" (March 31, 1994). Ministry of Culture and Education. In: *The News of the Seimas and Government of the Republic of Lithuania* 27/1994.

4. Adult Education in the Non-governmental Sector
   Governmental Decision:
   Decision No. 411 "On the Confirmation of Regulations of the Educational
   Institutions Register" (June 30, 1993). Government of the Republic of
   Lithuania. In: *Lietuvos Respublikos Auksciausiosios Tarybos ir Valstybès
   Zinios (The State News of the Republic of Lithuania)* 22/1993.
5. Agriculture / Economy
   Governmental Decision:
   5.1   Decision No. 935 "On Testing of the Minimal Knowledge of
         Farming; On the Creation of the System of Training of Farmers and
         the Counseling of Physical and Legal Persons Engaged in
         Agricultural Business" (December 9, 1992). Government of the
         Republic of Lithuania. In: *Lietuvos Respublikos Auksciausiosios
         Tarybos ir Valstybès Zinios (The State News of the Republic of
         Lithuania)* 1/1993.
   5.2. Amendment to above: Governmental Decision No. 846 (November
         16, 1993). In: *Lietuvos Respublikos Auksciausiosios Tarybos ir
         Valstybès Zinios (The State News of the Republic of Lithuania)*
         62/1993.
6. Agriculture / Economy
   Governmental Decision:
   Decision No. 394 "On the Establishment of the Labour Exchange of
   Lithuania under the Ministry of Social Protection and On the Confirmation
   of Normative Documents Regulating Employment", with supplement:
   "Rules Concerning Teaching, Teaching Anew and the Requalification of
   Unemployed Citizens" (December 29, 1990). Government of the Republic of
   Lithuania. In: *Lietuvos Respublikos Auksciausiosios Tarybos ir Valstybès
   Zinios (The State News of the Republic of Lithuania)* 3/1991.

Morocco

1. Population
   Policy Paper:
   "Stratégie d'information, d'éducation et de communication en planification
   familiale (IEC/PF)" (Strategy of Information, Education and Counselling on
   Family Planning). Ministry of Public Health. Rabat: 1992.
2. Adult Education in the Non-governmental Sector
   Policy Paper:
   "Projet pilote d'Imilchil, dossier secteur économique (La vallée d'Assif
   Melloul) Confins Haut et Moyen Atlas". Association ADRAR Maroc. 1991.
3. Population
   Policy Paper:

"Projet MOR 93/P07 : Intégration de l'éducation en matière de population dans les foyers féminins. Rapport d'activités mai 1993 - mai 1994" (Integration of Population Educationwithin Women Groups, report). Ministry of Youth and Sports and UNFPA. Rabat: 1994.

4. Literacy and Adult Basic Education
   Policy Paper:
   "Programme d'alphabétisation et d'éducation des adultes au Maroc" (Programme for Literacy and Adult Education in Morocco). Ministry of Employment, Crafts and Social Affairs. Rabat: 1992.

5. Agriculture / Economy
   Policy Paper:
   "Programme PEDAEX: Population Education Agricultural Extension". Ministry of Agriculture and Agrarian Reform. Rabat: 1991.

Namibia

1. Literacy and Adult Basic Education
   Policy Paper:
   "Literacy, Your Key to a Better Future. Guide to the National Literacy Programme in Namibia". Ministry of Education and Culture, Department of Adult and Nonformal Education. 1992.

Philippines

1. Local Governance / Community Life
   Legislation:
   Republic Act No. 7160 "Local Government Code" (Senate Bill No. 155, House Bill No. 31046), passed on October 8, 1991. Legislative Bodies of the Republic of the Philippines. 1991.

2. Agriculture / Economy
   Legislation:
   Republic Act No. 6657 "Comprehensive Agrarian Reform Law". Legislative Bodies of the Republic of the Philippines. 1988.

3. Language Education
   Legislation (Constitutional Provision):
   Constitution of the Republic of the Philippines, Art. XIV, Sect. 6-9 (adopted October 15, 1986; ratified on February 2, 1987). 1987.

4. Women
   Policy Paper and Governmental Decision:
   "Philippine Development Plan for Women, 1989-1992" (policy paper and compendium plan of the Medium Term Philippine Development Plan 1989-

1992); approved and adopted by Executive Order No. 348/February 17, 1989.

5. Indigenous Peoples and Minority Groups
   Legislation (Constitutional Provision and Laws) and Governmental Decision:
   5.1. Constitution of the Republic of the Philippines, Art. X, Sect. 15 (adopted October 15, 1986; ratified on February 2, 1987). 1987.
   5.2. Executive Order No. 220 (Decree creating the Cordillera Administrative Region). 1987.
   5.3. Republic Act No. 6734 (Organic Act for the Autonomous Region of Muslim Mindanao). 1989.
   5.4. Republic Act No. 6766 (Organic Act for the Cordillera Autonomous Region). 1990.

6. Civic Education
   Legislation (Constitutional Provision) and Governmental Decision:
   6.1. Constitution of the Republic of the Philippines, Art. III and XIII, Sect. 17-19 (adopted October 15, 1986; ratified on February 2, 1987).
   6.2. Executive Order No. 27 "On Education to Maximize Respect for Human Rights". (no date given).

7. Literacy and Adult Basic Education
   Policy Paper and Legislation:
   7.1. "Education for All - Philippine Plan of Action (EFA-PPA) 1991-2000". National Commission on Education for All. 1991.
   7.2. Republic Act No. 7165 "On Creating the Literacy Coordinating Council, Defining its Powers and Functions, Appropriating Funds Therefore and for Other Purposes" (Senate Bill No. 686 and House Bill No. 32276, passed October 1991). Legislative Bodies of the Republic of the Philippines. 1991.

Slovenia

1. Agriculture / Economy
   Governmental Decision:
   "Decree on the Prevention of Further Spreading of the *Scolytidae* Bark Beetle and Extermination Measures for 1994". Ministry of Agriculture and Forestry. In: *Official Gazette* RS 14/1994, pp. 778-781. 1994.

2. Health
   Policy Paper:
   "Slovenian Health Care Plan to the Year 2000". Ministry of Health. April 1993.

3. Agriculture / Economy
   Legislation:

"Law on Employment and Unemployment Insurance". National Assembly, Republic of Slovenia. In: *Official Papers of the Republic of Slovenia* 5-223/1991. (revisions and amendments: ibid. No. 17/1991; 12-672/1992; 71-2575/1993; 2/1994). 1991-1994.

4. Agriculture / Economy
   Legislation:
   "Law on Labour Relations". National Assembly, Republic of Slovenia. In: *Official Gazette* RS 14-696/1990.

5. Adult Education (General)
   Policy Paper and Legislation:
   5.1. Proposal for an "Adult Education Act" (July 5, 1994). Ministry of Education and Sports. 1994.
   5.2. "Law on Adult Education" of February 14, 1996. National Assembly, Republic of Slovenia. In: *Official Gazette* RS 10-602/1996.

6. Vocational Education and Training
   Policy Paper (White Paper):
   "Vocational Education and Training. Proposals for Developing a Conception". In: *Ministry of Education and Sports: White Paper on Education in the Republic of Slovenia.* Ljubljana: 1995. pp. 197-233.

Spain

1. Adult Education (General)
   Legislation:
   "Titulo Tercero de la Educación de las Personas Adultas de la Ley Orgánica 1/1990 de 3 de octubre, de Ordenación General del Sistema Educativo (LOGSE)" (Organic Law 1/1990, Title 3 on Adult Education). Legislative Bodies of the State of Spain. 1990.

2. Adult Education (General)
   Policy Paper:
   "Manifesto a Favor de un Modelo de Educación de las Personas Adultas que Garantice el Acceso de Todos a la Educación en Condiciónes de Calidad" (Model for an Adult Education System Guaranteeing Access for All under Conditions of Quality). Mesa de los Agentes por la Educación de Personas Adultas (Board of Adult Education Agents). January 1993.

Switzerland

1. Adult Education (General)
   Policy Paper:
   "Rechtsgutachten zu einer neuen Förderungsstruktur für die

Erwachsenenbildung" (Legal Appraisal of a New Structure for the Promotion of Adult Education). Koordinationskonferenz verschiedener Behörden, Schweizerische Vereinigung für Erwachsenenbildung (Swiss Association for Adult Education). 1993.

2. Adult Education (General)
   Legislation (regional law):
   "Gesetz über die Förderung der Erwachsenenbildung - EFG - vom 10. Juni 1990", revised version (Law on the Promotion of Adult Education). State Council, Canton of Bern. 1990.

3. Adult Education (General)
   Policy Paper:
   "Konzept zur Einrichtung von sechs regionalen Weiterbildungszentren im Kanton Schwyz - WEBIZ" (Conceptual Draft for the Establishment of Six Regional Centres of Further Education in the Canton of Schwyz), revised version. WEBIZ-Konzeptgruppe. Canton of Schwyz: December 1993.

4. Adult Education (General)
   Policy Paper:
   "Konzept für die Förderung der Erwachsenenbildung im Kanton Solothurn. Entwurf vom 1. Juni 1993" revised version (Conceptual Draft for the Promotion of Adult Education in the Canton of Solothurn). J. Federer and Projektgruppe Erwachsenenbildungs-Konzept.1993.

5. Adult Education (General)
   Legislation (regional law):
   "Kanton Luzern: Erziehungsgesetz vom 28. Oktober 1953, Änderung vom 3. Juli 1984" (Regional Law on Education). State Council, Canton of Luzern. 1984.

6. Culture
   Legislation (federal law):
   "Bundesgesetz über eine Stiftung des öffentlichen Rechts, bezweckend die schweizerische Kulturwahrung und Kulturförderung sowie die Pflege der kulturellen Beziehungen mit dem Ausland"; Main Document: "Botschaft über die Finanzhilfe an die Stiftung Pro Helvetia in den Jahren 1992 - 1995 vom 18. März 1991"; Additional Document 2: "Bundesgesetz betreffend die Stiftung Pro Helvetia vom 17. Dezember 1965" revised version of April 1,1984 (Creation of the Swiss Cultural Heritage Foundation Pro Helvetia). Federal Council, Swiss Confederation. Bern: 1991.

7. Agriculture / Economy
   Legislation (federal law) and Governmental Decisions:
   7.1.   "Bundesgesetz über die Förderung der Landwirtschaft und die Erhaltung des Bauernstandes - Landwirtschaftsgesetz - vom 3. Oktober 1951. Änderung vom 18. Dezember 1992" (Federal Law on the Promotion of Agriculture). Federal Council, Swiss Confederation. 1992.

7.2. "Verordnung über Beiträge an Vergütungen nach Landwirtschaftsgesetz - Landwirtschaftliche Vergütungsverordnung - vom 26. November 1990" (Decree regulating the reimbursement of agricultural production). Federal Department of Agriculture. 1990.

7.3. "Verordnung über die landwirtschaftliche Berufsbildung - VLB - vom 13. Dezember 1993" (Decree on Professional Training in Agriculture). Federal Department of Agriculture. 1993.

8. Vocational Education and Training
   Legislation (federal law):
   8.1. "Bundesgestz über die Berufsbildung - BBG - vom 19. April 1978" and "Verordnung vom 7. November 1979" (Federal Law on Vocational Education and Training). Federal Council, Swiss Confederation. 1979.

   8.2. "Botschaft über Sonderausgaben zugunsten der beruflichen und universitären Weiterbildung sowie zur Förderung neuer Technologien vom 28. Juni 1989" (Allocation of funds for vocational and post-secondary education). Federal Council, Swiss Confederation. 1989.

9. Adult Education (General)
   Policy Paper:
   "Leitideen zur Förderung der Erwachsenenbildung im Kanton Aargau" (promotion of adult education). Interessengemeinschaft der Erwachsenenbildungs-Organisationen (Syndicate of Adult Education Organisations). Lenzburg: 1993.

10. Access to Education
    Legislation (federal law) and Governmental Decisions:
    10.1. "Bundesgesetz über die Invalidensicherung - IVG - vom 19. Juni 1959. Stand 1. Januar 1994" (Federal Law on Aid for Invalid Persons). Federal Council, Swiss Confederation. 1994.

    10.2. "Verordnung über die Invalidensicherung - IVV - vom 17. Januar 1961. Stand 1. Januar 1994". Federal Department of Social Security. 1994.

    10.3. "Kreisschreiben über die Beiträge an Organisationen der privaten Invalidenhilfe" (January 1, 1994). Federal Department of Social Security. 1994

11. Vocational Education and Training
    Legislation (regional law):
    "Loi vaudoise du 19 septembre 1990 sur la formation professionnelle (LVFPr). Section 3, organes de concertation." (Regional Law on Vocational Education). State Council, Canton of Vaud. 1990.

12. Adult Education (General)
    Governmental Decisions and Legislation (regional law):
    12.1. "Règlement du Conseil d'état du Canton de Genève (C/2/7) de février 1974 instituant un Conseil de la formation continue des adultes"

(Decree Creating the Council for Adult Continuing Education). State Council, Canton of Geneva. 1974.
12.2. "Loi sur le Conseil de l'éducation continue des adultes (C/2/6) du 14avril 1989" (law on same). State Council, Canton of Geneva. 1989.
12.3. "Règlement d'application de la loi sur le Conseil de l'éducation continue des adultes du 20 novembre 1991" (Decree on application of above law). State Council, Canton of Geneva. 1991.
13. Adult Education (General)
Governmental Decision:
"Arrêté du 19 mars 1985 instituant une Commission de la formation des adultes" (Decree Establishing a Commission for Adult Education). State Council, Canton of Fribourg. 1985.

United Kingdom

1. Vocational Education and Training
Policy Paper (White Paper):
"A New Training Initiative: A Programme for Action". Department of Employment and Department of Education and Science. London: HMSO. 1981.
2. Vocational Education and Training
Policy Paper (White Paper):
"Education and Training for the 21st Century". Department of Employment. London: HMSO. 1988.
3. Vocational Education and Training
Policy Paper (White Paper):
"Employment in the 1990s". Department of Employment. London: HMSO. 1988.
4. Adult Education in the Public Sector
Governmental Decision:
"The Careers Service: Requirements and Guidance for Providers" (Guidance on the Implementation of the 1993 Trade Union Reform and Employment Rights Act). Department of Employment. London: HMSO. 1993.
5. Adult Education in the Public Sector
Policy Papers:
5.1. "A Review of Adult Education". Education Committee, Council of the Wakefield District. January 28, 1992.
5.2. "Adult and Community Education in the Wakefield District: An Adequacy Statement". Education Committee, Council of the Wakefield District. March 1993.

6. Adult Education in the Public Sector
   Policy Papers:
   6.1. "Strategic Plan for the Development of Community Education in the Calderdale Metropolitan District, 1994-1997". Council of the Calderdale Metropolitan District. (1993).
   6.2. "Evaluation of the 1993 Adult Education Programme in the Autumn Term of 1993 by the Continuing Education Sub-Committee" (report). Council of the Calderdale Metropolitan District. December 1993.
7. Adult Education in the Public Sector
   Policy Paper:
   "Community and Continuing Education Service" (review of community education in action). Education Committee, City Council of Bradford. 1993
8. Adult Education in the Public Sector
   Policy Paper:
   "Statement of Intent in Terms of 1992 Legislation Affecting Provision of Non-Accredited Courses for Adults". Sub-Commission of the Education Committee, Council of Leeds Metropolitan District. 1994.

United States of America

1. Vocational Education and Training
   Legislation:
   "Job Training Partnership Act". Congress of the United States, Public Law No. 97-300 (specifically titles II-A Training for Disadvantaged Youth and Adults; III Dislocated Workers; IV-B Job Corps), 96 Stat. 1322. Washington D.C.: 1982.
2. Access to Education
   Legislation:
   "Tribally Controlled Community College Assistance": Title 25, Chapter 20, Sub Chapter 1 - Tribally Controlled Community College Grant Program; Sub Chapter II - Tribally Controlled Community College Endowment Program (Public Law 95-471, October 17, 1978, now Public Law 98-1992, December 1, 1983). Washington D.C.: 1983.
3. Agriculture / Economy
   Legislation:
   "National Volunteers Anti-Poverty Programs":
   3.1. "Domestic Service Act" of 1973. Congress of the United States, Public Law 93113, Title 1.
   3.2. "National Community Services Trust Act" of 1993 (amendment to 3.1) Subtitle B, Chapter 1. Washington D.C.: 1993.
4. Culture
   Legislation:

4.1. "The National Endowment for the Humanities". Congress of the United States, Public Law 89-209, 1965. Washington D.C.: 1965.

4.2. "Support and Scholarship in Humanities and Arts", Congress of the United States Public Law 103-219, March 9, 1994. Washington D.C.: 1994.

5. Vocational Education and Training
Legislation:
"Family Support Act" of 1988, Title II: "Job Opportunities for Basic Skills (JOBS)". Congress of the United States, Public Law 100-485 (Welfare Reform Act). Washington D.C.: 1988.

6. Health
Legislation:
"The Public Health and Welfare. Sexually Transmitted Diseases: Prevention and Control Projects and Programs". Congress of the United States, United States Code, Title 42. Washington D.C.: 1994.

7. Civic Education
Legislation:
"United States Institute of Peace". Congress of the United States, Public Law 98-525, Title XVII, Para. 1702. Washington D.C.: 1984.

8. Agriculture / Economy
Legislation:
"Renewable Resources Extension Act". Congress of the United States, Public Law 95-306. Washington D.C.: 1978.

9. Literacy and Adult Basic Education
Legislation:
"National Literacy Act". Congress of the United States, Public Law 102-73. July 25, 1991. Washington D.C.: 1991.

Vietnam

1. Adult Education (General)
Policy Paper:
"Continued Renovation of the Education and Training Cause". Resolution adopted by the 4th Plenary Session of the Central Committee of the Communist Party of Vietnam (CVP). Hanoi: January 1993.

2. Population
Policy Papers and Governmental Decision:
"Population and Family Planning" programmes:

2.1 Central Secretariat of the Communist Party of Vietnam Instruction of September 19, 1985, and CVP V, VI, VII Congress. 1985.

2.2. Joint Instruction of Ministry of Education and Trade Union of Education on Population Education and Family Planning of July 4,

1987 (N. 13 CTLT). 1987.
2.3.   Council of Ministers (HDBT) Decision No. 162 (October 10, 1988).
1988.

2. Country Studies:

All country studies originally were prepared under the general title *The Expanding Legislation and Policy Environment of Adult Education and Training* and were presented at a UNESCO Institute for Education seminar held in Hamburg, Germany, in October 1994. In some cases, however, authors have adopted different titles indicating the more specific scope of their studies.

Some of the studies are unpublished conference papers. Manuscripts can be obtained from the UNESCO Institute for Education documentation centre (Feldbrunnenstrasse 48, 20148 Hamburg, Germany; for more information see also the Institute's data bank ALADIN: http:/www.unseco.org/education/aladin).

Australia
Mason, R. 1996. In: *International Review of Education* Vol. 42 (1-3). pp. 11-28.

Belgium
Bosselaers, L. *Socio-Cultural Education in Associations and Institutions in Flanders (Belgium).* (unpublished, 1994). 30 pp.

Brazil
Haddad, S. 1996. In: *International Review of Education* Vol. 42 (1-3). pp. 29-40.

Canada
Paquet, P. 1993. "L'évolution des politiques canadiennes et québecoises de formation des adultes depuis 1960". In: P. Dandurand et al. *Enjeux actuels de la formation professionnelle.* Quebec: Institut québecois de recherche sur la culture.

Czech Republic
Hubik, S. (unpublished, 1995). 26 pp.

Germany
Rohlmann, Rudi. 1994. *Gesetzgebung und Politik zur Erwachsenenbildung in Deutschland.* Bonn: Institut für Internationale Zusammenarbeit des Deutschen Volkshochschul-Verbandes.

Greece
Trantallidi, M. (unpublished, 1998). 36 pp.

Hungary
Harangi, L., and Tóth, J.S. 1996. In: *International Review of Education* Vol. 42 (1-3). pp. 59-74.

India
Patel, I. 1996. In: *International Review of Education* Vol. 42 (1-3). pp. 75-96.

Ivory Coast
Cisse, M. 1996. In: *International Review of Education* Vol. 42 (1-3). pp. 41-58.

Japan
Sato, K., Kakiuchi, E., and Fujimura, Y. *Development of Lifelong Learning Policies and the Social Education System in Japan.* (unpublished, 1995). 46 p.

Lithuania
Normantas, E. (unpublished, 1995). 19 pp.

Morocco
Belarbi, A. 1996. In: *International Review of Education* Vol. 42 (1-3). pp. 97-108.

Namibia
Namene, J. (unpublished, 1995). 23 pp.

Philippines
Canieso-Doronila, M.L. 1996. In: *International Review of Education* Vol. 42 (1-3). pp. 109-129.

Slovenia
Drofenik, O. (unpublished, 1996). 48 pp.

Switzerland
Rohrer, C., and Sgier, I. 1996. In: *International Review of Education* Vol. 42 (1-3). pp. 131-150.

United Kingdom
Raggatt, P., and Edwards, R. 1996. In: *International Review of Education* Vol. 42 (1-3). pp. 151-165.

United States of America
Cunningham, P.M. 1996. In: *International Review of Education* Vol. 42 (1-3). pp. 167-186.

Vietnam
Truong, N. (unpublished, 1995). 15 pp.

3. Other Policy Documents

Australia. 1991. *Come in, Cinderella. The Emergence of Adult and Community Education*. Canberra: Senate Employment, Education and Training Committee.

Australia. 1994. *Working Nation. Policies and Programme*. (White Paper on Employment and Growth). Canberra: Department of Employment, Education and Training, Commonwealth of Australia.

Australia. 1997. *Beyond Cinderella. Toward a Learning Society*. Canberra: Senate Employment, Education and Training Committee.

Canada. 1989. *S'adapter pour gagner* (Report). Ottawa: Conseil consultatif sur l'adaptation.

Canada. 1992 a. *Les chemins de la compétence. Education et formation professionnelle au Canada*. Ottawa: Conseil économique du Canada.

Canada. 1992 b. *Accroître l'accessibilité et garantir l'adaptation. L'éducation des adultes dix ans après la Commission Jean*. (s.l.): Conseil supérieur de l'education.

CEFA. 1982. *Apprendre: Une action volontaire et responsable* (White Paper). Québec: Commission d'étude sur la formation professionnelle et socio-culturelle des adultes.

Club of Rome. 1979. *No Limits to Learning* (Report). Oxford, New York: Pergamon.

European Commission. 1994a. *Growth, Competitiveness, Employment. Challenges and Ways into the 21st Century* (White Paper). Luxembourg: Office for Official Publications of the European Communities.

European Commission. 1994b. *European Social Policy. A Way Forward for the Union* (White Paper). Luxembourg: Office for Official Publications of the European Communities.

European Commission. 1996. *Teaching and Learning. Towards the Learning Society (White Paper).* Luxembourg: Office for Official Publications of the European Communities.

FSEA. 1998. *Principes de politique de formation.* (s. l.): Féderation suisse pour l'éducation des adultes.

Germany. 1994. *Erklärung der 2. Europäischen Weiterbildungskonferenz in Dresden.* Bonn: Bundesministerium für Bildung, Wissenschaft, Forschung und Technologie.

Hudson Institute. 1988. *Opportunity 2000: Creative Affirmative Action Strategies for a Changing Workforce.* Washington/D.C.: Department of Labor, Employment Standards Administration.

ICEA. 1994. *Apprendre à l'âge adulte.* Montréal: Institut canadien d'éducation des adultes.

Keating, P. 1994. *Working Nation. Primeministerial Statement to the House of Representatives.* Canberra: Australian Government.

Mali. 1995. *"Perspectives de Ségou". L'intégration sous-régionale par l'éducation de base* (Final Report). (s.l.): Ministère de l'éducation de base.

Morocco. 1997. *Education pour tous. Projet d'éducation sous forme de stratégie globale.* (s.l.): Ministère de l'éducation nationale.

Minedaf. 1998. *Septième Conférence des Ministres de l'éducation des Etats membres africains. Rapport final.* (Durban, South Africa, 1998). Paris: UNESCO.

Netherlands. 1994. *Naar Eigen Vermogen.* Rijswijk: Ministerie van Volksgezondheid, Welzijn en Sport.

Nordic Council. 1995. *The Golden Riches in the Grass. Lifelong Learning for All.* Arhus: The Nordic Council of Ministers.

OECD. 1973. *Recurrent Education: A Strategy for Lifelong Learning.* Paris: Organisation for Economic Co-operation and Development.

Quebec. 1991. *Partenaires pour un Québec compétent et compétitif.* Montréal: Ed. Officielles.

Quebec. 1998. *Vers une politique de la formation continue.* Québec: Ministère de l'éducation, Gouvernement du Québec.

South Africa. 1997. *A National Multi-year Implementation Plan for Adult Education and Training: Provision and Accreditation.* Pretoria: Directorate of Adult Education and Trainig, Department of Education.

Sweden 1996. *A Programme for Halving Open Unemployment by 2000.* (s.l.): Swedish Government.

UNESCO. 1976 a. *Recommendation on Participation by the People at Large in Cultural Life and their Contribution to it.* Paris: UNESCO.

UNESCO. 1996. *Education: A Treasure Lies Within.* (Report by the "Delors Commission"). Paris: Odile Jacob.

UNESCO. 1997. *Hamburg Declaration* and *Agenda for the Future.* Hamburg: UNESCO Institute for Education.

Unicef. 1990. *World Declaration on Education for All / Framework for Action to Meet Basic Learning Needs* (Report on the Jomtien Conference, March 1990). New York: Unicef House.

United Kingdom. 1997. *Learning for the Twenty-First Century. First Report of the National Advisory Group for Continuing Education and Lifelong Learning.* London: Department for Education and Employment.

World Bank. 1990. *Skills for Productivity: Policies for Vocational and Technical Education and Training in Developing Countries.* Washington/D.C.: World Bank.

4. Literature (Monographs and Articles)

Abrahamsson, K., Hultinger, E.S., and Svenningson, L. 1990. *The Expanding Learning Enterprise in Sweden.* Stockholm: Swedish National Board of Education.

Adorno, T.W. 1991. *The Culture Industry.* (ed. by J.M. Bernstein). London: Routledge.

Ahluwalia, M., and Sharma, A. 1995. *A Study of the Phenomena of Drop-Outs in the Literacy Campaign. A Field Experience.* Chandigarh/India: Regional Resource Centre for Adult and Continuing Education, Panjab University.

Ahmed, M. 1991. *Basic Education and National Development. Lessons from India and China.* New York: Unicef House.

Alheit, P. 1994. *Taking the Knocks. Youth, Unemployment and Biography.* London: Cassell.

Ander Egg, E. 1984. *Historia del trabajo social.* Alicante/Spain: Humanitas.

Ant, M. 1997. "Jobrotation - ein neues Zeitmodell zur Bekämpfung der Arbeitslosigkeit". In: *Grundlagen der Weiterbildung* Vol. 8 (4), pp. 160-163.

Aronowitz, S., and Di Fazzio, W. 1994. *The Jobless Future. Sci-Tech and the Dogma of Work.* Minneapolis/Minn.: University of Minnesota Press.

Aronowitz, S., and Giroux, H.A. 1988. "Schooling, Culture, and Literacy in the Age of Broken Dreams: A Review of Bloom and Hirsch". In: *Harvard Educational Review* Vol. 58 (2) pp. 172-194.

ASTAT. 1996. *Nachfrage in den Bereichen Weiterbildung und Kultur in Südtirol (ASTAT Information).* Bozen: ASTAT (Italy).

Atala, L. 1992. *European Approaches to Lifelong Learning. Trends in Industry Practices and Industry-University Co-operation in Adult Education and Training.* Bruxelles: CRE-ERT, European University Forum.

Australia. 1995. *Snapshots: A Statistical Profile of Adult Students and their Opinions.* Victoria: Adult, Community and Further Education Board.

Barbe, L. 1998. "Pour une relecture du référentiel des politiques de lutte contre l'illetrisme". In: C. El Hayek Caravansérail (ed.). *Illetrisme: de l'enjeu social à l'enjeu citoyen.* Paris: Groupe permanente de lutte contre l'illetrisme, Ministère de l'emploi et de solidarité, France. pp. 35-48.

Barton, D., and Hamilton, M. 1990. *Researching Literacy in Industrialized Countries: Trends and Prospects.* Hamburg: UNESCO Institute for Education.

Beck, U. 1988. *Gegengifte. Die organisierte Unverantwortlichkeit.* Frankfurt/Main: Suhrkamp.

Beck, U. 1992, *Risk Society: Towards a New Modernity.* Cambridge: Polity Press.

Beck, U. 1995. *Ecological Politics in an Age of Risk.* Cambridge: Polity Press.

Beck, U. (ed.). 1997. *Politik der Globalisierung.* Frankfurt/Main: Suhrkamp.

Beck, U., and Beck-Gernsheim, E. 1990. *Das ganz normale Chaos der Liebe.* Frankfurt/Main: Suhrkamp.

Beck, U., and Beck-Gernsheim, E. (eds.). 1994. *Riskante Freiheiten. Individualisierung in modernen Gesellschaften.* Frankfurt/Main: Suhrkamp.

Beck, U., Giddens, A., and Lash, G. 1994. *Reflexive Modernization.* Cambridge: Polity Press.

Beder, H. 1991. *Adult Literacy: Issues for Policy and Practice.* Malabar/Fa.: Krieger.

Bélanger, P. 1992. "L'éducation des adultes et le vieillissement des populations: tendances et enjeux". In: *International Review of Education.* Vol. 38 (4). pp. 343-362.

Bélanger, P. 1994. "Lifelong Learning: The Dialectics of 'Lifelong Education'". In: *International Review of Education.* Vol. 40 (3-5). pp. 353-381.

Bélanger, P., and Bochynek, B. 1999. *Financing of Adult Education in European Civil Society.* Hamburg: UNESCO Institute for Education.

Bélanger, P. and Mobarak, H. 1996. "UNESCO and Adult Education". In: A. Tuijnman (ed.). *International Encyclopedia of Adult Education and Training* (2nd edition). Oxford, New York: Pergamon. pp. 717-723.

Bélanger, P., and Tuijnman, A. (eds.).1997. *New Patterns of Adult Learning: A Six-Country Comparative Study.* Oxford, New York: Pergamon.

Bélanger, P., and Valdivielso, S. (eds.). 1997. *The Emergence of Learning Societies: Who Participates in Adult Learning?* Oxford, New York: Pergamon.

Belgium. 1999. *Etats des lieux: Communauté française de Belgique.* Namur: Ministère de la Communauté française.

Belisle, R. 1997. "Question de compétence. The Competence Issue: A Tool for Women (Quebec/Canada)". In: Mauch, W., and Papen, U. (eds.). *Making a Difference: Innovations in Adult Education.* Frankfurt/Main: Peter Lang. pp. 62-81.

Bell, D. 1976. *The Coming of the Post-industrial Society.* Harmondsworth: Penguin.

Benevolo, L.1993. *La città nella storia d'Europa.* Bari: Laterza.

Bengtson, V., Rosenthal, C., and Burton, L. 1990. "Families and Aging: Diversity and Heterogeneity". In: R.H. Binstock and L.K. George (ed.). *Handbook of Aging and the Social Sciences.* San Diego/Cal.: Academic Press. pp. 263-287.

Benton, N. 1992. *The Accreditation of Prior Learning: Recent Developments in Australia and New Zealand and Challenges for the 1990s* (unpublished paper). Geelong (Australia): 2nd AARE/NZARE Conference.

Benton, L., and Noyelle, T. 1992. *L'illetrisme des adultes et les résultats économiques.* Paris: OECD.

Berman, M. 1982. *All That Is Solid Melts Into Air.* New York: Verso.

Bernardo, A.B., 1998. *Literacy and the Mind: The Contexts and Cognitive Consequences of Literacy Practice.* Hamburg and Wiltshire/United Kingdom: UNESCO Institute for Education and Luzac Oriental.

Bernier, C. 1990. *Le travail en mutation.* Montréal: Saint-Martin.

Bernstein, B. 1990a. *Poder, educación y conciencia. Sociologia de la transmisión cultural.* Barcelona: El Roure.

Bernstein, B. 1990b. *The Structuring of Pedagogic Discourse.* London, New York: Routledge.

Blid, H. 1990. *Education by the People. Study Circles.* Oskarshamn: ABF.

Bloom, A. 1987. *The Closing of the American Mind: How Higher Education Has Failed Democracy and Impoverished the Souls of Today's Students.* New York: Simon & Schuster.

Bogard,G. 1992. *Pour une éducation socialisatrice des adultes. Constituer l'éducation des adultes en système autonome pour resocialiser les adultes en permanence.* Strasburg: European Council.

Bourdieu, P., and Passeron, J.-C. 1979. *The 'Heritors: French Students and their Relation to Culture.* Chicago/Ill.: University of Chicago Press.

Bourdieu, P., and Passeron, J.C. 1977. *Reproduction in Education, Society and Culture.* London, Beverly Hills/Cal.: Sage.

Braverman, H. 1974. *Labor and Monopoly Capital. The Degradation of Work in the Twentieth Century.* London, New York: Monthly Review Press.

Bron, A. 1998. "The Changing Agenda on Research in the Education of Adults and the Issue of Citizenship". In: A. Bron, J. Field and E. Kurantowicz (eds.) *Adult Education and Democratic Citizenship* (Vol. II). Kraków: Impuls. pp. 11-26.

Brookfield, S. 1985. *Self-directed Learning. From Theory to Practice.* San Francisco/Cal.: Jossey-Bass.

Caffarella, R.S. 1993. "Self-directed Learning". in: S.B. Merriam (ed.). *An Update on Adult Learning Theory.* San Francisco/Cal.: Jossey-Bass. pp. 25-35.

Canada. 1995. *Etats des lieux: Canada.* Ottawa: Commission nationale canadienne pourl'UNESCO.

Canadian Center on the Labor Market and Productivity. 1993. *1991 National Training Survey.* Ottawa: Canadian Center on the Labor Market and Productivity.

Canieso-Doronila, M.L. 1997. *Landscapes of Literacy. An Ethnographic Study of Functional Literacy in Marginal Philippine Communities.* Hamburg and London: UNESCO Institute for Education and Luzac Oriental.

Carnoy, M. and Samoff, J. 1990. *Education and Social Transition in the Third World.* Princeton, N.J.: Princeton University Press.

Castels, M. 1996. *The Rise of the Network Society*. Oxford : Blackwell.

Caulley, D.N. 1982. "Legislative History and Evaluation". In: *Evaluation and Program Planning* (Vol. 5). Oxford, New York: Pergamon. pp.45-52.

Cedefop. 1994. *Continuum entre l'enseignement obligatorie, la formation initiale et continue, et l'éducation des adultes.* Berlin: Centre européen du développement de la formation professionnelle.

Centre INFFO. 1990. "Le droit à la participation". In: *INFFO Flash*, July 1990.

Centre INFFO. 1992. *Reconnaissance des acquis.* Paris: Centre INFFO.

Centre INFFO. 1994. *Bilan des compétences.* Paris: Centre INFFO.

Chadwick, A., and Stannett, A. 1998. *European Perspectives on Museums and the Education of Adults.* Leicester: National Institute of Adult and Continuing Education.

Christiansen, L. 1995. "Exclusion sociale, chômage et vie quotidienne des femmes". In: M. Trantallidi (ed.). *L'éducation des adultes. Instrument de développement des ressources humaines dans l'Union européenne de l'an 2000.* Athènes: Secretariat général à l'éducation des adultes, Ministère de l'éducation nationale et des cultes. pp.143-150.

Cipolla, C. 1969. *Literacy and Development in the West.* Harmondsworth: Penguin.

Cohen, M.D., and Sproull, L.S. (eds.). 1995. *Organizational Learning.* Thousand Oaks, London, New Delhi: Sage.

Coombs, P.H., and Manzoor, A. 1974. *Attacking Rural Poverty.* Baltimore, London: Johns Hopkins UP.

Cornia, G.A., Van Der Hoeven, R., and Mkandawire, M. (eds.). 1992. *Africa's Recovery in the 1990s - From Stagnation and Adjustment to Human Development.* New York: St. Martin's Press.

Courtney, S. 1992. *Why Adults Learn.Towards a Theory of Participation in Adult Education.* London, New York: Routledge.

Cross, K.P. 1981. *Adults as Learners.* San Francisco/Cal.: Jossey-Bass.

Darcy de Oliveira, M., and Tandon, R. 1994. *Citizens Strengthening Global Civil Society*. Washington: Civicus.

Dave, R.H., Ouane, A., et Perera, D.A. 1989. *Learning Strategies for Post-Literacy and Continuing Education: A Cross-National Perspective* (2nd edition). Hamburg: UNESCO Institute for Education.

David, H. (ed.). 1990. *Le vieillissement au travail. Une question de jugement* (Actes du Colloque, mars 1989). Montréal: Institut de recherche appliquée sur le travail.

De Bandt, S., Dejours, C., and Dubar, C. 1995. *La France malade du travail*. Paris: Fayard.

De Brie, C. 1999. "Dans l'opacité des tractions transatlantiques, l'AMI nouveau va arriver". In: *Le Monde Diplomatique* 5/1999. p. 13.

De Puellez Benitez, M. 1993. *Estado y educación en el desarrollo historico de las sociedades europeas*. In: *Estado y Educaion. Rivista Ibero Americana de Educaion* 1/1993.

De Sanctis, F.M. 1975. *Educazione in età adulta*. Firenze: La Nuova Italia.

De Sanctis, F.M.1988 *Verso un duemila educativo*. Prato: Università degli studi di Firenze, Comune di Prato.

De Tommasi, L., Warde, M.J., and Haddad, S. 1996. *O Banco Mundial e las Politicas Educacionais*. Sao Paulo do Brasil: Cortez Editora.

Dejours, C. 1993. *Travail: Usure mentale. Essai de psychopathologie du travail* (new edition). Paris: Centurion.

Denmark. 1999. *Evaluation of the Regional Cultural Development Projects*. Nelleman Consultants.

Diop, A.M. 1989. "La place des anciens dans la société africaine". In: *Impact* No. 39. pp. 101-107.

Dominice, P. 1990. *L'histoire comme processus de formation*. Paris: L'Harmattan.

Dong, M. C. 1996. "China: People's Republic". In: A. Tuijnman (ed.). *International Encyclopedia of Adult Education and Training* (2nd edition).

Oxford, New York: Pergamon. pp. 768-772.

Doray, P. 1989. *Formation et mobilisation: Le cas d'aluminium Pechiney.* Lille: Presses Universitaires de Lille.

Doray, P. and ICEA. 1995. *La participaqtion des adultes à l'éducation au Québec.* Montréal: Université du Québec and Institut canadien d'éducation des adultes.

Draves, W.A. 1995. *Energizing the Learning Environment.* Manhattan/Kans.: Learning Resources Network.

Dubar, C. 1991. *La socialisation. Construction des identités sociales et professionnnelles.* Paris: Armand Colin.

EAEA. 1995. *The Roles and Functions of the System of Adult Education in the General Education System Including Vocational Training.* Barcelona: European Association for the Education of Adults.

EAEA. 1997. *Older Adults as Educators.* Barcelona: European Association for the Education of Adults.

EBAE. 1985. *Survey of Adult Education Legislation.* Amersfoort: European Bureau of Adult Education.

Egidi, V. 1990. "Vieillissement de la population et évolution des modes de vie en Europe". In: *Séminaire sur les tendances démographiques actuelles et modes de vie en Europe* (conference paper). Strasburg: European Council.

Elley, W.B. 1992. *How in the World Do Students Read?* Hamburg: The International Association for the Evaluation of Educational Achievement.

European Commission - Human Resources Task Force. 1994. "Analyse des pratiques de formation menées dans les entreprises pour l'adaption des travailleurs aux mutations industrielles". In: *Force-Euroform. Analyse des besoins en formation.* 6 oct. 1994, para. II.

Eurydice. 1993. *The Federal Republic of Germany.* Bruxelles: Eurydice, National Dossiers.

Eyerman, R., and Jamison, A. 1991. *Social Movements. A Cognitive Approach.* Pennsylvania/Penn.: Pennsylvania State University Press.

Fabbri Montesano, D., and Munari, A. 1984. *Strategie del sapere. Verso una psicologia culturale.* Bari: Dedalo.

Federighi, P. 1990. *Legislative and Administrative Measures in Favour of Adult Education.* Firenze: Università degli studi.

Federighi, P. 1996. *Strategie per la gestione dei processi educativi nel contesto europeo.* Napoli: Liguori.

Field, J. 1992. *Learning through Labour, Training, Education and the State, 1890 - 1939.* Leeds: University Press.

Fingeret, H.A. 1992. "Literacy in the U.S.A.: The Present Issues". In: UIE. *The Future of Literacy and the Literacy of the Future.* Hamburg: UNESCO Institute for Education.

Fingeret, H.A., and Jurmo, P. (eds.). 1989. *Participatory Literacy Education.* San Francisco/Cal.: Jossey-Bass

Forrester, V. 1999. *The Economic Horror.* Cambridge: Polity Press.

Franchi, A.M. 1999. *Regard sur l'éducation des adultes en France. Evaluation et perspectives.* Paris: Documentation française.

Freire, P. 1972. *Pedagogy of the Oppressed.* Harmondsworth: Penguin.

Freire, P. 1993. *Pedagogy of the City.* New York: Continuum.

Frischkopf, A. (ed.). 1994. *Weiterbildung und Museum.* Soest/Germany: Landesinstitut für Schule und Weiterbildung, Nordrhein-Westfalen.

Furet, F., and Ozouf, J. 1977. *Lire et écrire. L'alphabétisation des Français de Calvin à Jules Ferry* (2 vol.). Paris: Editions de Minuit.

Gayfer, M. (ed.). 1987. *Literacy in the Industrialized Countries: A Focus on Practice.* Special Issue of *Convergence* Vol. XX (3/4). International Council for Adult Education.

Gelpi, E. 1990. *Educaçion permanente. Problemas laborales y perspectivas educativas.* Madrid: Ed. Popular.

255

Gibbons, M. et al. 1994. *The New Production of Knowledge. The Dynamics of Science and Research in Contemporary Societies*. London, Thousand Oaks, New Delhi: Sage.

Giddens, A. 1990. *The Consequences of Modernity*. Cambridge: Polity Press.

Giddens, A. 1992. *The Transformation of Intimacy*. Cambridge: Polity Press.

Giddens, A. 1994. *Beyond Left and Right*. Cambridge: Polity Press.

Giere, U., and Hautecœur, J.-P. 1990. *A Selected Bibliography on Literacy in Industrialized Countries*. Hamburg: UNESCO Institute for Education.

Giere, U., Ouane, A., and Ranaweera, A.M. 1990. *Literacy in Developing Countries : An Analytical Bibliography*. (=*Bulletin of the International Bureau of Education*. Vol. 64. No. 254-257).

Giere, U., Ouane, A., Hautcœur, J.P., and Smuthá-Deutschmann, H. 1992. *Die Welten der Wörter - World of Words - Mondes des mots - Mundos de la palabras*. Hamburg: UNESCO Institute for Education.

Gnamus, O. 1990. "Literacy at the Threshold of the 21st Century". In: P. Bélanger, C. Winter and A. Sutton (eds.). *Literacy and Basic Education in Europe on the Eve of the 21st Century*. Amsterdam/Lisse: Swets & Zeitlinger.

Gorz, A. 1980. *Farewell to the Working Class: En Essay on Post-industrial Socialism*. London: Pluto Press.

Gorz, A. 1988. *Métamorphoses du travail, quête du sens*. Paris: Galilée.

GPLI. 1999. *Etats des lieux: France*. Paris: Groupe permanente de lutte contre l'illetrisme, Ministère de l'emploi et de solidarité, France.

Graff, H.J. 1979. *The Literacy Myth. Literacy and Social Structures in the 19th Century City*. New York: Academic Press.

Gramsci, A. 1986. *Selections from the Prison Notebooks of Antonio Gramsci* (ed. and transl. by Q. Hoare and G.N. Smith). London: Lawrence & Wishart.

Groothoff, H.-H. 1973. *Das Fischer Lexikon Pädagogik* (new edition). Frankfurt/Main: Fischer.

Guillemard, A. M. 1980. *La vieillesse et l'Etat*. Paris: P.U.F.

Guillemard, A. M. 1983. "Politique de désemploi des travailleurs vieillissants et remodelage du parcours des âges". In: *Gérontologie et Société* 24: 6-21.

Guillemard, A. M. 1995. "Le cycle de vie en mutation". In: Dubet, F., and Wieviorka, M. (eds.) *Penser le Sujet*. Paris: Fayard.

Guo-Dong, X. 1994. "Lifelong Education in China: New Policies and Activities". In: *International Review of Education*. Vol. 40 (3-5). pp. 271-282.

Habermas, J. 1987. *The Theory of Communicative Action* (2 vol., transl. by T. McCarthy). Boston: Beacon Press.

Habermas, J. 1990. *Strukturwandel der Öffentlichkeit: Untersuchungen zu einer Kategorie der bürgerlichen Gesellschaft* (new edition). Frankfurt/Main: Suhrkamp.

Hammink, K. 1990. *Functional Illiteracy and Adult Basic Education in the Netherlands*. Hamburg : UNESCO Institute for Education.

Hasan, A., and Tuijnman, A. 1997. "Adult Education Participation: A Policy Overview". In: P. Bélanger and A. Tuijnman (eds.). *New Patterns of Adult Learning: A Six-Country Comparative Study*. Oxford, New York: Pergamon. pp. 229-247.

Hautcœur, J.-P. (ed.).1997. *Alpha 97: Basic Education and Institutional Environments*. Hamburg and Toronto: UNESCO Institute for Education and Culture Concepts.

Havelock, E.A. 1976. *Origins of Western Literacy. Four Lectures at the Ontario Institute*. Toronto: Ontario Institute for Studies in Education.

Held, D. 1980. *Introduction to Critical Theory. Horkheimer to Habermas*. Berkley/Cal.: University of California Press.

Hirsch, E.D. 1987. *Cultural Literacy: What Every American Needs to Know*. Boston/Ma.: Houghton Mifflin.

Holland, C. 1998. *Literacy and the New Work Order. An International Literature Review*. Leicester: National Institute of Adult and Continuing Education.

Hoppers, W. 1999. "A Good Place for All? Nonformal Education, Distance Education and the Restructuring of Schooling: Challenges for a New Basic Education Policy". In: *International Review of Education* Vol. 46 (1).

Hunter, C. St.J., and Harman, D. 1985. *Adult Literacy in the United States*. New York et al.: MacGraw-Hill.

Huntington, S.P. 1996. *The Clash of Civilizations and the Remaking of World Order*. New York: Simon & Schuster.

ICEA. 1982. *Du point de vue des adultes*. Montréal: Institut canadien d'éducation des adultes.

IFFS. 1987. *La carta dei diritti del pubblico*. Roma: Federazione Internazionale dei Circoli del Cinema.

ILO. 1991. *African Employment Report*. Addis-Ababa: International Labour Office.

Issacs, S. 1997. "Global Indicators to the Transition of Lifelong Learning in South Africa". In: NIER and UIE (eds.). *Comparative Studies of Lifelong Learning Politics*. Tokio: National Institute for Educational Research. pp. 268-282.

Janne, H. 1976. "Theoretical Foundations of Lifelong Education: A Sociological Perspective". In: R. H. Dave (ed.). *Foundation of Lifelong Education*. Oxford, New York: Pergamon. pp. 129-185.

Jay, M. 1973. *The Dialectical Imagination. A History of the Frankfurt School and the Institute of Social Research 1923-1950*. Boston/Ma.: Little, Brown & Co.

Jung, I., and King, L. (eds.). 1999. *Gender, Innovation and Education in Latin America*. Hamburg: UNESCO Institute for Education and Deutsche Stiftung für Internationale Entwicklung.

Kayembe, N.B. 1988. *Accueil et référence en éducation des adultes au Québec*. Montréal: Institut canadien d'éducation des adultes.

King, L. 1994. *Roots of Identity. Language and Literacy in Mexico*. Stanford/Mass.: Stanford University Press.

Knox, A.B. 1993. *Synergistic Leadership for Adut Education*. San Francisco/ Cal.: Jossey-Bass

Korsgaard, D. 1998. *The Struggle for Enlightenment. Danish Adult Education during 500 Years*. Copenhagen: AWL.

Lash, S., and Urry, J. 1994. *Economics of Signs and Space*. Thousand Oaks, London, New Delhi: Sage.

Lawten, D. 1992. *Education and Politics in the 1990s*. London: Falmer Press.

Lengrand, P. 1994. "L'homme de la réponse et l'homme de la question". In: *International Review of Education* Vol. 40 (3-5). pp. 339-342.

Leroy, R. 1990. *The Financing of Continuing Vocational Training in Belgium*. Berlin: Centre européen du développement de la formation professionnelle.

Lévy, P. 1997. *Collective Intelligence: Mankind's Emerging World in Cyberspace* (transl. by R. Bononno). London: Plenum Press.

Lind, A. 1996. *"Free to Speak Up". Overall Evaluation of the National Literacy Programme in Namibia*. Windhoek: Directorate of Adult Basic Education, Ministry of Basic Education, Namibia.

MacDonald, C., and Munn, P. 1988. *Adult Participation in Education and Training*. Edinburgh: The Scottish Council for Research in Education.

Maheu, L. 1995. *Late Modernity*. London, New York: Routledge.

Matelard, A. 1994. *L'invention de la communication*. Paris: La Découverte.

Mathews, J. 1989. *Tools of Change*. Sydney: Pluto Press.

Medel-Añonuevo, C. 1995. *Women, Education and Empowerment*. Hamburg: UNESCO Institute for Education.

Medel-Añonuevo, C. 1996. *Women Reading the World. Policies and Practices of Literacy in Asia*. Hamburg: UNESCO Institute for Education.

Medel-Añonuevo, C. 1999. *Breaking Through. Engendering Monitoring and Evaluation in Adult Education*. Hamburg: UNESCO Institute for Education.

Meghnagi, S. 1995. "De l'éducation des adultes à la formation des compétences". In: A. Jobert, C. Marry and L. Tanguy (eds.). *Education et travail en Grande-Bretagne, Allemagne et Italie*. Paris: Armand Colin. pp. 332-354.

Molyneux, F., Low, G., and Fowler, G. (eds.). 1988. *Learning for Life. Politics and Progress in Recurrent Education*. London: Croom Helm.

Morin, E. 1977. *La méthode: La nature de la nature*. Paris: Seuil.

Mulenga, D. 1994. *Coping with Economic Crisis: Structural Adjustment and Education and Training and its Implications for Adult Education in Africa*. Northern Illinois University (Etats-Unis): Center for Governmental Studies.

Nagashima, M., Koji, K., and Hiroshi, S. 1994. *The State of Continuing Education in Japan*. Tokyo: Nippon University.

National Literacy Mission. 1999. (unpublished and untitled report from 13th July 1999 on the Federal Education Budget). New Delhi: National Literacy Mission, India.

Nuissl, E. 1994. *Adult Education in Germany*. Frankfurt/Main: Deutsches Institut für Erwachsenenbildung.

Odora Hoppers, C.A. 1996. *Adult Learning for Change and Sustainable Human Development: Mandate for Action from Five World Conferences*. Hamburg: UNESCO Institute for Education.

OECD. 1991. *Further Education and Training of the Labor Force: A Comparative Analysis of National Training Strategies for Industry Training*. Paris: Organisation for Economic Co-operation and Development.

OECD. 1996. *Lifelong Learning for All* (Report). Paris: Organisation for Economic Co-operation and Development.

OECD-CERI. 1992. *City Strategies for Lifelong Learning*. Paris: Organisation for Economic Co-operation and Development - Center for Educational Research and Innovation.

OECD-CERI. 1995. "The Lifelong Learner in the 1990s". In: D. Atchoarena (ed.). *Lifelong Education in Selected Industrialized Countries* (rev. edition). Paris: International Institute for Educational Planning, UNESCO. pp. 201-231.

OECD and HRDC. 1997. *Literacy Skills for the Knowledge Society. Further Results from the International Adult Literacy Survey.* Paris: Organisation for Economic Co-operation and Development and Human Resources Development Canada.

OECD and Statistics Canada. 1995. *Literacy, Economy and Society: Results of the First International Adult Literacy Survey.* Paris and Ottawa: Organisation for Economic Co-operation and Development and Statistics Canada.

Offe, C. and Heinze, R.G. 1992. *Beyond Employment.* Cambridge: Polity Press.

Okamoto, K. 1994. *Lifelong Learning Movement in Japan. Strategy, Practices and Challanges.* Tokyo: Ministry of Education, Science and Culture, Japan.

Ollivier, B. 1995. *L'acteur et le sujet. Vers un nouvel acteur économique.* Paris: Desclée de Brouwer.

Orefice, P. 1978. *Educazione e territorio.* Firenze: La Nuova Italia.

Orefice, P. 1991. *Politiche e interventi culturali e formativi in Italia nel secondo novecento.* Napoli: Ferraro.

Osorio, J., and Rivaro, J. (eds.). 1996. *Construyendo la modernidad educativa en América latina. Nuevas desarrollos curriculares en la educacion de personas jovenes adultas.* Santiago di Chile, Lima: UNESCO/OREALC and Tarea.

Otala, L. 1993. "Lifelong Learning Based on Industry-University Cooperation". In: *Lifelong Learning* 1/1993. Espoo: Centre for Continuing Education, University of Technology, Finland.

Ouane, A. (ed.). 1995. *Towards a Multilingual Culture of Education.* Hamburg: UNESCO Institute for Education.

Ozaki, M. et al. 1992. *Technology and Change and Labor Relation 1992.* Geneva: International Labour Office

Paci, M. 1995. "Il nostro lavoro e il tempo del benessere". In: *l'Unità 2.* 18th March 1995. p.1.

Palmade, G. (ed.).1975. *Das bürgerliche Zeitalter (Fischer Weltgeschichte* Vol. 27). Frankfurt/Main: Fischer.

Paquet, P. 1987. "Adults in Higher Education: The Situation in Canada". In: H.G. Schütze (ed.) *Adults in Higher Education. Politics and Practices in Great Britain and North America.* Stockholm: Almquist and Wiksell International. pp. 121-180.

Paul, J.J. 1991. *Formation continue. L'exemple du congé individuel de formation.* Dijon: IREC.

Péarker, H., Leplatre, F., and Ward, Ch. 1994. *Identification et validation des savoirs-faire et des connaissances acquises dans la vie et les expériences de travail. Rapport comparatif France – Royaume-Uni.* Berlin: Centre européen du développement de la formation professionnelle.

Petit, M. 1998. "Les bibliothèques des quartiers 'sensibles': des passerelles vers un droit de cité". In: C. El Hayek Caravansérail (ed.). *Illetrisme: de l'enjeu social à l'enjeu citoyen.* Paris: Groupe permanente de lutte contre l'illetrisme, Ministère de l'emploi et de solidarité, France. pp. 105-112.

Pieck, E. 1999. "Work-Related Adult Learning". In: M. Singh (ed.) *Poverty Alleviation, Work and Adult Learning.* Hamburg: UNESCO Institute for Education. pp. 10-17.

Pineau, G. 1994. "Histoires de vie et formation de nouveaux savoirs vitaux". In: *International Review of Education.* Vol. 40 (3-5). pp. 299-312.

Piore, M.J., and Sabel, C.F. 1984. *The Second Industrial Divide: Possibilities for Posterity.* New York: Basic Books.

Piotte, J.M. 1990. *Sens et politique. Pour en finir avec le grand désarrois.* Outremont/Québec: VLB.

Pöggeler, F. 1996. "History of Adult Education". In: A. Tuijnman (ed.). *International Encyclopedia of Adult Education and Training* (2nd edition). Oxford, New York: Pergamon. pp. 135-139.

Probyn, E. 1993. *Sexing the Self. Gendered Positions in Cultural Studies.* London, New York: Routledge.

Psacharapoulos, G., and Velez, E. 1992. "Does Training Pay, Independent of Education? Some Evidence from Columbia". In: *International Journal of Educational Research.* Vol. 17 (6). pp. 581-592.

Quigley, B. A. 1997. *Rethinking Literacy Education. The Critical Need for Practice-based Change.* San Francisco/Cal.: Jossey-Bass.

Reich, R. B. 1991. *The Work of Nations. Preparing Ourselves for 21st Century Capitalism.* New York: Knopf.

Reimers, F., and Tiburcio, L. 1993. *Education, ajustement et reconstruction: Option pour un changement.* Paris: UNESCO.

Requejo Osorio, A. (ed.) 1994. *Politica de Educaión de Adultos.* Santiago de Compostela: Torculo.

Ribero, J. H. 1993. *Educación de Adultos en América Latina. Desafíos de la Equitad y la Modernización.* Lima: Tarea.

Rifkin, J. 1995. *The End of Work.* London: Tarcher Putnam.

Roche, M. 1992. *Rethinking Citizenship.* Cambridge: Polity Press.

Roemer, J. E. 1996. *Theories of Distributive Justice.* Cambridge/Mass.: Harvard University Press.

Rogers, C. 1972. *Liberté pour apprendre?* Paris: Dumond.

Rubenson, K. 1989. "Swedish Adult Education Policy in the 1970s and 1980s". In: S. J. Ball and S. Larson (eds.). *The Struggle for Democratic Education.* New York: Falmer Press.

Rubenson, K. 1994. "Adult Education Policy in Sweden, 1967-1991". In: *Policy Studies Review* Vol. 13 (3/4). pp. 367-390.

Rubenson, K., and Xu, D. 1997. "Barriers to Participation in Adult Education and Training: Towards a New Understanding" In: P. Bélanger and A. Tuijnman (eds.). *New Patterns of Adult Learning: A Six-Country Comparative Study.* Oxford, New York: Pergamon. pp. 77-100.

Sainsaulieu, R. 1995. "Postface". In: B. Ollivier. *L'acteur et le sujet. Vers un nouvel acteur économique.* Paris: Desclée de Brouwer. pp. 457-464.

San Román Vazquez, A., and Ibarrola , C.C. 1994. *Historia de la Alfabetización y de la Educación de Adultos en México* (Vol. 1= *Del México prehispánico a la Reforma liberal*). San Angel/Mexico: Instituto Nacional para la Educación de los Adultos.

Sargant, N. 1991. *Learning and "Leisure". A Study of Participation in Learning and its Policy Implications*. Leicester: National Institute of Adult and Continuing Education.

Sargant, N. 1997. *The Learning Divide* (Report). Leicester: National Institute of Adult and Continuing Education.

Schütze, H.G. 1996. "Paid Educational Leave through Legislation and Collective Bargaining". In: A. Tuijnman (ed.). *International Encyclopedia of Adult Education and Training* (2nd edition). Oxford, New York: Pergamon. pp. 303-310.

Schuller, T. 1993. "Citizenship, Rights and Education" (Paper presented at the Conference *Adult Education and Social Change* held by the European Council, 22 to 25 March 1993). Strasburg: European Council.

Schuller, T. 1995. "Images of the Life Course". In: P. Alheit et al.(eds.) *The Biographical Approach in European Adult Education*. Wien: Verband Wiener Volksbildung. pp. 25-43.

Schuller, T. 1996. "Learning Generation: Age and Education". In: Walker, A. (ed.) *The New Generational Contract, Intergenerational Relations, Old Age and Welfare*. London: UCL Press.

Schwartz, B. 1972. *L'éducation demain*. Amsterdam: Fondation européenne de la culture.

Schwartz, B. 1994. *Moderniser sans exclure*. Paris: La Découverte.

Serres, M. (ed.). 1992. *Le rapport de mission sur l'université à distance*. Paris: UNESCO.

Singh, M. (ed.). 1997. *Adult Learning and the Changing World of Work*. Hamburg and Berlin: UNESCO Institute for Education and UNEVOC.

Sirvent, M. T. 1994. "The Politics of Adjustment and Lifelong Education: The Case of Argentina". In: *International Review of Education*. Vol. 40 (3-5). pp. 195-208.

Sirvent, M.T. 1999. *The Potential, Actual and Social Demand for Adult Education in Argentina*. Hamburg: UNESCO Institute for Education.

Sohlmann, A. 1998 a. "The Adult Education Initiative in Sweden". In: *Golden Riches* 1/1998, pp. 22-26.

Sohlmann, A. 1998 b. "The Culture of Adult Learning in Sweden: What Makes a Learning Society". In: *How Adults Learn: An International Conference.* Washington D.C.: Georgetown University Centre. pp. 8-11.

Standing, G. 1986. *Unemployment and Labour Market Flexibility: The United Kingdom.* Geneva: International Labour Office.

Steele, T., and Taylor, R. 1995. *Learning Independance. A Political Outline of Indian Adult Education.* Leicester: National Institute for Adult and Continuing Education.

Street, B. 1995. *Social Literacies: Critical Perspectives on Literacy Development, Ethnography and Education.* London: Longman.

Street, B. 1996 a. "Academic Literacies". In: Baker, D.J. Clay and C. Fox (eds.). *Alternative Ways of Knowing: Literacies, Numeracies, Sciences.* London: Falmer. pp. 101-134.

Street, B. (ed.). 1996 b. *Cross-cultural Approaches to Literacy.* Cambridge: Cambridge University Press.

Suchodolski, B. 1993. *Education permanente en profondeur.* Hamburg: UNESCO Institute for Education.

Sue, R. 1994. *Temps et ordre social.* Paris: P.U.F.

Sue, R. 1995. "Qualifications et compétences sociales". In: M. Trantallidi (ed.). *L'éducation des adultes. Instrument de developpement des ressources humaines dans l'Union Européenne de l'an 2000.* Athènes: Secretariat général à l'éducation des adultes, Ministère de l'éducation nationale et des cultes. pp. 70-76.

Sutton, P. 1992. *Basic Education in Prisons. Interim Report.* Hamburg: UNESCO Institute for Education.

Sweden. 1995. *Non-formal Education in Sweden.* Stockholm: Adult Education Council.

Swiss Commission for UNESCO. 1998. *'Eine Stunde lernen pro Tag' – Umsetzung in der Schweiz.* Bern: Swiss Commission for UNESCO.

Swiss Commission for UNESCO. 1999. *Alphabétisation – Francophonies – Pays industrialisés. Réponses au questionnaire: Suisse.* Bern: Commission nationale suisse pour l'UNESCO.

Tait, A. 1996. *Facts and Figures 1995.* Cambridge: The Open University.

Tandon, R. 1988. "Social Transformation and Participatory Research". In: *Convergence: Focus on Participatory Research* Vol. XXI (2/3). pp. 5-18.

Titmus, C. 1985. "General Introduction". In: EBAE (ed.). *Survey of Adult Education Legislation.* Amersfoort: European Bureau of Adult Education.

Titmus, C. 1990. "The System of Adult Education". In: ECLE (ed.). *International Handbook of Adult Education* (Vol. II). Prague: European Centre for Leisure and Education, UNESCO. pp. 197-206

Tornstam, L. 1989. "Aide formelle et informelle aux personnes agées. Analyses des structures actuelles et des options futures en Suède". In: *Impact* Vol. 39 (1). pp. 63-71.

Touraine, A. 1988. *Return of the Actor: Social Theory in Postindustrial Society.* Minneapolis/Minn.: University of Minnesota Press.

Touraine, A. 2000. *Can We Live Together? Equal and Different.* Stanford/Cal.: Stanford University Press.

Tuijnman, A. 1991. "Lifelong Education: A Test of the Cumulation Hypothesis." In: *International Journal of Lifelong Education.* Vol. 10 (3).

UIE. 1992. *The Future of Literacy and the Literacy of the Future: Report on the Seminar on Adult Literacy in Industrialized Countries, 1991.* Hamburg: UNESCO Institute for Education.

UIE. 1999. "Workshop 3: Ensuring Universal Rights to Literacy and Basic Education" (Fasc. a.-g.). In: UIE (ed.). *Adult Learning and the Challenges of the 21st Century. A Series of Booklets Documenting Workshops Held at the Fifth International Conference on Adult Education.* Hamburg: UNESCO Institute for Education.

UIE and NIACE. 1999. *Promoting Learning - United Nations Adult Learners' Week.* Hamburg: UNESCO Institute for Education and National Institute for Adult and Continuing Education.

266

UNDP. 1993. *Build Anew: United Nations Development Program* (Annual Report 1992/93). New York: United Nations, Public Relations Division.

UNESCO. 1972. *Third International Conference on Adult Education (Confintea): Final Report.* Paris: UNESCO.

UNESCO. 1976 b. *The Experimental World Literacy Programme: A Critical Assessment.* Paris : UNDP and UNESCO Teheran Institut.

UNESCO. 1985. *Fourth International Conference on Adult Education (Confintea): Final Report.* Paris: UNESCO.

UNESCO. 1993. *World Education Report 1993.* Paris: UNESCO.

UNESCO. 1994. *Education-for-All Summit of Nine High-Population Countries (New Delhi 1993). Final Report.* Paris: UNESCO.

UNESCO-APPEAL. 1997. *Asia-Pacific Regional Consultation on Adult Education* (Report on the Jomtien meeting, September 1996). Bangkog: UNESCO-APPEAL.

UN. 1987. *Global Estimates and Projections of Population by Sex and Age. The 1984 Assessment.* New York: United Nations.

Valdivielso, S. 1997. "Beyond the Walls of the Household: Gender and Adult Education Participation". In: P. Bélanger and A. Tuijnman (eds.). *New Patterns of Adult Learning: A Six-Country Comparative Study.* Oxford, New York: Pergamon. pp. 209-228.

Venezky, R.L., Wagner, D.A., and Ciliberti, B.S. 1990. *Toward Defining Literacy.* Newark/N.J.: International Reading Association.

Verhaagen, A. 1999. *Alphabétisation 1919-1999. Mais...que sont devenues nos campagnes?* Hamburg: UNESCO Institute for Education.

Vinkour, A. 1976. "Economic Analysis of Lifelong Education". In: R. H. Dave (ed.). *Foundations of Lifelong Education.* Oxford, New York: Pergamon. pp. 286-337.

Wagner, D.A. 1987. "Literacy Futures". In: D.A. Wagner (ed.). *The Future of Literacy In a Changing World.* Oxford: Pergamon. pp. 3-16.

Wagner, S., and Grenier, P. 1990. *Analphabétisme de minorité et alphabétisation d'affirmation nationale: à propos de l'Ontario français.* Rockland/Ontario: Prosario Inc.

Walker, A. (ed.) 1996. *The New Generational Contract. Intergenerational Relations, Old Age and Welfare.* London: UCL Press.

Walters, S. (ed.). 1995. *Adult Education and Training in South Africa, a Selected Chronology from 1910 to 1995.* Belleville/South Africa: Center for Adult and Continuing Education.

Warwick, B.E. 1992. *How in the World Do Students Read?.* Den Haag: International Association for the Evaluation of Educational Achievement.

Watkins, K.E., and Marsick, V.J. 1993. *Sculpting the Learning Organization. Lessons in the Art and Science of Science Change.* San Francisco/Cal.: Jossey-Bass.

Westwood, S. 1991. "Constructing the Future: A Postmodern Agenda for Adult Education". In: Westwood, S., and Thomas, J.E. 1991. *The Politics of Adult Education.* Leicester: National Institute for Adult and Continuing Education.

Wikelund, K. R., Reder, S., and Hart-Landsberg, S. 1992. *Expanding Theories of Adult Literacy Participation: A Literature Review.* Philadelphia/Penn.: National Center on Adult Literacy, University of Pennsylvania.

Wilson, W.J. 1987. *The Truly Disadvantaged: The Inner City, the Underclass and Public Society.* Chicago/Ill.: Chicago University Press.

World Bank. 1999. *Knowledge Sharing – Knowledge Management. Example: Education.* http://www.worldbank.org.

Index

access *12f., 19, 28, 32, 34, 42f., 46, 51, 64, 83, 88ff., 95, 98f., 102, 106f., 116, 123, 125, 129, 131, 133, 135, 147f., 160, 167f., 172, 178ff., 184, 190, 194, 211*
accessibility measure *49, 102ff.*
accreditation
    of prior learning (see also: *recognition of p. l.*) *51, 125, 133, 137, 144, 181ff., 191, 193*
    of qualifications *125*
accumulation of skills / competencies (see also: *synergie...*) *85, 101, 120, 129, 206*
active citizenship *46, 112, 119n., 197n.*
admission *14, 20f., 123, 125*
adult eduction
    agency *144, 158, 171, 191*
    association *115*
    centre *19, 128, 194*
    general *49, 59, 118, 136, 181n., 207n.*
adult educator *56, 155*
adult learners' week *108n., 209*
adult learning,
    economics of *17, 33, 72, 153, 155f.*
    work-related *7, 10, 17f., 21, 23, 31, 50, 78ff., 123, 153, 200*
agricultural extension (see also: *agricul. education*) *14, 31, 76, 172, 194, 207*
agriculture *16, 18, 62, 104f., 173*
AIDS *58, 68, 119*
allocation (per student; see also: *financial support; grants; scholarships; subsidies*) *79, 111*
andragogy *179, 182*
Australia *6, 8, 10f.. 15f., 31, 40, 61, 64, 78, 82, 92, 99, 106f., 108f., 123, 127f., 133, 144f., 160, 171, 190*
Bangladesh *188*
basic competencies *167, 170, 184, 189, 193, 204*
basic education (see also: *literacy*) *3, 6f., 9, 11, 14, 24, 33, 79, 95, 99, 101, 107, 120, 123, 126ff., 130, 139f., 147f., 164-195, 204, 207, 210*

basic skills (see: *b. competencies*) *33, 98, 126, 164, 166, 168, 171, 174n., 187, 189f., 191n.*
Belgium *7, 15, 24, 108n., 116, 124, 140, 182f., 192*
Benin *108n., 190*
Botswana *108n.*
Brazil *7, 16, 33, 39, 62, 64f., 79f., 119, 123, 126, 128f., 134, 143, 150, 169, 172, 174, 180, 183, 191f., 195*
Burkina Faso *107, 186*
Canada *5, 7f., 12, 14f., 21, 23, 79f., 82, 92, 104, 106, 115, 133, 171, 177, 182f., 190f., 201*
Caribbean *124*
Catalonia *3, 41, 54, 136, 150, 162, 210*
China *108n.*
civic education *11, 22*
civil society *7, 17, 27f., 32, 36, 40, 50, 54, 56, 58, 68ff., 83, 91, 99, 117, 145-152, 156, 167ff., 185, 188, 195-197, 208, 210f.*
collective actors *27, 29, 32, 67, 89, 112, 195f.*
community
    development *139, 168, 210*
    education *8, 11, 19, 128, 136, 143*
    service *96*
continuing education *8, 10, 12f., 16-20, 22, 41, 48, 50, 52f., 56, 68, 75, 79, 82, 94, 104, 109, 121-25, 131f., 138f., 171, 180f., 183, 201, 209*
continuing training (see also: *in-company / in-house t.*) *79, 201n.*
correspondence course *15, 123*
counselling (see also: *guidance; information services; orientation*) *17, 22, 108, 131, 143, 208*
Cuba *164*
cultural
    identity *173, 181*
    rights *148, 193*
culture industry *72, 209*
Czech Republic *7f., 22, 62, 64, 82*
decentralisation *47, 81, 101, 148, 150-153, 210*
democratisation (of education) *14, 38, 99, 166, 212*